Researching
YOUTH

Edited by
Julie McLeod and Karen Malone

Australian Clearinghouse for Youth Studies

ACYS
GPO Box 252–64
Hobart, Tasmania 7001

Cover design by Geraldine Burke, Gardenvale, Victoria
Printed by Advance Publicity, Hobart

ISBN 1 875236 48 1

Researching Youth is an important book, which deserves to be read and studied beyond the borders of Australia. Indeed, it demonstrates amply the breadth and the theoretical depth of Australian research on that much maligned, romanced, researched and imagined group, "Youth". It is sometimes said (by publishers, particularly in their marketing departments) that work which is only about Australia cannot be sold abroad; it is "niche"; it is simply not relevant. Here is a book which, by rights, ought to prove these pessimists wrong.

Escaping the charge that work about "youth" is almost always work about young men, *Researching Youth* moves with polished ease between discussions of young women and femininity, young men and masculinity and gender as relational. It avoids the trap of romanticising working-class lads as heroes of the class struggle, or readers against the grain of popular cultural pap. Rather, it explores in some detail the ways in which young people, men and women, are mythologised, even demonised, *and* the ways that young people make themselves (but not in conditions of their own choosing). Many of the themes arising from the empirical studies in which most of the book is grounded resonate with issues for/about youth in countries other than Australia. The spatial relations of fear, for example, or the role of the police, are themes that can be found in literature about youth from the US, the UK, New Zealand and South Africa. Similarly, policy issues relating to the absence or narrowing of provision for young people do not belong to Australia alone. Neither do questions about class (however understood), sexuality, nation or ethnicity. Of course, the Australian experience is inflected by the particular conditions of that country at this historical moment, and we cannot transport (so to speak) that experience, lock, stock and barrel, to other countries and believe that things are "just the same" everywhere in this increasingly globalised world. But that does not mean that those of us in other countries cannot learn from the work in this book.

Another important aspect of the book is its reflexivity about research methods. Indeed, the questioning of the whole nature of the endeavour of "youth studies" constitutes a significant theme for the book's contributors. One of my doctoral students has recently commented to me on the difficulty of finding anything new to say about research methods as she approaches the writing of her methodology chapter for her thesis. But here is an example of the kind of work and thought which does not simply recycle old feminist thoughts about research, but picks them up, interrogates them, puts them to good use and develops new ideas of its own.

Finally, this is an edited collection that reflects its origins in a research conference. The articles speak to each other, even when the links are not explicitly made. The reader feels as if s/he is taking part in an ongoing, an important, conversation. It would be invidious to pick out any one article in a collection that is so even. Every article is worth reading and makes a contribution to the debate. Youth studies is a burgeoning field, and one which raises significant questions for the social sciences and for research in education. *Researching Youth* makes a significant and timely contribution to it.

Debbie Epstein
Reader in Education
Centre for Research and Education on Gender
Institute of Education
University of London
October 2000

contents

Jennifer Angwin is a Senior Lecturer in the Faculty of Education, Deakin University. Her research interests include adult and community-based education for early school leavers of all ages, and the possibilities for this sector of educational provision. She is also developing online professional development activities for isolated rural and regional teachers working in the post-compulsory sector of education and training.

Catherine Beavis is a Senior Lecturer in the School of Social and Cultural Studies in the Faculty of Education, Deakin University. Her teaching and research focus on literacy, postprimary English, literature, popular culture and reading. Special interests include the implications of popular culture for the curriculum, and the use of contemporary literary theory in the secondary English classroom.

Gerry Bloustien is a Lecturer in the School of Communication and Information Studies, University of South Australia. She has published internationally on youth and gender issues and is the editor of *Musical Visions*, a book on popular music. Apart from her work on youth, her most recent work has extended into projects that explore the impact of new communication technologies on film, music, youth leisure activities and health industries.

Lindsay Fitzclarence is currently working in the Division of Education, Arts and Social Sciences at the University of South Australia. Prior to this, Lindsay worked in Education at Deakin University and was also a physical education teacher. He continues to maintain an interest in the study of sport and physical activity and at the same time has published in the areas of education and violence, and youth culture.

Lyn Harrison is a Lecturer in Health and Physical Education at Deakin University. Previous to this she was a Research Fellow at the Australian Research Centre in Sex, Health and Society / National Centre in HIV Social Research, La Trobe University, Melbourne. For the past five years she has been involved in research on adolescent risk-taking and HIV/AIDS, and community and school-based sexuality education.

Christopher Hickey is a Lecturer in the Faculty of Education at Deakin University and has a strong research interest in the education and socialisation of young males. This work has focused on the links between identity formation, masculinity and the role played by sport, physical activity and popular culture. He has undertaken extensive research around the behaviours and rationalisations of young males as members of peer groups.

Peter Kelly is currently a Lecturer in Social and Behavioural Studies at the University of Queensland. His intellectual interest is in the forms and processes of institutionalised intellectual abstraction which take Youth as their object, and the consequences for Youth, in terms of surveillance, intervention and regulation, which flow from this expert problematisation of all aspects of their lives.

Julie McLeod is a Lecturer in the Faculty of Education, Deakin University, where she has also been a Lecturer in Women's Studies. She has taught and published on the sociology of gender and the social, historical and cultural context of education. Her research interests include feminist and social theory in educational research, and studies of subjectivity. She is conducting (with Lyn Yates) a qualitative, longitudinal study of secondary school students.

Karen Malone is Asia-Pacific Director, UNESCO-MOST Growing Up In Cities project and Senior Lecturer in Science and Environmental Education at Monash University. She has taught and published widely in the multidisciplinary field of children's environments, urban planning and participatory action. Recently she was editor of a special edition of the international journal *Local Environment*, focusing on children, youth and urban environments.

Maria Pallotta-Chiarolli is Lecturer in the School of Health Sciences at Deakin University and has published widely on ethnicity, gender, sexuality and HIV/STDs in education and health. Her publications include *Someone You Know* about a friend with AIDS (Wakefield Press, 1991; new edition, August 2000); *Girls Talk: Young women speak their hearts and minds* (Finch Publishing, 1998); and *Tapestry* (Random House, 1999).

Johanna Wyn is Associate Professor and Director of the University of Melbourne's Youth Research Centre. She has published widely in her main areas of research on the educational needs and career pathways of young people, and in youth health promotion. Her most recent book is called *Rethinking Youth* (co-authored with Rob White 1997) published by Sage, and Allen and Unwin.

Lyn Yates is Professor of Teacher Education at the University of Technology, Sydney, and convenor of the Change and Education Research Group (CERG) in that faculty. Her main research interests are in inequalities, social change, subjectivities and Australian education policy and practice. She is currently completing (with Julie McLeod) a seven-year qualitative, longitudinal study of young people from 12 to 18.

Julie McLeod and Karen Malone

introduction

How do we "do" research on and about young people? What interpretative and methodological dilemmas are raised by taking "young people" as a focus of inquiry? Does youth research entail distinctive approaches, questions and modes of analysis? And what are the specific characteristics, and truth claims, of the field of inquiry described as youth research or youth studies?

These are some of the questions that prompted this collection of essays, shaped by initial conversations among the contributors. The volume grew out of a research conference held in the Faculty of Education at Deakin University in 1998, where a number of scholars were invited to discuss their own research projects on – or about or with – young people, or on the category of "youth" and "youth studies". Participants critically reflected on methodological and interpretative dilemmas explored in their research, and considered how their research experience might illuminate broader debates in youth research. This collection thus explores methodological issues in the field of youth studies, interrogates how we research youth, and links these discussions to contemporary theoretical debates in the social sciences. It includes papers presented at the conference as well as chapters subsequently requested.

Attending to questions of how "youth" is researched and represented underlines that youth is not a self-evidently natural category, that it is "produced", and that it signifies as much a focus for inquiry and category of concern (popular, policy, adult, etc.), as it does a period in people's lives. At the same time, we are cognisant that, as a description of young people, youth has strong connotations, evoking persistent gender and class-based images – typically of working-class and/or delinquent young men. In this sense, the terms "youth" or "youths" seem unable to capture the specificity of young women's experiences, and therefore risks eliding the feminine. While youth is a term now used increasingly to denote both male and female young people, its masculine lineage persists. It is quite uncommon to hear youth as a noun on its own to describe young women – when it refers to one gender, it is invariably male. Groups of young women are more likely to be described as "girls", an infantalising description that also suggests some of the difficulties in representing youthful femininity. Further, the discursive association of youth with "delinquent" or undesirable young men, is also underlined (unwittingly) by certain kinds of youth research that have sought to document (celebrate, bemoan) the dangerous, reckless and risky conduct of young people.

Yet, despite such problematic connotations, the term "youth" is a powerful signifier, and has strong currency in academic, policy and popular discussions about young people. What it means to research, to construct, to analyse, to represent "youth" – and all the complexity, elisions, ambiguities and resonances this involves – are key questions for this book.

While each of the chapters in this volume considers and works with different methodologies, the book is not intended as a research manual, a kind of "how to do it in six easy steps" tool kit for researchers. Rather, each of the chapters addresses the framing questions in a different way, illustrating some of the possibilities, as well as problems and dilemmas, in researching youth. Most chapters include a discussion of a particular research project, question or methodology, that is located not only in relation to larger social, empirical or theoretical debates, but also keeps in focus the specific challenges posed by researching or theorising about young people today.

Research on young people encompasses a diverse range of topics and interests, including youth and popular culture, labour market and school participation, and studies of young people "at risk". Work on "youth" continues to proliferate, as is evident in the recent publication of numerous overviews and edited collections (e.g. Skelton & Valentine 1998; Wyn & White 1997; Cohen 1997) and the establishment of a new international journal dedicated to scholarship in youth studies (*Journal of Youth Studies*). Further, the growing interest in youth studies is not confined to the halls of academia, though they remain important sites for the production of knowledge about young people. Youth studies is also marked by a strong "will to know", animated by the concerns and questions of policy-makers, youth advocacy workers and agencies, educators, labour market analysts as well as academics. This range of interests (with all its intended or unintended, desirable or dangerous effects) is central to the formation of the field of "youth studies". The chapters here are interdisciplinary, engaging with youth studies, with related fields of inquiry, such as education and cultural studies, and with theoretical debates from, for example, feminist, postcolonial, poststructuralist or Foucauldian work. These chapters thus represent work on diverse projects. However, once assembled, several thematic clusters or foci emerge around identity, gender, educational experiences and pathways, disadvantage and risk, dangerous spaces, and discussions of how to represent social, sexual and class relations among young people.

In the opening chapter, Gerry Bloustien explores the representation and constitution of the (gendered) self as it is negotiated through the lens of a video camera. She draws upon an intensive 14-month ethnographic study of a disparate group of female adolescents in Adelaide, South Australia, who documented on video what they saw as important facets of their lives. The videos crossed between private and public space, but she focuses the discussion primarily on the realm of the domestic, looking closely at the way perceptions and negotiation of private space, particularly bedroom space, are managed in very different social contexts and by girls from quite diverse cultural backgrounds. Processes of selfrepresentation are also addressed by Lyn Harrison in her chapter on 'Representing sexual hegemony: Focus groups and governmentality'. She notes the popularity of focus groups as a strategy for investigating opinions and attitudes, and argues that we need now to consider the specific types of knowledge and power relations produced within focus groups. Using data from single-sex focus groups conducted by researchers at the National Centre in HIV Social Research, Harrison examines the ways in which young people represent their sexuality as well as the ways in which researchers use these data to re-present "truths" about young people's identities.

In 'Coming out/going home: Australian girls and young women interrogating racism and heterosexism', Maria Pallotta-Chiarolli focuses on young women and girls' written and visual representations of self, and explores how they negotiate their sexuality, ethnicity and gender. The chapter analyses the processes of "coming out" and "going home" in the lives of young women and illustrates the public and private strategies girls and young women are devising in order to resist ethnocentric, racist and heterosexist educational structures and pedagogies. It offers rich insights into the ways in which young women represent their multi-layered lives and identities. Julie McLeod's chapter reflects on the popularity of both "identity" as an object of inquiry, and of research interviews as a favoured strategy for investigating identity. Drawing on interviews conducted for a longitudinal study of young people, McLeod discusses a number of interpretative dilemmas encountered in trying to represent identity as "in process" and in attempting to combine both a developmental and sociological perspective on the self. The chapter particularly focuses on gender identity, and this theme is also developed by Johanna Wyn in her discussion of 'The post-modern girl'. Wyn explores how girls' identities are constructed in relation to schooling and to their experiences and expectations of educational success. A particular focus of the chapter is the intersection of class and gender relations in constructing the idea of the "clever girl", and Wyn examines what is distinctive about processes and patterns of identity construction today compared to growing up as a young woman in the 1950s or 1970s. She also considers how the changes associated with "late modernity" have disrupted linear views of the transition from youth to adulthood or from school to work force, arguing that: "Young identities are formed in relation to the relationships young people have with consumption, leisure, family and work, as well as education, *while they are still at school*" (p.68 in the text).

Perceptions of cleverness and academic success are also examined by Georgina Tsolidis in her discussion of the "relationship between processes of ethnic identification and educational aspiration, attainment and experience" (p.71 in the text). Drawing on a school-based study (with findings derived from both surveys and interviews), Tsolidis analyses the ways in which young people construct a dichotomy between being "cool" and being academically successful. This study raises a number of issues concerning ethnic minorities and academic achievement, the effects of globalisation, and diasporic communities and education. She argues that young people from communities with a historic experience of diasporic existence hold the possibility of creating a third space between the academic and mainstream popular culture, a space in which academic success is not seen as inevitably at odds with popular culture's demand to be cool. Jennifer Angwin's chapter provides a further perspective on notions of educational success and young people's identity formation through education and training. She discusses a research project undertaken in a Victorian provincial city with young people enrolled in VET (Vocational Education and Training) programs, and with VET providers, and reflects on some of the dilemmas encountered in trying to develop a participatory action research approach when working with young people for whom educational failure, rather than success, was a common experience. She poses the question: "Within the totalising research and policy discourses which dominate VET, is it possible to present the voices of disengaged and educationally disadvantaged young people?" (p.97 in the text). She asks whether even the best-intentioned project can only "yet again, reproduce a deficit view of early school leavers, and continue to marginalise young people ..." (p.97 in the text).

In 'Youth as an artefact of expertise', Peter Kelly draws on Foucauldian analyses to argue that adult anxieties about youth as "dangerous" and expert knowledges (including academic

and policy research) about youth have been central in producing youth as a site of governmental regulation. He proposes that the representation of youth, and the attendant
construction of truths about youth, are implicated in the regulation of populations of young
people, populations which are rendered knowable in all their diversity only through these
processes of representation. Kelly focuses particularly on the institutional and abstract nature
of these processes. Adult concerns about young people often fixate on the feared effects of
risky and dangerous behaviours. Catherine Beavis, in her chapter 'Youth culture and the texts
of the new technologies', analyses the dominant debates about young people's engagement
with digital texts – from the representation of computer games as signifying violence and
danger, and threatening to corrupt and undermine young people and families, to the representation of new technologies as sites for generating new forms of literacy and cultural
practice. In both cases, Beavis discusses the alleged effects – detrimental, emancipatory – of
digital culture on identity formation, particularly in relation to the representation and
formation of young men and of masculinity. She analyses policy and popular discourses as
well as the claims of poststructuralist research for the possibilities afforded by techno-literacy.

Christopher Hickey and Lindsay Fitzclarence also explore constructions of masculinity,
looking particularly at generational difference and at patterns and processes of socialisation
and of communication. They suggest that for many young people, and especially for young
men, there has been a "communication breakdown" and, drawing on elements of "narrative
therapy" they propose a pedagogy for developing "conversational flow". A particular focus of
the chapter is the relationship between masculinity, sport and violence. Drawing on their own
classroom research, they illustrate how their pedagogical approach can help young people to
develop new ways of seeing and talking about gender and violence, and encourage more open
and respectful dialogue. Working with young people to effect change is also a focus of Karen
Malone's chapter. Using a multidisciplinary and multi-method approach to data collection,
and drawing from findings from two Australian sites of an international participatory action
research project, Malone explores the impact of a "climate of fear" on young people's spatial
behaviour. She discusses how "moral panics" informed by "underclass ideologies" have
brought into focus conflicts over space use and the introduction of forces to segregate and
purify space. Malone argues that, fuelled by stereotypical representations of urban youth as
dangerous predators, this global phenomenon of segregation is a product of late modernity
and is determined in terms of age, ethnicity and class. She proposes that in order to reveal the
multiplicity of the youth environmental experience, methods of enquiry need to be designed
that include mapping the micro-geographies of youth.

Lyn Yates considers some of the dilemmas involved in trying to focus on "class" in qualitative research and on the issue of what exactly it is that we are representing when we talk
about class, and how it compares to other social forms such as gender and ethnicity. She
considers such dilemmas in relation to debates and trends in recent qualitative research and
theorising on class, and in relation to a longitudinal qualitative study of young people that
she and Julie McLeod are conducting. Although what is meant by class, or how we represent
class when studying young people is problematic, nevertheless, Yates argues, "working with
the concepts and theories associated with 'class' does ... help to illuminate 'individual' ways
of being, and relationships between individuals and education" (p.160 in the text).

Together, the chapters in this volume engage with important methodological and interpretative questions concerned with how to "research youth", and offer reflective and
challenging responses. The empirical focus of the chapters offer insights about "Australian

youth" at the turn of the twentieth century, but the methodological and theoretical issues that are addressed resonate further afield, speaking across disciplines and national boundaries.

Acknowledgments

This volume of essays, and the conference which preceded it, were made possible by the generous assistance and support of many people. We would like to thank the conference participants and all the authors for their enthusiasm and patience, and for their willingness to respond promptly to the inevitable "deadline" calls. The conference was organised by Karen and Julie while they were both Postdoctoral Research Fellows in the Faculty of Education at Deakin University. The Deakin Centre for Education and Change provided financial assistance, as well as wonderful administrative support. We thank in particular the then Director of DCEC, Jane Kenway; and Angela Bloomer and Miranda Hughes for assistance above and beyond the call of duty. Miranda Hughes also provided valuable editorial assistance. We are grateful to the Graduate School of Research in the Faculty of Education and to the Director, Terry Evans, for their encouragement and financial support for the conference. The Deakin Youth, Physicality and Health Research Group contributed funds and has been an important forum for debating myriad issues about youth research. The early stages of planning the conference benefited from discussions with Jane Kenway and Peter Kelly. We thank Debbie Esptein for kindly accepting our invitation to write a Foreword for the volume. Geraldine Burke transformed the ideas from the book into a stunning collage, and we thank her for designing the cover. The editorial and publishing staff at the Australian Clearinghouse for Youth Studies, especially Sheila Allison and Sue Headley, offered clear guidance and expert advice. Finally, we would like to acknowledge the ongoing support for research provided by the Faculties of Education at Deakin and Monash universities, where Julie and Karen now respectively work.

References

Cohen, P. 1997, *Rethinking the Youth Question: Education, labour and cultural studies*, Macmillan, London.
Skelton, T. & Valentine, G. 1998, *Cool Places: Geographies of youth cultures*, Routledge, London.
Wyn, J. & White, R. 1997, *Rethinking Youth*, Allen & Unwin, Sydney.

Gerry Bloustien

Teddy bear chains and violent femmes: Play, video cameras and the negotiation of (gendered) space

This is my Lost Forest. It is not so much a place that is lost but a place where I can remember. This is where I can remember how to be a child

Hilary

THE central focus of this chapter draws on the serious nature of play,[1] together with the concept of "body-space" (see Duncan 1996) – that is, how play creates, enables, hinders and negotiates space through bodily praxis (Bourdieu & Wacquant 1992; Moore 1994). Specifically, it explores some of the ways in which a specific time and place can seem more "open" for play in what Battaglia (1995) describes as the "rhetorics of self-making" in the experiences of the young women in my fieldwork. Ten teenagers were participants in an intensive ethnographic study, which took place over the period of three years, from when they were about 15 years old. The young women spent 14 months of this time videoing their own worlds, whenever and however they liked; they had complete control over the selection, filming and editing of their everyday lives.[2]

Research and methodology[3]

In the wider ethnographic research, from which this chapter is drawn, I was exploring the everyday lived experiences of 10 teenage girls through their own eyes.[4] The participants were deliberately drawn from diverse ethnic and socioeconomic backgrounds and all of the original 10 have stayed with the project, which began in 1993, until 1996.[5] The girls were invited to document on video any aspects of their lives that they considered important. I assured them that they would have complete control over the selection, filming, style, and editing and that if they wished, we would screen their edited videos publicly at a student film festival.[6]

The girls were given no funding or specific direction on ways of using the camera beyond the fundamentals.[7] It was emphasised that they were free to video what they liked and how they liked, although I would be willing to show them specific video techniques if they requested them. No-one requested help or any more guidance in how to use the camera. The camera, which was lent to them by the university free of charge, was a compact Hi8 "superior" domestic camera. I deliberately chose this camera for its low-light capacity, its near-broadcast video quality and its small size so that it would seem as unobtrusive as possible in the girls' lives.[8]

The research examined the way each girl chose to interpret, negotiate and challenge her perceptions; the way she explored her developing sense of self and her relationships with the various social institutions in which she was engaged. The range of stylistic approaches that each girl seemed to explore at different times was quite wide. I found that the girls' use of the medium reflected their knowledge of aspects of music video; parodies of David Attenborough-style documentaries, or mock current affairs formats investigating this strange human species: "the teenage girl". At other times, I noticed that there were more serious attempts to document the fun, the movement and excitement of their social engagements by using hand-held camera techniques. At these moments, the camera was in the middle of the activity rather than being the voyeur.

Significantly, what emerged from the videos and the filmic processes, through the perceptual frames and boundaries the individuals placed upon themselves, were the ways in which the girls acknowledged their particular social and cultural constraints. For the girls, the camera became a tool for interpreting and redefining their worlds. Not everything in their world was for public viewing. Not everything was selected for recording in the first place. Not everything was videoed in the same way. I argue that the selection, the filming and the editing processes highlighted the way the girls struggled to represent themselves in ways that cohered with their already established social and cultural frameworks. On the surface, such attempts at representation seemed like "just play", but under closer scrutiny we can see specific strategies, "the human seriousness of play" (Levi Strauss 1966; Goffman 1970; Turner 1982; Handelman 1990), providing insights as to the way gendered subjectivity is performed and simultaneously constituted. This indeed, is identity as *process* (Hall 1996) with popular culture (especially television, film and music) playing a vitally important role in its production.

Identity as process: play and mimesis

Engagement with popular culture, especially for young people, is a complex dialectic activity, one that oscillates repeatedly between total engagement and a balancing, knowing *distanciation* (Willett 1964).[9] From my observations and understandings of the young women in my study, I perceived this involvement with popular culture to be a deeply engrossing, *embodied* play – a "deep play" (Geertz 1975 (1973)), an experimentation with aesthetics, form and image that was infused with meaning. There was no total unthinking abandonment to pleasure, although there were moments of disengagement with the everyday. Nor was it the play of people who believe that their actions could be, in some way, ultimately politically subversive. I argue that a legitimate scepticism interfused this play. It was the scepticism of those who know that they too can create images and knowledge but that ultimately, the illusion was just that, "play". It was not so much about changing the rules, or of calculatedly implementing strategies, but rather, having "a sense of the game" (Bourdieu 1977, 1990; Bourdieu & Wacquant 1992). It was evidence of "the rhetorics of self-making" (Battaglia 1995) – deliberate and dramatic strategies employed for simultaneously representing and constituting the self. Seen in this light, we can see that play has a very serious function indeed.

Here, then, I am using the concept of *play* to describe a particular *process* of representation and identification; strategies that incorporate, reflect on and depict the individual everyday experiences and perspectives of growing up female in Adelaide, South Australia, in the mid 1990s. The introduction of the camera in my fieldwork, offered this "symbolic" space to play, to experiment – as I shall detail below – but, simultaneously, it highlighted the usual difficulties and constraints the girls experienced in their search for "alternative selves" (Schechner 1993, p.39).[10] The effect of such self-reflexivity and self-making, both on and off the camera, offered fascinating insights into the way each person negotiated and constituted her sense of (gendered) self. Obviously, this self-making occurred within both domestic and more public locales. Here, I am limiting my focus to only four of the participants, Hilary, Diane, Sara and Grace,[11] exploring the particular ways in which their bedroom spaces proved so central to the simultaneous constitution and representation of the self, both in front of, and away from the camera's eye.

My own private space

For all of teenagers involved in the study, their bedrooms represented an arena of great significance and personal reflexivity. It was "a place where you can really be yourself" (Belinda) or in Diane's words, "my own private space". Each participant's video included a section where she visually explored her own bedroom through the lens of the video camera. Sometimes this inquiry was quite explicit with a verbal commentary in voice-over and sometimes it was not remarked on, beyond the camera's gaze. In most cases, each person seemed to see her room as a reflection and extension of her own individual personality and taste. Yet, it was clear on closer observation, that the choices, which determined the style and ambience of the space, were very much in keeping with her familial and wider social values. That is, I argue that each bedroom reflected wider, underlying power relations within which the teenager was already enmeshed. Through her own distinctive appropriation of fantasy and play, each would carefully negotiate these relations from within these arenas of symbolic power. I begin with a brief visit to Hilary's room where, as cited above, she "could remember how to be a child".

Hilary's room: revisiting the Lost Forest

Although her house was quite small, Hilary had her own bedroom. Organised and academically-able, she portrayed this through the immaculate appearance of her room. Yet, among the academic books and the more adult icons, were hints of a childhood nostalgically idealised. There were, for example, several romantic images of fairies, wizards and pixies decorating this space. Significant in themselves, these little snippets of fantasy seemed to herald the greater importance of Hilary's "Lost Forest".

Under the built-in wardrobe in her bedroom lay a small, hidden, secluded cellar. Hilary had decorated this tiny area with rugs, candles and magical symbols. Naming it the Lost Forest,[12] she transformed the space into a dramatic room of fantasy. She would take her friends down there or used it as a place in which to be quietly alone.

Outside the Lost Forest, even within her bedroom proper, was an adult world of certainty, responsibility and order. Inside seemed richly dense with unspoken possibilities, a place still seemingly in the process of evolving into something else. Unlike her more "public" rational world of control, this area was self-consciously sensual, crowded with emotion and romance.

The rugs, semi-darkness of the candles, pungent odour of incense made a space of the body. This was where the "civilised" body experienced the sensations it had been encouraged to distrust and disregard (Elias 1978 (1939)). To reach the Lost Forest she had to enter through a trap door that was too small for adults to enter easily, perhaps reinforcing her self-awareness of her still young, physical immaturity. Yet this area, separated physically from her more "disciplined" self, was still kept neatly contained and containable. While seemingly dramatic and alternative, a manifestation of the "child" to Hilary's usual portrayal of the "adult", the contrast between this and the "everyday" seemed all too consciously articulated for it to be a repressed aspect of her psyche.

First, the Lost Forest represented a space that was, simultaneously, physical, mental and social (Lefebvre 1991, pp.11-12). It was simultaneously a "real-and-imagined space" (Soja 1985, 1996), both a place of liminoid mimetic blurring (the imagined, the "not-real") and yet also one that is carefully marked out as a discrete territory (the geographically "real"). Indeed, it seemed to demand a redefining of space and thus an unsettling of some of the frequently simplistic ways in which space is categorised.

Second, I would argue that the Lost Forest was a manifestation of the powerful quality of "serious play". It was a way of creating an idealised past in the middle of an uncertain and often scary future. This brief account of Hilary's "space to play" underpins the main arguments in this paper.

Place as spaces of power relations

Every geographical place is actually experienced as a space of power relations (Duncan 1996, p.4). Space cannot simply be understood as geographical or material boundaries, as "realities that can be touched with the finger" (Bourdieu & Wacquant 1992, p.228). Rather geographic space needs to be appreciated as "a space of relations", an arena of potential struggle for "symbolic power" (Bourdieu 1991). Inevitably, that means that space is implicitly gendered, exclusive and is frequently contradictory (see, for example, Massey 1994; Lefebvre 1991; Gregory & Urry 1985; Soja 1985, 1996) and can have far-reaching consequences in the way specific individuals experience their surroundings.

Even within the home, conceptions of what constitutes "private space" are not uniform. In my research, it was clear that teenagers from less affluent families had less physical domestic space at their disposal than those from more materially privileged homes. The teenagers from separated homes or blended families, where they occupied two or more dwelling places, thought of their bedroom spaces in different ways from the those who had only one such space to call their own. Most of the Aboriginal teenagers shared their rooms with other members of their family or were expected to give up their rooms regularly for a visiting relative. So, clearly a particular room, such as a bedroom, was not necessarily equally "private" for all people in the household. Equally, the concept of "private space" itself is not a universal, understood across all cultures or even within one culture. An individual's social positioning within her micro-culture of family or immediate social networks affects her under-standing of space. For some, the notion of personal or individual "private space" is a right. For others, the concept just does not exist (Sciama 1993, p.87). Some of this complexity and paradox underlies the words of 15-year-old Diane, as she described her room as "her own private space".

Diane's room: teddy bear chains and Peter André

Both on and off camera, Diane seemed quite restrained in her demeanour and in her activities, and yet she believed that she was not confined at all. In describing her bedroom as her "own private space" she seemed to believe that she possessed her own exclusive arena where she could be free to experiment, where "I can do literally what I want to". Yet in many ways, Diane's room seemed far from an independent "free space". It was, for example, manifestly cluttered with many artefacts and consumables common to an Anglo-Australian 1990s girlhood; there were pink and white china ornaments, dolls, a teddy-bear chain and several posters of neat male pop stars decorating the walls and surfaces of her room. This "private space" seemed to reflect a very conventional, heterosexually-oriented female childhood or early teenage-hood rather than be an area in which to test out any ideas that were different from her family's.

Furthermore, due to limited space, Diane's bedroom seemed to be all too easily accessible to others to be truly "a room of her own" (Woolf 1929; Rose 1993). Seemingly, then, this was hardly an expression of adolescent experimentation; there were no rebellious images of teenage-hood here![13] Rather, her room portrayed both nostalgic images of childhood while simultaneously cohering with the particular adult values in which she was enmeshed.

I turn now to Sara's room. She too constituted her sense of self through a distinctive use of fantasy while reflecting the established values of her own familial and immediate social networks.

Sara's room: into the dragon's lair

Sara's home was situated 45 minutes out of the city of Adelaide. The nearest public transport was more than another 45 minutes down a narrow country lane. This difficulty of access meant that while she could walk the long trek to the bus stop by day, night-time activities were severely curtailed.

The two-storey brick home itself was at the end of a private dirt road, atop a narrow winding, quite hazardous track. The house was in fact still being constructed; there were many pieces of equipment and building tools lying around the outside of the house.

The family of four lived in the small finished section of the house downstairs. The large main living room, which was used for cooking, eating, studying, talking, watching television and working on various assignments had all available areas cluttered with items. Books, papers, and tools were strewn around all possible surfaces. As this main living area led straight into Sara's bedroom, inevitably most of the household clutter spread itself into that room too.

Ostensibly, her door barely separated Sara's area from the rest of the house. It even lacked a handle. Yet there were several ways in which Sara did attempt metaphorically to carve out privacy for herself in a domestic arena, which was not able to offer her much material "space to play". First, on her bedroom walls were small photographs of close friends, a huge poster of the film *Chaplin* ("because Charlie Chaplin is such a great actor"), and a collection of magazine photos of Australian actor Gary Sweet. Above her bed, there was a very exotic poster of a ferocious dragon. Sara said that the dragon was, like herself, from Nepal and angry. Like Hilary's Lost Forest, it seemed that here was an alternative aspect of Sara's self that she wanted to explore and portray. She usually presented herself to me as very amicable and rarely ruffled, so apart from this statement, anger was not an aspect of her personality I had ever experienced, on or off camera.

Sara marked out her symbolic boundaries in several other ways too. First, she would physically shift her bedroom furniture around. Every time I visited I would find that the bed or cupboard would be moved so that the perspective of the room appeared to be completely new. Second, she created a mental space for her imagination. There was always loud music and the unusual pungency of the incense filling the physical spaces of her room, creating a distinctive aural and olfactory atmosphere. Then there was the deliberate use of her bed and the outside balcony that encompassed the house, as spaces "to think in". Sara drew attention to these areas through the video camera and still photographs

> I spend a great deal of time and enjoy thinking here. I can be private here.
>
> Sara

She would frequently sit outside on a huge chair looking at the surrounding bushland and sunsets. There were several still camera shots taken by her of the bed, the landscape and of the chair itself.

Yet at the same time, it is clear that the territory which Sara symbolically carved out as her own within the domestic arena, did not vary too greatly from her established familial values. It was "distinctive" in Bourdieu's (1984) terms while maintaining *"différance"* (as in the concepts developed by Derrida 1978; see also Hall 1996). Although Sara's parents were born in Australia, they had long been practising Buddhists. Their decision to adopt Sara from Nepal was part of their expression of attachment to that country and its values. Thus, the incense, the images and photos on her walls are all perfectly in tune with her adoptive parents' ideals and Buddhist affiliations. At the same time, there was just enough "playing" at the borders of these values through the loud music, the shifting furniture, the freedom to day-dream and fantasise on her bed and balcony to allow her to feel she had a room of her own. I will return to the importance of fantasy for creating symbolic boundaries, but first, there is a third room I want to visit. Like Sara, Grace had little physical space with which to play.

Grace's room: smelly teddies and violent femmes

Grace spent a great deal of her time looking after her younger brother. It was a duty she resented, unlike Diane, who when her mother had to go into hospital, was happy to "play mum for a while". She saw herself as emotionally independent of her mother, capable of making all her own decisions, even though at the beginning of the fieldwork period she was still living at home.[14] Unlike some of the teenagers, such as Hilary, who saw herself as an equal adult to her mother ("my Mum is my best friend"), Grace saw herself as parent within her family unit.[15] Yet, her own room revealed a fascinating juxtaposition of child and adult. Whereas Hilary kept these aspects of her self carefully separated, in Grace's room they seemed to collide with a disconcerting violence.

One of the first things that Grace decided to record of her room was her collection of toys, squashed together in an exuberant display on her bookcase shelves. Teddy bears, old dolls, soft furry animals were individually and lovingly introduced to the video camera.

> These are my smelly teddies [holding three tiny toys up to the camera]. They were given to me by my grandmother for my birthday. They each have a different smell.

Grace also spent a great deal of time carefully attempting to video the adhesive stars on her ceiling and her little statues of fairies. Like Hilary, Grace's bedroom was full of such icons of romance. And yet, interspersed with such magical visions were images of quite brutal violence. Grace was a fan of nihilistic and aggressive music with violent lyrics. Many of her posters, promoting the bands or the albums, depicted quite gruesome scenes. For example, one, of a band called Rage Against the Machine, included a graphic image of a Buddhist priest passively ablaze after immolating himself in a political protest.

This strange juxtaposition of romantic child-like images and adult aggression was further enhanced when Grace talked on camera about the illicit drug use of her social group. She sat facing the video chatting knowledgeably about the effects of particular amphetamines or hallucinogens, with carefully selected music of The Violent Femmes (her favourite rock band) playing from her tapes in the background. As she talked, she hugged her favourite large fluffy toy. The effect for me, an adult observer, was quite disturbing and surreal as I watched the careful balancing of contradictory worlds without any apparent sense of conflict or irony by the user.

So far, I have briefly described how four teenagers, Diane, Hilary, Sara and Grace, attempted to create symbolic boundaries within their domestic worlds. All the rooms I have described so far incorporated images of fantasy and the young women primarily focused on this iconography when they made their videos or talked about their rooms. These symbols can be considered as interrelated aspects of fantasy; as practical nostalgia, as New Age Romanticism and as Serious Play and Mimetic Excess. I will examine each more closely for the importance of such imagery within each cultural context.

Fantasy as practical nostalgia

On the one hand, it is clear that for each young woman such iconography represented a nostalgic return to childhood. If we understand that, for many, the move into adulthood represented an ambivalent process that was uncertain and in many ways, threatening, then such images can be seen to represent a desire for an idealised past. Such nostalgia may be more than a desire or a sentiment for something that has passed. It is embodied, efficacious and practical.[16]

Nostalgia may in fact be a vehicle of knowledge, rather than only a yearning for something lost. It may be practised in diverse ways. It is not simply longing or an imaginary step back to another time and place that seems more "real" or authentic, but an engagement with a different kind of "other" that opens up more possibilities. Because it seems a familiar, comfortable "other", it can reproduce emotions, which as Battaglia (1995, p.93) observes, "opens subjects to creative reconfiguration: nostalgic practice invites self-problematisation". Like mimesis, through which nostalgia is often realised, such revisiting of the past offers the power to reposition the individual with the present. It offers what both Michael Taussig (1993) and Homi Bhabha (1990) have called "slippage" and ambivalence, a temporary step into the subjunctive in order to reassess the material present.

The discourse of mimicry is constructed around an ambivalence; in order to be effective, mimicry must continually produce its slippage, its excess, its difference (Bhabha 1990, p.125).

The related way that the images of fantasy can be understood is as an aspect of New Age Romanticism.

Fantasy as new age romanticism

As indicated earlier, stylised pictures and posters of magical figures prominently decorated many of the teenagers' bedrooms. These images were quite sophisticated rather than childlike, straightforward representations. In their pastel colouring and wispy indeterminate outlines the characters were very other-worldly indeed. They were also minimally gendered and in fact, more often, androgynous in depiction. The figures seemed very much linked to a New Age Romanticism of spirituality and other "otherworldliness" with their flowing hair, medieval clothing and ethereal quality. For many of the young women, such aesthetics were perfectly in tune with their parents' ongoing adherence to "grass-roots" socialism and environmentalism. The New Age Movement, like the former Hippy movement of the 1960s, represented a desire to abandon materialism and embrace a new vision of what appeared to be a universal "communitas" (see, for example, Turner 1969, pp.94–164; Handelman 1990, pp.88).

Of course, fairies have long been associated with young girls and childhood, but these teenagers between the ages of 13 and 16 did not see themselves as children but rather as Douglas (1984 (1966), p.95) suggests "marginal beings; those left out from the patterning of society". In Allison James' (1986) words they are "nobodies"; that is, too old to be classified as children and too young to be considered adults. These teenagers were young women hovering on the brink of adulthood, as it were, developing physiologically but not quite there emotionally yet! Their age and personal circumstances meant that some had far more freedom of movement and choice than others. The iconography and discourses, drawn from the New Age movement and expressed in the posters and drawings that decorated some of their bedrooms, seemed to allow a certain symbolic bridging between childhood and adulthood. They seemed to permit an expression and exploration of this liminoid stage of their lives. New Age symbolism often embodies, in the words of Dennis Hall (1994, p.13), "a self-conscious experience of the indeterminate, the decentred and the transitional ... that deliberately eludes the chains of definition".

In the bedrooms of many of the participants of my research project, such symbolism very distinctively lined their walls. The fairy figures in these posters were all young adults with long flowing blond hair and waif-like ethereal bodies in the midst of pastoral forests and idyllic greenery. Complementing such images were usually many colourful candles, music, incense and adhesive tiny florescent stars on the ceilings. Thus, the magical element in their pictures seemed to be part of a much larger representation of fantasy – a semi-mysterious world that often seemed to sit uneasily with the newly acquired demands and responsibilities of imminent adulthood. It was another aspect of the management of uncertain subjectivities

Music associated with New Age ideology also reflects the desire to "confuse boundaries", and as Hall (1994, p.17) indicates, "exhibits the spirit of playfulness, the taste for irony and the penchant for quotation or textual looting associated with postmodernism". Other writers have noted the links between the New Age movement and concepts of "wholeness, spirituality, relationships, self healing, universal brotherhood and sisterhood, creativity and oneness of the universe" (see, for example, Grove Hall 1994, p.23). These qualities, together with the many references to idealised childhood in popular music, suggest that the images of fairies and other remnants of childhood in the teenagers' rooms were not simply nostalgic. Rather they are "rooted in particular forms of ideology that have tended to elevate process over being, the inexplicable over the rational ... in a world where the self has become problematic" (Neustadter 1994a, p.65, 1994b).

Fantasy as serious play and mimetic excess

A third interrelated way of considering such iconography is to see it as representing another aspect of "serious play". The symbols of fantasy were a practical way of "feeling out" the ambivalent boundaries of the present either through the seemingly unchanging aesthetics and representations of a romanticised childhood past or through the fluid, ethereal quality of an idealised (spiritual) future. Either way, the shifting conceptions of time–space in these bedrooms through such symbolism, gave each place the necessary ambience of a "space to play". Yet, not every teenager drew upon such romantic imagery. Many had far more restrictions placed on them, either directly in terms of the decor of their rooms or in terms of the way they internalised the values within their homes. Sometimes in those situations, the symbolism had to be converted into dramatic excess, just as caricature can often more freely express and explore difference than realistic imagery can. Perhaps that is an explanation of Hilary's Lost Forest. Her carefully-delineated, recreated "childhood" can be interpreted as an example of mimetic excess (Taussig 1993). With others, such as Diane, the imagination is carefully contained within acceptable limits. As I indicated earlier, I will now return to Diane's room, which we visited previously. Now we can start to see how Diane's symbolic boundaries were also very carefully drawn indeed. Her bedroom was far more than simply an arbitrary reflection of a teenager's personal taste in music, fashion and style.

Diane's private space revisited

Diane began her video with a close reflexive look at her bedroom. As she filmed, she explained how her room reflected her interests and "obsessions" (her own word). She zoomed on the painted nameplate on her door and on to some old photos on her dressing table of herself at three and then at six, "at my mum's second marriage". Then she drew attention to her many posters of Peter André, Michael Jackson and other male pop stars. This was a very personal narrative.

As indicated earlier, her room was quite small, painted and decorated in pink and white. It had numerous soft fluffy toy animals and pretty china ornaments, but she did not comment verbally on these aspects. Rather, she used the camera to establish herself as "a really big fan" of her favourite musicians. She set up her tape-recorder to play their songs as background music as she filmed, turning down the volume at a strategic point so that she could then articulate her feelings of "fandom".

The gender relations in her family were very strictly defined and a very specific form of gendered identity was a constant topic of discussion. Even though finances were difficult, as her father was unemployed, the mother's role as housekeeper was considered paramount. Her parents described Diane to me as outgoing, sensible, domesticated and hard-working but perhaps too conscientious as far as school work was concerned; she was lauded and portrayed as an academic student, in contrast to the way in which her brother and most of her friends were discussed. Yet it was not considered particularly desirable for Diane to go on to tertiary studies. Rather Diane modelled herself along very traditional feminine lines, taking over the domestic routine when her mother was ill, "being Mum for a while" or looking after her brother who was older than she was.

These sharply delineated gender relations were constantly reinforced in family conversations. I was told of her brother's boss who continually "humiliated" the boys at work by calling them "hopeless girls". There were concerned, anxious family conversations around the kitchen table about teachers or students who were rumoured to be homosexual. Her brother and her father would frequently tease Diane about Peter André, whom they said "looked like a 'poof'". She herself was described by her parents through numerous little anecdotes (usually while she was in the room and part of the conversation) as extremely attractive.

The world outside the house was drawn for me in family discussions as morally lax, dangerous and violent. Most of Diane's acquaintances and school friends were described as being risk-takers and potentially antisocial because they drank and took drugs. The girls were "backstabbers" and their behaviour was promiscuous. Boyfriends were always represented as difficult conquests that had to be held on to like property or possessions. Boyfriends were also the means of cultural capital or status in Diane's world.

So in the discursive context of Diane's immediate social world it seems that what the teenager *did* have, in her "own private space", was the freedom to engage in particular teenage fantasies – but only as circumscribed by her familial situation. Her room reflected and reinforced these familial values of ideal womanhood and romanticised femininity through its pink colour, softness and prettiness, through the soft toys and ornaments. The fact that her room was only decorated with *male* stars was also significant. To be constituted firmly within female and feminine culture, as it was defined in her immediate world, there could be no hint or suggestion of an alternative sexual orientation. In Diane's home environment, judging by those intensive conversations around the kitchen table, this would be unthinkable and certainly unsayable.

Conclusion: containing the fantasy of private spaces

In this paper, I have explored the material and symbolic spaces which the teenagers in my fieldwork created as their own familial (and familiar) arenas for play. I drew together the significance and role of place in the process of play and the constitution of self, arguing that play is a negotiation of space, since space itself is a manifestation of power relations.

My particular research methodology, the use of the camera by the girls as a means to "play with" and "explore" possible identities through particular generic styles and televisual forms, was integral to this investigation. It provided insights into the girls' use of particular frameworks to explore their worlds and revealed why and when one particular style and narrative form was deemed appropriate at a particular time and why another was discarded. Rather than seeing these generic choices as arbitrary, a closer look reveals these aspects of play and fantasy as mimesis, as strategies to explore and constitute identity.

In this analysis I am rejecting the usual way of analysing film texts – even such home-produced artefacts – through film theory which draws on semiotic and psychoanalytic concepts (see, for example, Modleski 1988; Penley 1989; Williams 1983, 1989). Rather, I am exploring the relationship between identity and the camera through a different prism, drawing on notions of identity as *process* and utilising the concepts of play and mimesis.

I am emphasising the phenomenological and physiological effect that underlies film-making and viewing, rather than the cognitive and psychological.[17] Both the combined video and the huge amounts of individual raw footage from which the final film was compiled, facilitated each girl's own exploration and constitution of her sense of self. The small domestic video camera she used became a means of framing and reconstituting reality. The cinematic apparatus in this paradigm was not creating "an impression of reality" (Baudry 1986) but a palpable and disturbing power. Walter Benjamin calls this "the physical shock effect" which "disrupts the traditional, historically sedimented habits and expectations of vision; it undoes the transcendental and phenomenological structures that claimed to regulate perception and to ground and unify the ego" (quoted in Shaviro 1993).

Childhood and adolescence usually allows licence to play, and experiment and play, as we have seen, is a very serious, sometimes desperate, venture – a testing and stretching of boundaries to harness a sense of certainty. For the teenage participants in this study, their engagement with narrative style, genre and form in their own film-making indicated their searching for and struggle with their sense of shifting possible identities. Hilary's own reflective comments confirm such interpretation. At the end of the filming process she stated: "The film has shown me that change is the only certainty in life."

Play in this conception then becomes an integral aspect of self-making, However, such an understanding is complicated by the different ways each young woman experienced her own "microworld" and her own place within it. For some, these domestic arenas and their own bedrooms within the home, were described as their "own private space", a place where they believed they could experiment and explore other possible selves. This belief was reflected symbolically in the decor of their bedrooms such as the posters on their walls. Often it was manifested in the contents of their diaries, their cupboards and wardrobes, their activities and in the video footage. For others, this kind of "privacy" manifested through serious play was not possible or contemplated as "desirable". In the home, certainty reigned, manifested by an adherence to a particular and naturalised expression of values and behaviour. Experimentation outside of that discursive sphere was therefore limited.

In this way, I argue that for each young woman the concept of privacy was relative and symbolically bound by what her family and immediate social networks considered appropriate in her world. One teenager may believe she truly has a "private space" in spite of the fact that she has no desire or expectancy of experimenting anything else. In each case, it seemed, that the "individual" selves they attempted to reflect, by the choices in the decor of their rooms and by their activities within those spaces, reinforced familial values rather than challenged them.

References

Bateson, G. 1972, *Steps to an Ecology of Mind*, Chandler Publishing Company, SF.

—— 1979, *Mind and Nature*, Fontana, UK.

Battaglia, D. (ed.) 1995, *Rhetorics of Self-making*, University of California Press, Berkley, LA.

Baudry, J-L. 1986, 'Ideological effects of the basic cinematic apparatus' in *Narrative Apparatus and Ideology: A film theory reade*r, ed. P. Rosen, Columbia University Press, New York.

Bhabha, H. 1990, 'On mimicry and man: The ambivalence of colonial discourse', *October*, n.28, pp.125-33.

Bloustien, G. 1998, 'It's different to a mirror cos it talks to you' in *Wired Up: Young people and electronic media*, ed. S. Howard, Falmer Press, London.

—— 2001, 'Ceci n'est pas une jeune fille' in *Hop on Pop: The politics and pleasure of popular culture*, eds H. Jenkins, J. Feuer & T. Macpherson, Duke University Press, Durham, NC.

Bourdieu, P. 1977, *Outline of a Theory of Practice*, Cambridge University Press, Cambridge.

—— 1984, *Distinction: A social critique of the judgment of taste*, Harvard University Press, Cambridge, Mass.

—— 1990 (1980), *The Logic of Practice*, Polity Press, Cambridge.

—— 1991, *Language and Symbolic Power*, Polity Press, Cambridge.

Bourdieu, P. & Wacquant, L.J.D. 1992, *An Invitation to Reflexive Sociology*, University of Chicago Press, Chicago.

Caillois, R. 1961, *Man, Play and Games*, The Free Press, New York.

De Certeau, M. 1988, *The Practice of Everyday Life*, University of California Press, Berkeley.

Derrida, J. 1978, *Writing and Difference*, trans. A. Bass, Routledge, London.

Douglas, M. 1984 (1966), *Purity and Danger: An analysis of the concepts of pollution and taboo*, Routledge & Kegan Paul, London.

Drotner, K. 1994, 'Ethnographic enigmas: The everyday in recent media studies', *Cultural Studies*, v.8, n.2, pp.341-57.

Duncan, N. (ed.) 1996, *Body Space: Destabilizing geographies of gender and sexuality*, Routledge, London.

Elias, N. 1978 (1939), *The Civilizing Process Vol. 1: The history of manners*, Basil Blackwell, Oxford.

Fine, G.A. (ed.) 1987, *Meaningful Play: Playful meaning*, Proceedings of The 11th Annual Meeting of the Association for the Anthropological Study of Play (TAASP), Human Kinetics Publishers, Campaign, Illinois.

Geertz, C. 1975 (1973), 'Deep play: Notes on the Balinese Cockfight', in *The Interpretation of Cultures*, Hutchinson, London, pp.412-53.

Goffman, E. 1969 (1959), *The Presentation of Self in Everyday Life*, The Penguin Press, London.

—— 1970, *Strategic Interaction*, Blackwell, Oxford.

—— 1974, *Frame Analysis: An essay on the organisation of experience*, Harper & Row, New York.

Gregory, D. & Urry, J. (eds) 1985, *Social Relations and Spatial Structures*, Macmillan, London.

Grove Hall, S. 1994, 'New age music: An analysis of an ecstasy', *Popular Music and Society*, v.18, n.2, pp. 23-44.

Hall, D. 1994, 'New Age Music: a voice of liminality in postmodern culture', *Popular Music and Society*, summer, v.18, n.2, pp.13-22.

Hall, S. 1996, 'Music and identity' in *Questions of Cultural Identity*, eds S. Hall & P. du Gay, Sage Publications, London.

Hall, S. & Jefferson, B. (eds) 1976, *Resistance through Rituals*, Hutchinson, London.

Handelman, D. 1990, *Models and Mirrors: Towards an anthropology of public events*, Cambridge University Press, Cambridge.

Huizinga, J. 1949 (1944), *Homo Ludens: A study of the play element in culture*, Routledge & Kegan Paul, London.

James, A. 1986, 'Learning to belong: Boundaries of adolescence', in *Symbolising Boundaries: Identity and diversity in British cultures*, ed. A.P. Cohen, Manchester University Press, Manchester.

Lefebvre, H. 1991, *The Production of Space*, Blackwell, Oxford.

Levi Straus, C. 1972 (1966), *The Savage Mind*, Weidenfeld & Nicholson, London.

Massey, D. 1994, *Space Place and Gender*, Polity Press, Cambridge.

Modleski, T. 1988, *Loving With a Vengeance: Mass produced fantasies for women*, Routledge, New York.

Moore, H.L. 1994, *A Passion for Difference*, Polity Press, Oxford.

Neustadter, R. 1994a, 'The obvious child: The symbolic use of childhood in contemporary popular music', *Popular Music and Society*, v.18, n.1, pp.51-68.

—— 1994b, 'Back to the future: Childhood as utopia', *Extrapolation*, n.35, v.2, pp.145-55.

Omvedt, G. 1966, 'Play as an element in social life', *Berkley Journal of Sociology*, n.11.

Penley, C. 1989, *The Future of an Illusion*, University of Minnesota, Minneapolis.

Rose, G. 1993, *Feminism and Geography: The limits of geographical knowledge*, University of Minnesota Press, Minneapolis.

Schechner, R. 1985, *Between Theatre and Anthropology*, University of Pennsylvania Press, Philadelphia.

—— 1993, *The Future of Ritual*, Routledge, London.

Schwartsman, H.B. 1978, *Transformations: An anthropology of children's play*, Plenum, New York.

Sciama, L. 1993, 'The problem with privacy in Mediterranean anthropology', in *Women and Space*, ed. S. Ardener, Berg, Oxford, pp.87-111.

Shaviro, S. 1993, *The Cinematic Body*, University of Minnesota Press, Minneapolis.

Soja, E.W. 1985, 'The spatiality of social life: Towards a transformative retheorisation' in *Social Relations and Spatial Structures*, eds D. Gregory & J. Urry, Macmillan, London.

—— 1996, *Third Space: Journeys to Los Angeles and other real-and-imagined places*, Blackwell, Cambridge, Mass.

Taussig, M. 1993, *Mimesis and Alterity*, Routledge, New York.

Turner, V. 1969, *The Ritual Process: Structure and anti-structure*, Aldine, Chicago.

—— 1982, *From Ritual to Theatre: The human seriousness of play*, Performing Arts Journal Publications, New York City.

Willett, J. (ed.), 1964, *Brecht on Theatre: The development of an aesthetic*, Eyre Methuen, London.

Williams, L. 1983, 'When a woman looks', in *Re-Vision: Essays in feminist film criticism*, eds M.A. Doane et al., University Publications of America, Frederick, Md., pp.83-99.

—— 1989, *Hard Core: Power, pleasure and frenzy of the visible*, University of California Press, Berkeley.

Winnicott, D.W. 1971, *Playing and Reality*, Tavistock, London.

Woolf, V. 1929, *A Room of One's Own*, Hogarth Press, London.

Notes:

[1]   There is a wealth of fascinating work on the seriousness of play, which I am utilising here (see, for example, Bateson 1972, 1979; Caillois 1961; Fine, 1987; Goffman 1969 (1959), 1974; Handelman 1990; Huizinga 1949 (1944); Omvedt 1966; Schechner 1993; Schwartsman 1978; Turner 1982).

[2]   It took them a further two years to select and edit some of their footage into a 20-minute documentary for public viewing. It is important to understand that not everything in their lives was selected for filming. Not everything that was videoed was edited for later (public) viewing.

[3]   See Bloustien (1998 & 2000) for more detail on this research project.

[4]   Here I use the term to describe the way individuals *perceive and engage in* their worlds. It is a *perception* of the world rather than just a sphere of existence. Drotner summarises it thus: "Everyday life is a means to create some certainty in a world of ambivalence" (1994, p.352; see also Elias 1978; De Certeau 1988).

[5]   The names used here are of course not their real names. In their videos where they had complete control over what would be portrayed for an audience and what would not be

revealed they have retained their real names.

6   The festival was held in December 1996. The video was awarded two prizes – best documentary and best editing out of 140 entries.

7   As a production "company" *Femco* (Female Co-operative) formed for the express purpose of making the documentary, the young women and I were able to attract funding from the Australia Council, Community Arts Project, purely to cover the cost of post-production.

8   Now even more advanced, lightweight digital cameras are available on the market but at this time the Hi8 camera was the most appropriate model of video camera for my purposes.

9   The dramatist Bertolt Brecht first coined this term to discuss the political use of his style of drama (see Willett (ed.) 1964). German film-maker, Rainer Werner Fassbinder drew upon Brecht's aesthetics to employ the same technique to underpin a similar political concern in his film-making. I use the same term here as I contend that is exactly what the girls were doing. They would be aware of the *personal* affects of such strategies although, no doubt, without full realisation of the *political* implications of such representations.

10 Elsewhere Schechner (1985, p.110) reminds us that the psychologist Winnicott (1971, pp.177-93) utilised notions of play that parallel the ideas of Van Gennep, Turner and Bateson. All of these theorists in different ways recognise that though play "transitional phenomena take place". The child and later the adult recognise certain situations and events as "not me ... not not me". During the process of this recognition, however, a blurring occurs, the "dance goes into the body" (Schechner 1985, p.110).

11 These are not their real names.

12 The Lost Forest was the name of an imaginative (and expensive) toyshop in the city during the time of my study. The shop specialised in soft toys and in their "serious" attitude towards their potential customers. Any child purchasing a toy had to be assessed by the vendors as to the suitability of their role as a "parent". The point about the name is of course that it connotes a nostalgic return to the idealistic, fantasy realm of childhood, rather like Never Never Land.

13 Ideas of what constitutes "teenage rebellion" are of course specific to particular cultures, eras and places. In some times and places the concept does not exist.

14 For example, she chose her own high school at the age of 12, a school that required her catching two or three buses across town, arranging all the enrolment and practical details.

15 Of course a major difference was that Diane could see her activity as temporary ("playing mum for a while") whereas for Grace it was an onerous and ongoing situation until she moved out of home.

16 Battaglia (1995) has argued that use of nostalgia in this way can be read as a way of simultaneously representing and constituting the self in a self-affirming past.

17 See Shaviro (1993) for interesting utilisation of Benjamin's and Taussig's insights in relation to contemporary film.

Lyn Harrison

chapter 2

Representing sexual hegemony:
Focus groups and governmentality

SOCIAL research into HIV/AIDS, Sexually Transmitted Infections (STIs) and blood-borne viruses as they affect young people in the general population and groups defined as "at-risk" (e.g. homeless, intravenous drug users, young men who have sex with men) is generally concerned with identifying the factors at work in determining what young people do which puts them at risk of contracting these diseases.

More recently, the emphasis has shifted to obtaining "more subtle and detailed social and cultural data for use in designing educational interventions" (Dowsett et al. 1998). This has been in response to the recognition that simply providing knowledge about safe sex without paying attention to gender power relations and the social and cultural context of young people's sexual decision-making – including the production of desire – is ineffective. It is within this context that focus discussion groups have achieved popularity as a means of gaining more in-depth qualitative information.

When conducting social research in the area of HIV/AIDS, issues around (sexual) difference and its representation become central. Discourses about HIV/AIDS[1] have not only been successful in making people aware of HIV as a disease entity, but have also opened up new ways of talking and thinking about sex and sexuality. In this process, sexual differences have become more transparent. How these differences are represented by those who do research is (or should be) a central element in academic debates that focus on identity formation.

Drawing on data from a focus group with young men aged 15–16 years conducted by researchers at the National Centre in HIV Social Research, this paper explores the production of specific forms of knowledge-power-desire in focus groups. In particular, the discussion addresses the ways in which these young men, together with the focus group facilitators, reproduce (often unconsciously) heteronormativity and dominant discourses of masculinity and femininity.

Focus groups: strengths and weaknesses

Much of the literature on focus groups concerns itself with techniques for improving interaction. However, some researchers have given consideration to the specific types of knowledge and power relations produced within focus groups. Tulloch and Lupton (1994) have argued that researchers need to remind themselves that they are not producing "truth" when they engage in research but particular versions of truth "in which the politics of their position as researchers is inevitably implicated" (p.130). David Morgan (1997), provides a comprehensive overview of focus group research. There is not enough space here for a detailed summary of his account but a few general points can be made about the identified strengths and weaknesses of this qualitative method.

Strengths

Morgan argues that focus groups provide a rapid method for data gathering which obviates lengthy field observations and are a useful method for projects with limited resources. Focus group discussions can also provide immediate data on similarities and differences in the opinions and experiences of participants without post hoc analysis of individual statements (Morgan 1997, p.10). He notes that there is less interviewer control in focus group discussions (which can also be seen as a weakness in some circumstances) and that this means, at least notionally, that participants are free to talk about experiences which are meaningful to them.

Weaknesses

Focus groups are seen as "unnatural" social settings in that they are "(a) limited to verbal behaviour, (b) consist only of interaction in discussion groups, and (c) are created and managed by the researcher" (Morgan 1997, p.8). Although Morgan notes that all research is an intrusion, he argues that participant observation achieves a degree of naturalism and also provides "relatively uncontaminated statements" (p.9) from participants and that this cannot be captured in focus group studies. As well, focus groups provide less depth and detail about opinions and experiences than do one-to-one interviews.

A reliance on group interaction to produce data can be seen as both a strength and a weakness. Although group interaction can produce informative debate, there is a tendency towards conformity, with participants withholding thoughts they may have in private. Alternatively, participants may exhibit a polarisation of views, with individuals expressing more extreme views in the focus group than they hold in private (Morgan 1997, p.14). Morgan further argues that the presence of a moderator in a discussion of a pre-selected topic means that there is a possibility of bias toward the researcher's (perceived) views. This, of course is a possibility with all research, both qualitative and quantitative.

There has been some discussion in the literature about whether focus group members should be strangers or acquaintances. Morgan rightly points out that either of these two scenarios will generate different group dynamics and that the main criterion for selection should be "Can the group comfortably discuss the topic in ways that are useful to the researcher?" (Morgan 1997, p.38). Some researchers favour strangers because, even though acquaintances can converse more readily, groups formed on this basis rely on "taken-for-granted assumptions that are exactly what the researcher is trying to investigate" (Morgan 1997, p.37). Examining the production of power-knowledge-desire in focus groups about sexual health and sexuality with young men makes problematic considerations about group membership and participants' levels of comfort.

Our research in secondary schools in Victoria has been conducted against the backdrop of a gender debate about boys/young men and their perceived "underachievement" at school, and/or their violent behaviours (including self-harming behaviours). As part of this debate, the processes of achieving a masculine identity are often brought into focus. In the case particularly of sexuality education, hegemonic masculinity (Connell 1995) and its effects on relationships and sexual practices can become more transparent and open to scrutiny. Our research on sexuality in schools has also been conducted with the ever present "white noise" of homophobia, expressed more publicly and emphatically by young men than young women. Researchers in Britain and Australia have documented young men's homophobic attitudes (Wood 1984; Van der Ven 1994; Hillier, Harrison & Warr 1998) and their relationship to the production of hegemonic masculinity. Nayak and Kehily (1977), for example, have written recently on "the culture of masculinity and its significance for the production of homophobia" (p.138). The focus in this paper is on the ways in which the male researchers and participants in this focus group work together to produce the "truths" of (hetero)sexuality and hegemonic masculinity. This raises some questions about the effects of gender on the production of knowledge in this context. It is argued that young men have a strong social and psychological investment in presenting themselves publicly as heterosexual and that, because of this, focus group discussions with male facilitators and participants can reinforce and actively reproduce heteronormativity.

Theoretical framework

I have found *governmentality* a useful concept when trying to work through and make sense of young men's identity work in focus group discussions. For Foucault, government is defined as "the conduct of conduct" (in Burchell 1993, p.267). According to Mitchell Dean (1995), *conduct* in the first instance means to lead or direct. In the second instance, the reference is to *human* conduct. Here the *liberal* government of conduct presupposes a free subject. *Free* here is in the sense of being a "self-governing actor replete with a repertoire of choice" and a *subject* is in the sense of someone "whose subjection works through the promotion and calculated regulation of spaces in which choice is to be exercised" (Dean 1995, p.526, see also Foucault 1983, pp.220-21). Within this framework of meaning, focus groups can be viewed as a site of governmentality. The Foucauldian formulation moves away from more conventional notions of government by bringing "issues of the regulation of conduct into focus" (Dean 1995, p.561). Foucault has suggested that government is a "contact point" where techniques of domination – or power – and *techniques of the self* "interact" (Burchell 1993, p.268). Extending Foucault's work, Dean employs the terms "practices of governmental self-formation" and "practices of ethical self-formation". The first term is related to

> *the ways in which various authorities and agencies seek to shape the conduct, aspirations, needs, desires and capacities of specified political and social categories, to enlist them in particular strategies and to seek definite goals; ethical self-formation concerns practices, techniques and rationalities concerning the regulation of the self by the self, and by means of which individuals seek to question, form, know, decipher and act on themselves* (Dean 1995, p.563).

Dean is careful, however, to indicate that the distinction between these two forms of government is not absolute. "To say that a practice is one undertaken by 'self upon self' is not to exclude the possibility that this practice is authorised by a particular agency, and transmitted and learnt within particular cultural forms" (Dean 1995, p.563). Both of the practices identified by Dean become transparent when critically examining the production of power-knowledge-desire in focus group discussions on sexuality. Foucault (1980) has asked "what kind of body [does the] ... current society" need? (p.58). This question is of particular relevance when examining the production of heterosexuality in the context of the HIV/AIDS pandemic.

Methods

This paper draws on data from a focus discussion group with male students collected as part of the Youth/General Population Program at the National Centre in HIV Social Research over the past three years. Single sex focus groups with students in Years 8, 9 and 10 (aged 14–16) have been used, often in concert with surveys and, in some cases, other qualitative methods, as a primary source of data for a range of projects which have explored sexual health issues for young people. The transcript from one focus group with young men in Year 10 conducted in a rural town in Victoria is used here as a primary source because this focus affords a more thorough examination of group interaction. I wish to emphasise however that although the recruitment for and composition of this focus group differed from others, focus groups conducted with young men across a range of studies over the past three years, produced consistent patterns of knowledge-power-desire. The recruitment for this focus group was carried out by the community health worker in the town. The discussion was facilitated by a male researcher at the National Centre and a young man in his twenties who was a volunteer at the local youth drop-in centre where the focus group discussion took place. The young men were drawn from a range of different schools but, living in a small town, they all knew each other. In all the other cases, focus group participants were recruited by teachers and the discussions were held at schools.

Transgressing boundaries: acquaintances versus strangers

As noted above, when researchers make decisions about the selection of focus group participants, there is an assumption that acquaintances can converse more readily. Considering that the primary *raison d'etre* for conducting focus group research is to facilitate group interaction, it would seem reasonable to assume that recruiting acquaintances should assist this process. However, this assumption becomes problematic when investigating sensitive issues such as sexuality. Young people have a large investment in presenting their sexual selves in particular ways, and transgressing the public/private boundaries in focus group discussions with people you may see everyday can be threatening and often dangerous. Morgan alludes to this when he points out that what participants tell researchers is shared with the rest of the group, raising serious invasion of privacy concerns that limit the topics researchers can pursue (Morgan 1997, p.32). Tulloch and Lupton (1994) argue that: "Focus groups generate particular issues of power and reflexivity of their own" (p.133). They argue that the proliferation of research into sexual practices prompted by the HIV/AIDS pandemic, while progressive in the sense that it has alerted us to previously unexplored health-threatening sexual attitudes and behaviours, has also further extended, "the network of surveillance that surrounds and continually monitors sexual activity, serving to cast certain practices as "deviant" or "risky" and therefore drawing boundaries between groups and individuals and making moral judgements" (p.135).

Shared meanings: the assumption of heterosexuality

Some researchers prefer to recruit strangers as focus group participants because acquaintances more readily rely on taken-for-granted assumptions in their interactions. By inference, this assumes that strangers do not, which is simply not the case when you are investigating issues around (hetero)sexuality, masculinity and femininity. Debbie Epstein and Richard Johnson (1994), for example, have written about the assumption of heterosexuality in school-based sex education where heterosexuality remains the silent term against which all other forms of sexuality are measured (and found deviant). In this context, where broader discourses of sexuality structure the way we experience our own sexuality, there is a sense in which there is no such thing as a "stranger". Because of the pervasiveness of heterosexuality, even those who do not identify as heterosexual learn how to "pass" in the school context because it is often dangerous to do otherwise.

(Re)producing heterosexuality and hegemonic masculinity in focus groups

A colleague and I recently submitted a paper to a journal for review in which we examined the meanings of sex for rural youth and used data from focus groups as well as quantitative and qualitative data from open-ended questions from a national survey of rural young people (Hillier, Warr & Haste 1996). One reviewer made the following comment on method:

> I was surprised at the homogeneity of the young people's responses. This is not just a general point … This should be thought through. Is the apparent homogeneity an effect of the methods? (Anonymous reviewer, 7 Aug. 1998)

The short answer to this question is "Yes". In seeking to provide some explanations as to why this is the case, this section examines the verbal interactions between researchers and participants in their joint project of heterosexual identity work.

Epstein and Johnson (see also Mac an Ghaill 1996; Wood 1984; Nayak & Kehily 1997) have written about the pervasiveness of heterosexism and homophobia in schools, suggesting that:

> At its most general level, there is a presumption of heterosexuality that is encoded in language, in institutional practices and the encounters of everyday life … It is not necessary for homophobia to be expressed for heterosexism as a cultural structure to be active in a particular moment. It operates through silence and absences as well as through overt discrimination (Epstein & Johnson 1994, p.198).

The following examples of questions asked by the facilitators illustrate how the presumption of heterosexuality is encoded in language which produces silences about other sexualities:[2]

1 Living in [name of town] how do you meet girls?
2 Do you ever meet girls at school?
3 Who do you talk to or what do you read or whatever if you want to know about ah … boyfriends, girlfriends or sexually transmitted diseases or pregnancy, contraception?

4 Say your girlfriend or someone else's girlfriend got pregnant and didn't know
   what to do about it, what would you say?

The first two questions were asked as precursors to talking about sexual relationships.
These questions assume that any relationships these young men have will be heterosexual.
There is simply no room here for discussing same sex relationships. The young men also
assume the naturalness of these questions and go on to talk about the places where they are
likely to meet girlfriends.

Questions 3 and 4 were asked in order to find out what sources of information these young
men accessed and their knowledge of available services. There is some attempt to be inclusive
in question 3 although the hesitancy ("ah …") before the facilitator mentions boyfriends
suggests he is uncomfortable with this inclusion. Before providing answers about girlfriends
the boys engage in talk and laughter that is not decipherable on the tape and despite the facilitator asking "Sorry, what was that?" the boys start talking about sources of information. We
have written elsewhere (Hillier, Harrison & Warr 1998) about the pressures on young men in
group situations to conform publicly to heterosexual norms when questions about sexual
difference are raised. In the example above, where the only reference to sexual difference is
preceded by an uncomfortable hesitation the imperative for these young men to reaffirm their
heterosexuality is even more acute. The emphasis in Question 4 is again on heterosexual relationships which in a sense confirms the previous reference to "boyfriends" as a glitch in an
otherwise seamless heterosexual narrative.

(Re)producing hegemonic masculinity

The privileging of penetrative hetero sex is an important component in the reproduction of
what Connell (1995) has referred to as hegemonic masculinity, and the reproduction of
inequality in gender power relations is integral to this process. The excerpt below is but one
example of the reproduction of these power relations through discourse:

> *Say you've scored a girl at a party, or it's a girlfriend and you might be interested in*
> *having sex with her, who decides how far it will go? Do girls around here say no?*
> "Yep."
> "Yeah."
> "Usually."
> "Yeah."
> "Yep, a lot of the time."
> *What else do they do?*
> "Boys don't."
> "No."
> *Boys don't?*
> "Boys don't say no."
> *Boys don't say no, so they just wait for the knock back?*
> "Yeah."
> "Yeah."
> *How do girls give the knock back around here?*
> "They'll say no."
> *Say no?*

"Pull their jeans back up." [Laughter]
"Yeah, that sounds about right."

The facilitator's use of the word "scored" as a way of describing what happens when a young man is successful in attracting a young woman at a party, is indicative of shared cultural understandings and values about what are appropriate male behaviours in this context. Elsewhere we have discussed how young men's standing in their peer group is enhanced by their ability to attract sexual partners, the opposite being true for young women who risk damaging their reputation as "nice" girls (Hillier, Harrison & Warr 1998).

The reference to "scored" does not only relate to "winning" a social partner for the night but is intimately tied to the prospect of sex, as the facilitator also acknowledges. In this scenario, girls say "no" but boys never do. The stereotypes of young men as sexual predators, always ready for sex, and young women as undesiring, not really wanting sex are reproduced. In a similar way, when speaking about oral sex, these young men talk about it as something that is done to them and, as a group, laughed at the idea that they would give a "head job" to a young woman. As one young man pointed out: "Mostly what you hear at school is just head jobs and stuff, you don't hear about the guy doing anything to the girl though, it's just mostly what the girl does." In this example not only is the young woman there to provide pleasure but this young man cannot even conceive of man to woman oral sex as a "head job". After this comment, the facilitator asks: "Is it more just sex or is it head jobs as well?". This comment indicates that he too defines "sex" as heterosexual intercourse; head jobs are something else.

This discourse of predatory male sexuality is not seamless, however, and young men have to work hard to maintain it. At one point in this interview the young men acknowledge this. Immediately after the discussion on head jobs one young man stated: "It could be a lot of crap you know" and the group went on to talk about young men who "big note" their sexual exploits, asserting that only about half of the young men who bragged about their exploits were telling the truth.

Hegemonic masculinity and discourses of female sexuality: victimisation and violence

Michelle Fine, writing about young women and what she calls the missing discourse of desire in school-based sex education, has identified several prevailing discourses about female sexuality. Two of these, *sexuality as violence* and *sexuality as victimisation* where "female adolescent sexuality is represented as a moment of victimisation" (Fine 1992, pp.33-34), are traces in the following extract. The questions asked by the facilitator in this instance were part of a longer discussion which sought to elicit how much these young men knew about available sexual health services in their town.

What about … say someone's girlfriend got raped or your girlfriend got raped?
"Go looking for them with a gun."
What else could you do?
"Pull the trigger." [General laughing]
"Probably get all your mates to go after whoever it was."
"Bash the shit through them."

The choice of this example by the facilitator is consistent with previous questions about service provision in its emphasis on the dangers of heterosex for young women: pregnancy, rape, STIs. While these dangers are real, rarely are young men assumed to want or need sexual health services except as a post hoc solution to unprotected or violent sex. There is no suggestion for instance, that these young men might want to access these services for information about responsible contraception, alone or with their female partners. Elsewhere these young men thought that young women who got pregnant "didn't know what they were doing" or were "not educated enough" or "too shy" to ask if their partner had a condom. These comments imply that contraception is a young woman's responsibility, despite these young men's insistence elsewhere that using condoms was a dual responsibility in sexual relationships.

The facilitator's question about rape also invokes a violence advocating response from these young men, typical of the macho culture that is part of hegemonic masculinity. Whether these young men would actually take this course of action or not, the point is that the discourse of young women as victims and young men as heroic warriors (and sometime rapists) is embedded in the story-lines of heterosexuality, making this response the only one that makes sense.

Of course, none of these discourses are produced in a social vacuum. The ways in which young men, for example, speak dominant forms of masculinity and femininity in focus groups mirror broader cultural forms. In this sense *practices of governmental self-formation* at the institutional level and *practices of ethical self-formation* at the interpersonal level work together to produce heterosexuality as the (only) "truth" of these young people's sexual identities.

Some reflections on practice

The examples given in this paper illustrate how the male facilitators and the young male participants engaged in joint identity work which actively reproduced heterosexuality and hegemonic masculinity as the norm. Discourses about sexual difference, young women as active and desiring sexual beings and different ways of being masculine are missing from this interview. It is often presumed that using male facilitators in male focus groups will facilitate rapport and make participants more comfortable. These are important goals when discussing sensitive issues but, as the data suggest, the techniques for gaining rapport can see facilitators using hyper-masculine patterns of communication which produce attitudes and behaviours that many sexuality educators are trying to challenge. How to move beyond these patterns of communication in our work with young men is an issue that needs to be addressed.

As a researcher, I have acted as a facilitator in focus group discussions with young people and ruminated over endless transcripts in the pursuit of more certain knowledge about the "truths" of young people's sexuality. In the process I have often expressed concerns about the partial truths these data tell and the consequences for our representations of young people's sexual lives. My concerns have arisen from the realisation that data from focus group discussions produce only partial and imperfect knowledge and often say a great deal about dominant discourses but very little about whether these discourses are reproduced and/or transformed in the private spaces of young people's relationships and sexual practices. However, I am reminded here of Foucault's warning that everything is dangerous, a point suggested earlier in relation to Tulloch and Lupton's (1994) description of focus groups as an "extension of the network of surveillance that surrounds and continually monitors sexual activity". Peter Kelly's chapter in this book develops similar arguments in relation to the production of a range of expert knowledges about youth.

The young men in the focus group discussed in this chapter (and those in many others) show an awareness of this network of surveillance in their hesitations, often monosyllabic answers, aggressive humour (Haywood 1996), and expressions of homophobia and misogyny. Nayak and Kehily (1997) have pointed to the complex social and psychological investment that young men have in presenting themselves as heterosexual, a process that actually requires the sort of identity work discussed here. My colleagues and I have often expressed frustration at the interactions produced in focus groups with young men, pondering ways in which we can obtain "better" raw data for our task of representation. In contrast, young women, more often than not, are happy to talk at length about sexuality and relationships, discussing stereotypes and gender expectations and acknowledging the contradictions and uncertainties in current gender power relations. Attempts at discussing these issues with young men often result in silences and/or reiterations of heteronormativity, the very thing that researchers are seeking to deconstruct. One of the consequences of these gender differences in communication is that the network of surveillance is extended more and more into the sexual lives of young women while young men are able to, often quite effectively, resist these incursions.

References

Burchell, G. 1993, 'Liberal government and techniques of the self', in *Economy and Society*, v.22, n.3, pp.267-82.

Connell, R.W. 1995, *Masculinities*, Allen & Unwin, Sydney.

Dean, M. 1995, 'Governing the unemployed self in an active society', in *Economy and Society*, v.24, n.2, pp.559-83.

Dowsett, G.W., Aggleton, P., Abega, S., Jenkins, C., Marshall, T.M., Runganga, A., Schifter, J., Tan, M.L. & Tarr, C. 1998, 'Changing gender relations among young people: The global challenge for HIV/AIDS prevention', *Critical Public Health*, v.8, n.4, pp.291-309.

Epstein, D. & Johnson, R. 1994, 'On the straight and narrow: The heterosexual presumption, homophobias and schools', in *Challenging Lesbian and Gay Inequalities in Education*, ed. D. Epstein, Open University Press, Buckingham.

Fine, M. 1992, *Disruptive Voices: The possibilities of feminist research*, University of Michigan Press, USA.

Foucault, M. 1980, 'Body/power', in *Power/Knowledge: Selected interviews and other writings 1972–1977 by Michel Foucault*, ed. C. Gordon, Harvester Wheatsheaf, Hertfordshire.

—— 1983, 'Afterword: The subject and power', in *Michel Foucault: Beyond structuralism and hermeneutics*, eds H.L. Dreyfus & P. Rabinow, University of Chicago Press, Chicago.

Haywood, C. 1996, 'Out of the curriculum: Sex talking, talking sex', *Curriculum Studies: Special Issue on Sexuality*, v.4, n.2, pp.229-49.

Henriques, J., Holloway, W., Urwin, C., Venn, C. & Walkerdine, V. 1984, *Changing the Subject: Psychology, social regulation and subjectivity*, Methuen, London & New York.

Hillier, L., Harrison, L. & Bowditch, K. 1999, '"Neverending love" and "Blowing your load": The many meanings of sex to rural youth', in *Sexualities: Studies in Culture and Society*, v.2, n.1, pp.69-88.

Hillier, L., Harrison, L. & Warr, D. 1998, '"When you carry a condom all the boys think you want it": Negotiating competing discourses about safe sex', *Journal of Adolescence*, v.21, pp.15-29.

Hillier, L., Warr, D. & Haste, B. 1996, *The Rural Mural: Sexuality and diversity in rural youth,* Research Report, Centre for the Study of Sexually Transmissible Diseases, La Trobe University, Melbourne.

Hollway, W. 1995, 'Feminist discourses and women's heterosexual desire', in *Feminism and Discourse: Psychological perspectives,* eds S. Wilkinson & C. Kitzinger, Sage Publications, London.

Mac an Ghaill, M. 1996, *Understanding Masculinities,* Open University Press, Buckingham.

Morgan, D. 1997, *Focus Groups as Qualitative Research,* Sage Publications, London.

Nayak, A. & Kehily, M. 1997, 'Masculinities and schooling: Why are young men so homophobic?', in *Border Patrols: Policing the boundaries of heterosexuality,* eds D.L. Steinberg., D. Epstein & R. Johnson, Cassell, London.

Tulloch, J. & Lupton, D. 1994, 'Health communication after ICA/ANZCA '94: Some issues of theory and method', *Australian Journal of Communication,* v.21, n.2, pp.122-37.

Van der Ven, P. 1994, 'Comparisons among homophobic reactions of undergraduates, high school students, and young offenders', *Journal of Sex Research,* v.31, n.2, pp.117-24.

Wood, J. 1984, 'Groping towards sexism: Boys' sex talk', in *Gender and Generation,* eds A. McRobbie & M. Nava, Macmillan Education, Basingstoke.

Acknowledgments

I wish to thank the research team (in its various guises) who have worked with me on projects in the Youth/General Population Program at the National Centre in HIV Social Research, La Trobe University over the last three years. I would also like to thank Dr Lynne Hillier and Dr Peter Kelly for providing valuable feedback on drafts of this paper.

Notes

[1] Following Henriques et al. (1984) every discourse is understood as:

the result of a practice of production which is at once material, discursive and complex, always inscribed in relation to other practices of production of discourse. Every discourse is part of a discursive complex; it is locked in an intricate web of practices, bearing in mind that every practice is by definition both discursive and material (p.106).

Within this understanding of discourse the interrelationship between language, subjectivity, social organisation and power is emphasised. Wendy Hollway has recently made the case for using discourse analysis in concert with a psychodynamic account of positioning in discourses as well as a consideration of the part played by individual history (1995). Even though these last two are often hard to "get at", their influence in shaping sexual identities needs to be acknowledged.

[2] The questions are numbered for ease of reference but are not in strict chronological order because they were interspersed with more general questions about living in a rural town.

Maria Pallotta-Chiarolli

"Coming out/going home": Australian girls and young women interrogating racism and heterosexism

IN a collection of diary entries written during her adolescence and entitled 'Coming Out/Going Home', Jess Langley (1998) writes about her coming out as a young lesbian. It necessitates her move to inner-city Melbourne to "be with people like myself and feel more comfortable in my surrounds". She pays rent while she continues with her schooling and runs a support group for other young lesbians. Hence, "coming out" has led to the establishment of a new cultural, sexual and socioeconomic home as well as setting up a support base, another "home" others like herself can go to. She also presents another "going home", regularly visiting her mother in the outer suburban area where she was born and raised. Langley soon finds that this is also a "coming out" as she and others around her become aware of how different her life and her aspirations actually are as a young lesbian completing school in an inner urban, lower socioeconomic area. Thus, her life is a regular journeying to and from multiple homes, multiple "lifeworlds", where even the train journey itself is fraught with fears of violence because she dares to be "out" as an independent young lesbian.

> As people are simultaneously the members of multiple lifeworlds, so their identities have multiple layers, each layer in complex relation to the others ... We have to be proficient as we negotiate these many lifeworlds – the many lifeworlds each of us inhabit, and the many life-worlds we encounter in our everyday lives (Cope & Kalantzis 1995, pp.10-11).

The interweaving of "lifeworlds"

Like Langley, many Australian girls and young women are "coming out" and "going home" in the negotiation of potentially homogenising and conflicting categories such as gender, sexuality, ethnicity, indigeneity and other factors such as class and disability. In other words, they are assertively interweaving "lifeworlds", positioning themselves and others as home-sites of confluence and intermixture, rather than as having to assimilate to one "world" or the social rules of one category at the expense of others. Nor are they "intersecting" within one self two or more neat and homogeneous "worlds" with distinct chasms between them. They are acknowledging the differences *within* as well as *between* categories. I use the word "interweaving" as it metaphorically represents fluidity, boundary-blurring, and the diversity of strategies girls and young women use to "come out", to negotiate, manoeuvre and resist the codes and identities of various categories.

The main questions then become to what extent schools are acknowledging and encouraging girls and young women's skills of critical perception, critical thinking, the negotiation of differences, and the passion for social justice, and the extent to which they engage with diversity rather than reconstruct it as homogeneity. For example, an increasing number of girls in our schools are finding that membership to several "lifeworlds" is apparently cancelled due to their making visible their lesbian or bisexual "lifeworld". Thus, although educational systems may be (far too) slowly shifting away from the denial of diverse sexualities in young women's lives, this previous invisibility may run the danger of being superseded by policies and programs that deal with non-heterosexual sexuality as something separate from, indeed somewhat "deviant" from, other aspects of girls' lives. Thus, just as educators have recognised the necessity of contextualising gender education programs and policies according to specificities such as class, ethnicity and geographical location, so, too, do sexuality education programs and policies need to be contextualised.

From 1996 to 1998, I worked with over 150 girls and young women from around Australia in the production and publication of writing, photography, cartoons and art that explored the multiple lifeworlds they belonged to and the impact of these "worlds" on issues such as bodies and health, school and friendship, love and sex. At the beginning of this project, I had just completed an autobiographical novel on five generations of women in my Italian family after undertaking ethnographic research and oral history interviews (Pallotta-Chiarolli, 1999a). Shifting and multiple constructs of "home", ethnic identity, gender and sexuality were very much my concerns and I was interested in working with young women in the analysis of their own "lifeworlds". Australian schools, youth organisations, young women's organisations, ethnic, lesbian and health organisations were informed of the project and girls and young women were invited to submit written and visual material that they wished to share, in the form of a book, with other girls and young women. As I explained in the introduction:

> *I set about collecting all sorts of girls' talk from around Australia for all sorts of girls from around Australia, from north Queensland to southern Tasmania, from Perth to Sydney. Some days I was floating around in this telephone space over deserts and tropical jungles, hearing the rain in the background at Daly River, Northern Territory, and feeling the heat of Oodnadatta in the dry outback of South Australia! I asked lots of girls, and lots of people living with and working with girls, what girls want to know and what girls want to say* (Pallotta-Chiarolli 1998, p.vi).

Their work was then framed by my own writings: introductions, commentaries and questions for girls to think and talk about. My sections were clearly marked with a particular title, 'Can I do some talking?', and an icon, and always positioned somewhat marginal to the main sections of the page and chapter which had been produced by the girls and young women. As I wrote in the introduction, "I'm one of the old girls who'll pop up regularly asking whether I can do some talking. (You can just say no and turn the page on me!)" (Pallotta-Chiarolli 1998, p.viii).

The call for submissions from girls for the eventual book, *Girls' Talk: Young women speak their hearts and minds* (Pallotta-Chiarolli 1998), was based on the premise that girls have much to teach us about the contextualisation and negotiation of categories such as ethnicity, gender and sexuality. Thus, alongside the pioneering work of educators such as Georgina Tsolidis (1986) which established a research model and theoretical framework for educating "Voula", or girls from non-English speaking backgrounds, I believe we need to consider how "Voula" or girls from culturally diverse backgrounds and of diverse sexualities can educate the educators and the wider society. Much of Tsolidis' work was based on listening to girls and their parents discuss their lived realities. It continues to be very relevant as multicultural and multisexual girls' voices are not being given equitable space and are not being listened to in many schools and in the wider society (Pallotta-Chiarolli 1997).

As Jess Langley's diary entries illustrate, girls growing up in Australia are undertaking three complex social processes of "coming out/going home" in relation to categories such as ethnicity, sexuality, gender, rural/urban sites, religion and class. These are: the critiquing and interweaving of socially ascribed categories and labels within themselves; the crossing, bridging and bordering of "worlds" and the regulations and codes of those "worlds"; and the employment of strategies of adaptation, negotiation and selection in order to live their lives as satisfactorily and successfully as possible. Girls are resisting being trapped in the duality of what they have inherited and what the dominant group wishes to enforce, or indeed resisting being defined by any single set of perceptions and ascriptions, bearing in mind that minority groups also tend to enforce their own conformist criteria for "belonging".

Postcolonial feminism and mestiza feminism, or the feminism of culturally-hybrid women such as Chicanas or Mexican-American women in Latin America, are gaining significance in Australia and informing second and third generation women living within, between and beyond the borders of two or more cultural backgrounds (Anzaldua 1987; Lugones 1994; Molina 1994; Trinh 1991). Postcolonial and feminist theorists represent individual identity as a site of the intermixture of ethnicity, sexuality and gender.

I am an act of kneading, uniting and joining that not only has produced both a creature of darkness and a creature of light [going home], but also a creature that questions the definitions of light and dark and gives them new meanings [coming out] (Anzaldua 1987, pp.80-81).

Before proceeding, I wish to point out three concerns in the way such arguments – including my own – are presented. First, the very language and categories used to articulate these debates are problematic. It is difficult to acknowledge and write about multiplicity and heterogeneity while using a language of potentially homogenising categories such as "Anglo-Australian", "non-English-speaking background", "Asian", "Middle-Eastern". Similarly, queer theory is interrogating the potential rigidity and limitations that labels such as "lesbian" and "bisexual" can imply.

Second, this system of categorisation also denotes hierarchical dualisms, as in the use of the words "mainstream" and "minority", "English-speaking backgrounds" and "non-English-speaking backgrounds", "heterosexual" and "lesbian". Diversity is recognised but it may be difficult to destabilise a perceived Anglo-centrism marked by class privilege and heterosexism.

Third, this system creates gaps and invisibilities where the realities of many girls are ignored, such as girls from non-Anglo cultural backgrounds whose first language was English, girls who are multi-cultural in ancestry rather than bicultural, girls who may be in loving relationships with other girls but find the Western construction of "lesbian" alienating or irrelevant in their cultural contexts. Further, the way in which factors such as class, urban/rural geographical background and present location, religion, level of education, ability/disability, age, sexuality influence and interweave with issues of migration, ethnicity, and language may also be ignored (Pallotta-Chiarolli 1995; 1996).

One path out of this "to label or not to label and what to label" impasse – one which Australian girls are increasingly aware of and negotiating – is to use these labels and categories critically and strategically. In other words, it is important to acknowledge the political use of these labels in addressing sociocultural specificities while simultaneously being aware of, and preventing the manipulation of, these categories to establish new artificial constructions of exclusion, invisibility and discriminatory boundary-marking. As Trinh T. Minh-Ha writes:

> *Multiculturalism does not lead us very far if it remains a question of difference only between one culture and another … To cut across boundaries and borderlines is to live aloud the malaise of categories and labels; it is to resist simplistic attempts at classifying; to resist the comfort of belonging to a classification* (Trinh 1991, pp.107-08).

Hence, in line with postcolonial and mestiza feminisms, girls' writings in *Girls' Talk* (1998) seem to illustrate the significance of five main points in articulating multiple identity and/or multiple oppression. They are:

- acknowledging intracategory differences within a group as well as intercategory diversity between social groups;
- exploring the relationships among various conditions and constructs such as ethnicity, class, gender, sexuality, religion, geographical location and education;
- understanding that racism, sexism and homophobia are interconnected, as are all forms of prejudices and discrimination;
- acknowledging definitions and identities as constantly shifting and in flux rather than as static, via contextualisation of time and place; and
- upholding one's own self-ascriptive perceptions, definitions and meanings and showing agency in resisting, subverting and negotiating externally assigned labels.

Australian girls and their journeys into cultural "lifeworlds"

From many submissions to *Girls' Talk*, it is apparent that by the late 1990s, many immigrant and second-generation girls *are* speaking various forms of feminism and *are* part of the multiplicity of feminism itself, and this does *not* require comparison to some "norm" of feminism as defined by a dominant group. Instead, it requires what Yuval-Davis (1994) terms "transversal politics", and what Lugones (1990) terms "world-travelling" in order to prevent antagonisms and misrepresentations. However, both of these feminists, as well as Australian feminists such as Ang (1996), concede that some differences and ambivalences may not be resolved but may be used creatively and strategically in order to reach and involve all girls within their own multiple locations.

Girls appear keen to explore five social processes:

1 cultures and cultural change within the broader framework (the political, social, economic contexts), and cultures being seen as continually reshaped and dynamic;
2 the impact of migration including identifying adaptation strategies; stages in the process of migration such as grieving, "culture shock", romanticising of the past culture, and how and why migrants might retain and cherish the past; and how and

why there is a strong identification with others of similar background;

3   the self of the first culture, the cultural framework of the early years of childhood and the present home culture, and identification of the values that are still relevant to their present lives and/or identification of the changed expressions of these deepest values;

4   the self of the second culture, the contributions and new outlooks, the reinforcement of the first culture perspectives and the points of contradiction and conflict;

5   the self in many cultures: the self that has continued to be, the self that becomes fragmented, the self that is lost, the self that is imposed; how to enjoy being multicultural and, indeed, value the psychological and social skills gained in negotiating differences and diverse situations.

In 'White, anglo and middle class', M.E. (1998) takes the very categories that have been constructed to position her within a notion of socioeconomic and cultural "mainstream" and deconstructs them to reveal the multiplicity within:

> *I refuse to accept a racist ideology that says all white experience is Anglo experience. It tears me apart when I see the way Australia is heading back to its genocide beginnings and constructing a white mainstream to support its racist policies. And it angers me even more when people assume I'm part of this racist Anglo majority based on the colour of my skin. White does not mean woman. White does not mean me. White means being racist and patriarchal.*

Identifying herself as a young feminist from a lower socioeconomic background, and with a Welsh migrant mother, M.E. demonstrates how those positioned as "white, Anglo and middle class" are not always so. She has "gone home" by looking into the label "British", finding the hierarchies within, and rejecting the standard denial of diversity within "white" people (M.E. 1998, p.232).

Young Muslim women and girls write of their need to understand the differences between and within Islam as a religion and Islam as a patriarchal culture before they could "come out" and "go home" as Muslim and female in Australia. This involves resisting the stereotype that is imposed from non-Muslim perspectives as well as internalised by Muslims in an effort to assimilate to Western constructions of feminist power and identity that the veil always signifies ignorance and oppression. In 'A metre of chiffon', Ayse Uyguntemur (1998), a young Sunni Muslim woman of Turkish descent and born in Australia tells of what made her "fall from the pedestal of ... Australian Turkish Modern Woman", not only in the eyes of the external Western world but also in the eyes of her Turkish migrant family: "I could never have imagined that a one metre square piece of chiffon could have made such a dramatic difference". Wearing the hijaab signifies for her that:

> *I believe in rights for women ... I am a feminist ... I am not a victim, and certainly not a second class citizen as you may think Islam classifies me ... I was born in Australia, have lived in Australia, in fact have never left the east coast of Australia but I'm too dark to be an "Aussie" I guess. And, well, I do wear the hijaab, so I am considered a "radical Muslim" by my family and Turkish community. Therefore, they don't consider me "one of them"* (Uyguntemur 1998, pp. 205-06).

She explains the fine lines that exist between and within Islamic cultures and Islamic religions and how, within the latter, the status of women was taken to be equal to that of men, while it is patriarchal control that has constructed unjust cultures.

Another young Muslim woman, Karima Moraby (1998) writes in her essay, 'I am me: an Australian muslim woman', of the multiplicity of being born to an Australian Catholic mother who later converted to Islam and a Lebanese Muslim father. Learning to negotiate these differences within her "home", she realises there is another world of school that also needs to be negotiated:

> *I think my first realisation that I was actually different or perceived to be different was when at eight I was told to stand in front of the class and my teacher said to the class, "This is what a Muslim girl looks like". I was not wearing a hijaab (a head scarf) and was in school uniform. So I looked just like everybody else. That day changed my life as I realised that even though I might look like everybody else, and feel like everybody else, this did not mean that everybody else saw me as the same* (Moraby 1998, p.209).

The next few years saw Moraby ping-ponging between a denial of her Islamic self, and a rejection of her Western self, and eventually fully blending "the Western" and "the Islamic" to suit herself, for example choosing not to wear a veil.

> *I am an Australian*
> *I am a Woman*
> *I am a Muslim Woman*
> *I am an Australian Muslim Woman…*
> *I am me…*
> (Moraby 1998, p.209).

Other girls and young women write of the impact of knowing about their parents' struggles as refugees and migrants, or as women growing up under oppressive political regimes. They needed to "go home" to understand the results of such experiences on family members before they were able to "come out" with aspirations and resolutions for their own lives. For example, Ruiyi writes about her mother's educational and career aspirations having been thwarted by the Cultural Revolution in China. Her tenacity in eventually returning to her studies and becoming an engineer and, as Ruiyi says, always trying to "master more knowledge" has deeply affected the way Ruiyi sees her own education and ambitions (Ruiyi 1998 p.99).

Similarly, young women of diverse Aboriginal backgrounds, such as the 1997 Human Rights Award Winner Tammy Williams (1998), reflect upon the struggles and determination of their forbears, and how these battles have provided the opportunities that Tammy's generation can use to continue working for equality and anti-racism:

> *As I look back on the lives of my grandparents, and even my mother's life, I realise I am speaking before you with thanks to their personal dedication and commitment to reconciliation. It is the struggle of our forbears, which has resulted in my generation [being able to] enjoy the right to have access to secondary and tertiary education. A right which not even my mother could enjoy* (Williams 1998, p.262).

Australian girls journeying against heterosexism

Girls are situating homophobia and heterosexism within the parameters of human experience of oppression and marginalisation, rather than positioning these prejudices as outside or deviant from the "usual" prejudices. They do not need to identify as lesbian or bisexual themselves to be affected by and/or actively challenge homophobia and heteronormativity. In her personal essay entitled, 'Are you the one with the gay brother?', Simone Garske (1998) reflects upon the homophobic harassment she experiences in high school because of her brother who had come out as gay and had left the school a few years before: "I was like a walking disease; I had the gay virus and I might pass it on to the heterosexual guys" (p.135). Homophobic graffiti appears on her house and she experiences abuse such as food being thrown at her on the bus. Despite parental support and complaints, the school offers minimal support.

> *I realised I was being ruled by these gutless wonders, both students and teachers, at school. I had a wonderful family who loved and supported me. My brother was a fabulous person who was gentle and caring* (Garske 1998, p.136).

She realises it is up to her to resist the homophobic harassment and "comes out" confidently and outspokenly as the sister of a gay brother within an unsupportive educational institution, as well as "goes home" to an appreciation of the "world" of acceptance and strength in her family environment. She also positions herself as "living in the real world" where sexual diversity is acknowledged and supported rather than the unreal world of homophobia and heterosexism in education. This successful personal negotiation of the tensions between her "worlds" of existence has her locating a space for herself where she can live "exactly the way I want and I'm extremely happy" (Garske 1998, p.137).

Girls with gay or lesbian parents are also aware of the need to negotiate and bridge the chasms between their "home" realities and the labels and ignorance of the worlds of school and society. Rebekah Venn-Brown (1998) writes about what happened when her father, a Christian minister, came out as gay and left her mother to live with a man when Rebekah was 15. In 'You can either get better or bitter', she stresses she had no support at school: "No-one recommended counselling, a support network – education and information – absolutely nothing." So she begins to educate others. When some students in her English Literature class are disgusted that one of the authors they are studying is gay, she asks the teacher if she can address the class for just a few moments.

> *He agreed. I told the class of my concern at their narrow-mindedness. And then I told everyone my father was gay and that if I could be accepting surely they could also. It left the class stunned – and I gave myself a pat on the back* (Venn-Brown 1998, p.92).

She is also aware of the social constructions of gender and sexuality as her father and herself move within and between their "lifeworlds":

> *I've also seen a strange parallel – as I was developing, physically and mentally, into a woman, Dad was changing also. He was dealing with changing into a gay man. Just as my changes were subtle and little by little, so were his* (Venn-Brown 1998, p.92).

In 'Your mum's a lezzo', 13-year-old Sally (Sally, Lacey & Grandma 1998) clearly understands that "the problem is not having a lesbian mum but having a lesbian mum in this homophobic world. So really everyone else has got the problem if they can't accept it" (p.106). She has developed what she calls "categories, the people who know and the people who don't know", slotting people into these categories in order to assist her in negotiating her "lifeworlds" of school, home, and small rural community in New South Wales (p.107). Again, the school environment is seen as perpetuating a heterosexist mythology about families that alienates some students who belong to a "home" reality that has no official place in school life.

Interviews with lesbian students conducted by Michelle Rogers (1998) reveal their strengths and resistances in negotiating their "lifeworlds" as they both "come out" to the wider society, in their schools, and "go home" to themselves, as young lesbians. They critically question and deconstruct institutional rhetoric as Lisa does: "I know one of the mottoes of our school is like 'enabling you to find out who you are' and I'm not sure how the school would react if someone was very openly 'out'" (p.139). And again, support in the family "home" compensates for and subverts the condemnation from school and society, as in Shaz's situation: "I've never really had a problem with my sexuality because my uncle's gay and my mum's, you know, like they are like really close so I was always taught that there was nothing wrong with it" (p.139). Questioning institutional rhetoric also involves the interrogation of fixed labels of the gay/straight binary divide that some school policies may be using to structure all antihomophobic work and yet which also do not encompass the broader dimensions of sexual diversity. For example, Cloe says,

> It doesn't really bug me who I am in love with as long as I am happy... I don't think any boxes can be put onto it [sexuality]. I don't really go, "OK, I am sleeping with a girl so I am gay", you know, I go, "I am totally in love with this person and that's what it means and that's what matters" (in Rogers 1998, p.71).

Hence, girls are thinking beyond homogenising and singular categories. In 'Take three steps back (into the closet)', Tamsin Dancer (1998) from Adelaide questions the homogeneity and exclusionary practices often at work within what she had thought was a safe, accepting "home", the lesbian community, when she has a "brief relationship" with a male. She writes: "I felt as though I was playing a board game and had turned up a card that read, 'You realise you are bisexual. Take three steps back (into the closet)'" (Dancer 1998, pp.157-58).

Dancer also challenges other forms of hierarchy and homogeneity within the lesbian and gay communities that imitate those of the heteronormative world:

> We need to question why the chic, white and well-dressed, lesbian image is so attractive. Is it a safe box for the mainstream to keep me in? There are a lot of young dykes, bi and queer women, like me, that will never fit that limited category – we are fat, or poor, or people of colour, or parents, or disabled (Dancer 1998, p.158).

Amanda (1998) writes in 'Political activism: isn't that a dirty word?' about "coming out" in Brisbane as a young lesbian looking for a space to get support for her multiple interconnected issues. She discovers no such site exists so "I decided to start one ... All of a sudden I had a political identity as the person who ran the young lesbian support group" (p.254). She had constructed a "home" for herself which would become a "home" others could also go to. Amanda concludes, "dreaming about the kind of world I want to live in is great, but getting out and helping to create it is even better" (p.255).

Helena, who is of Greek background, has challenged the boundaries and rules of the wider society, the school and her Greek family and community, and "gone home" to herself where she has stopped organising her life and actions according to heteronormative external ascriptions and definitions:

> They all go, "This is a heterosexual school and you shouldn't be here"... I don't see a name on the wall saying this is a heterosexual school (in Rogers 1998, p.140).

> Mum started yelling the house down ... that I needed psychiatric help...my dad spat on me

about five times and threw things on me … Coming out and accepting it myself made me feel better as a person … before I came out I used to always be rebellious, since I came out I've calmed down … everything has calmed down (in Rogers 1998, p.97).

Girls and young women are publicly resisting the combination of ethnocentrism and homophobic harassment in their schools and other public spaces. They reflect the impact of Australia's multicultural and immigration policies of the last 40 years in producing a generation born to migrant parents and negotiating their multiple life-worlds, resisting external racist and homophobic ascriptions which they perceive as linked, and claiming their particular spaces within their schools and within the wider Australian society.

In 'Wandering', Naomi Ullmann (1998) not only presents the contradictions and paradoxes inherent within her inheritance of the Palestinian/Israeli nationalist chasm, "a Jewish state – Palestinian land/Arab killing Jew – Jew killing Arab" and the added intricacies and insights of living in a multicultural Australia where she is forming friendships with Palestinian and other Arabic girls, such as Julieanne, Australian-born with Arabic grandparents, who tells her "it's important to me that the Jewish people have a safe place to live … have somewhere for their children … but it's just as important for everybody else too. No-one deserves it more than anyone else" (Ullman 1998, p.212).

Ullmann also presents the complexity of 'Jew killing Jew' by interrogating her ancestors' complicity in the condemnation and destruction of homosexual Jews.

"HOW CAN YOU, OF ALL PEOPLE, WHO HAS BEEN PERSECUTED YOURSELF, PERSECUTE OTHERS?"
I think to myself, and, out aloud,
"The Nazis also persecuted homosexuals" (Ullman 1998, p.211).

A young lesbian of Jewish background, Madelaine, in 'My mentor and friend', writes of her reaching a crisis-point in needing to negotiate and resist the codes and regulations emanating from all "lifeworlds": "I decided to have a mid-life crisis at age 16 … I suddenly realised everything was as my parents, school and Jewish background wanted me to be. It was not me. So I started from scratch. The new me." (Madelaine 1998, p.159).

She goes to a bookshop to get more information and there meets Jan, the lesbian bookshop owner, who becomes her mentor and friend, who "has great faith in me, and my ability to be anything I wanted to be" (Madelaine 1998, p.159). Many possibilities are opened to Madelaine through the worlds on the bookshelves and, affirmed with new knowledge from which to make decisions, she concludes that in her life "I will do all I can" (p.159).

In a poem 'Crimes of existence', young Aboriginal lesbian writer Romaine Moreton explores the parallels between racism and heterosexism, and the internal familial divisions external Christian and Western condemnations of homosexuality have created.

My mother also doesn't stop
        to consider,
that when Great Christian Leaders
   & other vilifiers of homosexuality
call society to attention
   & ask them to jail.
The queers, leso's & gays,

that what they really mean
  is for her
to
           incarcerate
  her very own daughter
& make sexuality
           her crime.
& place her daughter in the cell
next to
  her very own son,
for they have already made Blackness his.
                    (Moreton 1998, p.222)

Again, the contextualisation of lesbian sexuality according to other categories such as indigeneity, and the multiple identities many students have, are inadequately addressed in schools. As I have illustrated via the above examples, schools and teachers are in a significant position to act as cultural mediators between student and family/community, student and mainstream society, and student and social services/organisations/community groups that cater for their ethnic, gender and sexual identities in order to foster more just understandings and practices (Pallotta-Chiarolli 1995, 1996, 1999b, 1999c). And yet, this position is not acknowledged at all, or is reluctantly conceded, or faces tremendous obstacles in establishing viable policies, programs and practices with students.

Multicultural *does* mean multisexual

I do not believe it is blasphemous to compare oppressions of sexuality to oppressions of race and ethnicity: Freedom is indivisible or it is nothing at all besides sloganeering and temporary, short-sighted, and short-lived advancement for a few (Jordan 1996, p.12).

Girls of diverse sexualities and diverse cultures are cultural negotiators in the social processes of "coming out/going home". Australia is witnessing both confluence and conflict as the end-products of historical forces, and policies in relation to both multiculturalism and homosexuality are beginning new inscriptions and resistances to long-standing discriminatory institutions, such as education and Church. Culturally and sexually diverse girls and young women are coming forth/coming out as key agents in eroding long-standing exclusions and silences in relation to multicultural, multisexuality in Australian institutions such as education.

The publication of girls' writings constructs powerful sites of intervention and resistance into homophobic, racist and sexist discourses. More spaces need to be provided for girls to "come out" and "go home", to cross borderlines and expand boundaries, to explore the contradictions and confluences inherent in the construction of their multiple social positionings as both end-products of larger sociopolitical and cultural forces, and beginnings of new inscriptions into society, politics and culture. This recognition of multiple locations as sites of possible oppression, power and resistance can do much to challenge ethnocentric, sexist and heterosexist perspectives. Girls need to be encouraged to gain and articulate their visions of themselves and others who co-exist with them in their schools, their immediate worlds, and the worlds beyond their perception.

Their contributions to my book have exemplified girls' great potential to demonstrate and transcend categorical limitations, oppressions, and the splitting of concurrent realities inherent in the need to homogenise, categorise and simplify. Their recognition of themselves and others as multi-placed persons, constantly undertaking "coming out/going home" journeys can do much to challenge ethnocentric, sexist and homophobic perspectives. As Trinh T. Minh-Ha (1999, p.229) writes:

> *as long as the complexity and difficulty of engaging with*
> *the diversely hybrid experiences of heterogenous contemporary*
> *societies are denied and not dealt with ... the creative interval*
> *is dangerously reduced to non-existence.*

The "creative interval" between and within "coming out" and "going home" is becoming a larger and stronger base, constructed by Australian girls and young women. As 14-year-old Khizran Khalid (1998, p.265) writes,

> *I'm the voice of tomorrow.*
> *I'm the one who will make a difference.*
> *I'm the one who will see tomorrow.*
> *But can you take the time to listen?*

Acknowledgment

I wish to express my admiration and appreciation of the many girls and young women who submitted such thought-provoking and inspirational material to *Girls' Talk*. As a parent, educator and older woman, I am in awe of your strengths, insights and determination.

I also wish to thank Julie McLeod for her encouragement and patience in the development of this paper, and her warm welcome to my working life here at Deakin University; Lori Beckett whose passion and commitment encouraged the development of aspects of this paper for her book *Everyone is Special! A handbook for teachers on sexuality education* (1998, Association of Women Educators, Brisbane); and to Rex Finch of Finch Publishing who first approached me with the idea of compiling a book "for girls by girls".

This paper is a modified version of a paper published in *Women's Studies Journal (NZ)* 1999, v.15, n.2, pp.71-88.

References

Amanda 1998, 'Political activism: Isn't that a dirty word', in *Girls' Talk: Young women speak their hearts and minds*, ed. M. Pallotta-Chiarolli, Finch Publishing, Lane Cove, Sydney.

Ang, I. 1996, 'The curse of the smile: Ambivalence and the "Asian" woman in Australian multiculturalism', *Feminist Review*, n.52, pp.36-49.

Anzaldua, G. 1987, *Borderlands/La Frontera: The new mestiza*, Spinsters/Aunt Lute, SF.

Cope, B. & Kalantzis, M. 1995, 'Why literacy pedagogy has to change', *Education Australia*, n.30, pp.8-11.

Dancer, T. 1998, 'Take three steps back (into the closet)', in *Girls' Talk: Young women speak their hearts and minds*, ed. M. Pallotta-Chiarolli, Finch Publishing, Lane Cove, Sydney.

Garske, S. 1998, 'Are you the one with the gay brother?', in *Girls' Talk: Young women speak their hearts and minds*, ed. M. Pallotta-Chiarolli, Finch Publishing, Lane Cove, Sydney.

Khalid, K. 1998, 'The voice of tomorrow', in *Girls' Talk: Young women speak their hearts and minds*, ed. M. Pallotta-Chiarolli, Finch Publishing, Lane Cove, Sydney.

Jordan, J. 1996, 'A new politics of sexuality', in *Bisexual Horizons: Politics, histories, lives,* eds S. Rose et al., Lawrence & Wishart, London.

Langley, J. 1998, 'Coming Out/Going Home', in *Girls' Talk: Young women speak their hearts and minds*, ed. M. Pallotta-Chiarolli, Finch Publishing, Lane Cove, Sydney.

Lugones, M. 1990, 'Playfulness, "world"-travelling, and loving perception', in *Making Face Making Soul/ Haciendo Caras,* ed. G. Anzaldua, Aunt Lute Books, SF.

—— 1994, 'Purity, impurity, and separation', *Signs: Journal of Women in Culture and Society,* v.19, n.2, pp.458-79.

Madelaine 1998, 'My mentor and friend', in *Girls' Talk: Young women speak their hearts and minds*, ed. M. Pallotta-Chiarolli, Finch Publishing, Lane Cove, Sydney.

M.E. 1998, 'White, anglo and middle class', in *Girls' Talk: Young women speak their hearts and minds*, ed. M. Pallotta-Chiarolli, Finch Publishing, Lane Cove, Sydney.

Molina, M. 1994, 'Fragmentations: Meditations on separatism', *Signs: Journal of Women in Culture and Society*, v.19, n.2, pp.449-57.

Moraby, K. 1998, 'I am me: an Australian Muslim woman', in *Girls' Talk: Young women speak their hearts and minds,* ed. M. Pallotta-Chiarolli, Finch Publishing, Lane Cove, Sydney.

Moreton, R. 1998, 'Crimes of existence', in *Girls' Talk: Young women speak their hearts and minds,* ed. M. Pallotta-Chiarolli, Finch Publishing, Lane Cove, Sydney.

Pallotta-Chiarolli, M. 1995, 'Only your labels split me: Interweaving ethnicity and sexuality in English studies', *English in Australia*, n.112, pp.33-44.

—— 1996, '"A rainbow in my heart": Interweaving ethnicity and sexuality studies', in *Schooling and Sexualities: Teaching for a positive sexualities,* eds C. Beavis et al., Centre for Education and Change, Deakin University, Deakin University Press, Melbourne.

—— 1997, '"Educating Voula"/Voula educating: Interweaving ethnicity, gender and sexuality in education', *Education Links*, n.54, pp.16-18.

—— (ed.) 1998, *Girls' Talk: Young women speak their hearts and minds*, Finch, Sydney.

—— 1999a, *Tapestry: Interweaving lives*, Random House, Sydney.

—— 1999b, 'Diary entries from the "Teachers' Professional Development Playground": Multiculturalism meets multisexualities in education', in *Multicultural Queer: Australian Narratives,* eds G. Sullivan & P. Jackson, Haworth Press, New York.

—— 1999c, '"Multicultural does not mean multisexual": Social justice and the interweaving of ethnicity and sexuality in Australian schooling', in *A Dangerous Knowing: Sexual pedagogies,* eds D. Epstein & J.T. Sears, Cassell, London.

Rogers, M. 1998, 'Being on patrol and being patrolled', in *Girls' Talk: Young women speak their hearts and minds,* ed. M. Pallotta-Chiarolli, Finch Publishing, Lane Cove, Sydney.

Ruiyi 1998, 'My mother the student', in *Girls' Talk: Young women speak their hearts and minds,* ed. M. Pallotta-Chiarolli, Finch Publishing, Lane Cove, Sydney.

Sally, Lacey & Grandma 1998, 'Your Mum's a lezzo', in *Girls' Talk: Young women speak their hearts and minds,* ed. M. Pallotta-Chiarolli, Finch Publishing, Lane Cove, Sydney.

Tsolidis, G. 1986, *Educating Voula*, Ministerial Advisory Committee on Multicultural and

Migrant Education, Melbourne.

Trinh, T.M. 1991, *When the Moon Waxes Red,* Routledge, New York.

Ullmann, N. 1998, 'Wandering', in *Girls' Talk: Young women speak their hearts and minds,* ed. M. Pallotta-Chiarolli, Finch Publishing, Lane Cove, Sydney.

Uyguntemur, A. 1998, 'A metre of chiffon', in *Girls' Talk: Young women speak their hearts and minds,* ed. M. Pallotta-Chiarolli, Finch Publishing, Lane Cove, Sydney.

Venn-Brown, R. 1998, 'You can either get better or bitter', in *Girls' Talk: Young women speak their hearts and minds,* ed. M. Pallotta-Chiarolli, Finch Publishing, Lane Cove, Sydney.

Williams, T. 1998, 'A vision for the future', in *Girls' Talk: Young women speak their hearts and minds,* ed. M. Pallotta-Chiarolli, Finch Publishing, Lane Cove, Sydney.

Yuval-Davis, N. 1994, 'Women, ethnicity and empowerment', *Feminism and Psychology* v.4, n.1, pp.179-97.

Julie McLeod

chapter 4

Metaphors of the Self: Searching for young people's identity through interviews

REFLECTING on the contemporary popularity of memoirs and autobiographical writing, the Australian author Drusilla Modjeska eloquently describes some of the shifts this has wrought in collapsing simple distinctions between "fiction" and "non-fiction" and in situating the self as something to be remembered, re-told and re-created. "If the self is a lens", she writes, "then it is fractured, prismatic, contingent" (2000, p.7). The interest in memory and self is not, she argues, simply a return to older forms of biography and memoir, but rather suggests the emergence of another genre, a new way of figuring the self and its relation to the world in which it was formed: "The self is less a lens to look back on a different version of history than a prism. It breaks up the picture and reassembles it so that it is strange and at the same time utterly recognisable" (Modjeska 2000, p.7).

A fascination with the self and autobiography is evident too in much recent research in the humanities and the social sciences (Mansfield 2000; Rose 1998; Kuhn 1995). There has been a particular interest in subjectivity among feminist and poststructuralist researchers (Weedon 1999; Barrett 1999). Indeed, in the past decade or so, casting research projects in terms of what they can reveal about processes of gendered subjectivity has been a hallmark of much feminist sociological research. This can partly be explained by a feminist orientation to politicise the personal, and by the poststructuralist insistence on the "construction" of identity, the contingency of truth, and a privileging of partiality and perspective over omniscience and grand narratives. Identity is commonly represented as constructed, non-unitary, decentred, non-essential (e.g. Weedon 1999; Davies 1989, 1993; Kenway 1997; Hey 1997). Yet, at the same time, much of this kind of research pursues the question of how best to understand, to theorise, and to know the "truth" about that fragmented and elusive subjectivity. Assertions about the indeterminate character of subjectivity have thus been met by a proliferation of work that privileges subjectivity as a focus of inquiry and seeks to say more and more about its production.

What are some of the methodological and conceptual dilemmas raised by constructing research projects around the problematic of understanding "subjectivity"? In this chapter, I reflect on the interpretation of identity in an interview-based longitudinal study of young people (the 12 to 18 Project), that Lyn Yates and I began in 1993. Throughout this discussion, Modjeska's idea of the self as "prismatic" is an illuminating metaphor to keep in mind. In relation to research interviews, it reminds us that the self is not simply mirrored, directly revealed to the observer; and that the interview itself can offer only a partial angle onto the self – it too is prismatic and contingent.

This chapter begins with a brief outline of the design of the 12 to 18 Project, and an explanation of the focus of gender identity in this discussion. Some of the broader theoretical questions which frame the 12 to 18 Project are also addressed. Second, I consider the influence of poststructuralist claims about identity as discursively constructed, and identify some slippages and simplifications in these formulations. Third, I examine the popularity of interviews as a method for investigating identity, and note some dilemmas arising from the different ways of reading an interview text. I argue that interviews conducted longitudinally offer a rich source for interpreting the formation of identity "in process", and that in this task we need to work with both sociological and psychological understandings of identity. In the next section, I propose that Bjerrum Nielsen's (1996) reworked metaphor of the self as a "magic writing pad" offers us a way of representing identity that can account for change and continuity over time, and acknowledge both psychological and sociological dimensions, without falling into deterministic explanations either way. In the final section, I discuss these issues in relation to the self-representation of one young woman from the Project, and raise a number of issues about interpreting the significance of changes and continuities in her gender and class identity.

Designing an interview-based study of young people

The 12 to18 Project is a qualitative, longitudinal study of Australian school students as they progress from the end of primary school (12 years old) through to Year 12 and move into their first year post-school: or, if they have left school before Year 12, until they are 18.[1] Twice each year for seven years, Lyn Yates and I have interviewed the students, audio- and video-taping their responses. Students have attended four different kinds of school: two metropolitan schools, one of which is a co-educational private school and the other a state secondary college and two schools in a provincial town, a former technical school and a fairly traditional "academic" high school (see Yates & McLeod 1996; McLeod & Yates 1997).

We are examining both changing patterns over time among students from different schools and developments within individuals over the course of their secondary schooling and adolescent years. Comparisons are developed that are synchronic – across different groups of students at the same age level – and diachronic – developments and changes in individuals over time. The interviews focus on three themes in particular: the development of gendered subjectivity; young people's changing engagements with and attitudes to school; and students' thinking about their futures. This chapter explores questions concerning how to interpret the "production" or "development" of gender identity. It addresses how gender identity is represented – or negotiated – by young people in our study, and how it is represented as a concept in the research literature.

In terms of understanding "gender", we are observing both differences between girls and boys (what's changing, what's staying much the same), and the production of individual students as gendered (and classed) subjects (McLeod 2000; Yates 1999, 2000). In analysing interview responses, we have attended to what Harriet Bjerrum Nielsen calls "unacknowledged gender" (Bjerrum Nielsen 1996). Students are not explicitly asked to talk about how they think of themselves as a girl or a boy, or to respond to questions about their "genderedness" in direct and immediate ways. Rather, "gender subjectivity" is read off from the ways in which students respond to the full range of questions – even when gender is not for them an obviously foregrounded issue. Bjerrum Nielsen usefully suggests that:

> The gendered subjectivity is the gendered "being in the world" which consists of unacknowledged and to some extent unconscious gender (unconscious images/discourses and feelings attached to gender). Unacknowledged gender is the way gender is present as background when one reflects on something else, for example what kind of person one is, what kind of desires one has, what kind of feelings one experiences as having. Gender identity can then conversely be defined as the acknowledged gender (Bjerrum Nielsen 1996, p.11).

For example, in our study, there are patterns of gender difference in thinking about the future. In Year 7, many girls spoke with great optimism and energy about an adventurous and risk-taking future, whereas most boys were not thinking about the future in this way at all (Yates 1998; McLeod & Yates 1998). Or, during the middle years, many girls expressed an intense engagement with friends and of spending time talking and simply "hanging out" with them. For boys, friends were no less important, but, in general, friendship was conducted while engaging in more organised activity – sport, fishing, football, etc. (McLeod 1998a, 1998b; McLeod & Yates 1998). In other work, I have explored how the gender identity of two young people was shaped in interaction with class identifications and with the discourses and ethos of their particular school (McLeod 2000). Below, I briefly consider recurring concerns and patterns of thought in one young woman (Sue) attending a government secondary school in a provincial city. In the 12 to 18 Project, then, researching gender identity involves attention both to patterns of overt self-description and to more indirect expressions and representations of gendered conduct and attitudes.

The 12 to 18 Project examines the intersection of individual subjectivities and life histories with specific forms of schooling, acknowledging as well the effects on subjectivity of social differences and practices and of cultural discourses. Theoretically, and especially in terms of understanding identity, the Project has been shaped by the broad and diverse group of ideas described as "poststructuralism", including Foucauldian notions of "technologies of the self" (Foucault 1988; Rose 1998); by analyses of "habitus" – how dispositions are formed and transposed (Bourdieu & Wacquant 1992; Bourdieu 1998); and by work that explores both a sociological and psychological dimension to subjectivity (Hollway 1989, 1995; Walkerdine 1990, 1997; Donald 1991; Bjerrum Nielsen & Rudberg 1994).

The longitudinal design of the study allows us to observe the *development* of individual biographies, and to take seriously the (poststructuralist) injunction that the subject is "in process". This perspective also admits that "the psyche", as Wendy Hollway argues, is "something which is not a simple reflection of the social" (1995, p.92); and, broadly speaking, the self is viewed as constituted by both conscious and unconscious motivations and desires. At the same time, the Project is exploring what Bourdieu and Wacquant describe as a "relation of 'ontological complicity' ... between habitus as the socially constituted principle of perception and appreciation, and the world which determines it" (Bourdieu & Wacquant 1992, p.20). It addresses the performance of "habitus" as well as its inventiveness (Bourdieu & Wacquant 1992), looking at the formation and effects of "habitus" over time, rather than imagining it as a set of traits or relations once acquired or frozen in time.

Discourses and identities

Much recent research on young people, gender and identity in education has examined the micro-dynamics of gender relations, and explored what the particularity of interactions can tell us about the production of subjectivities, the operation of the broader gender order and the possibilities for deconstructing and reconstructing dominant discourses (e.g. Golden 1996; Jones 1996; Davies 1989, 1993; Gilbert & Taylor 1989; Kenway et al. 1993; Thorne 1993; Kamler et al. 1994; Hey 1997; Yates 1997).[2] A common task of such research projects, particularly those influenced by poststructuralism, is to identify the discursive practices that structure subject positions and the ways in which gendered subjects occupy/take-up/inhabit these positions.[3] So popular have these approaches become, that certain propositions about gender and identity now circulate as common-place and unquestioned truths – gender is constructed; people occupy multiple and even contradictory subject positions; discursive practices produce identities; and identities are non-unitary and de-centred.

On the one hand, then, there has been a proliferation of research on gender and identity and on the discursive production of identities. On the other hand, aspects of this work can sound formulaic, and offer relatively static, flat and one-dimensional accounts of identity. Further, in some forms of this research, there is a tendency to slip analytically from discourses to subjectivities as if they were the same thing: here subjects are principally understood as bearers of or effects of discourse. But, subjectivity is not coterminous with, and may exceed or disrupt, dominant cultural discourses (Bjerrum Nielsen & Rudberg 1994, 1995). In the 12 to 18 Project, the subject is conceptualised as "becoming" rather than fixed, as being a psychological as well as a sociological category, and consequently, a distinction is maintained between discourses and subjectivity because, as Harriet Bjerrum Nielsen and Monica Rudberg advise "[P]sychological life stories and cultural discourses are not reducible to one another" (1995, p.86).

In addition, the "discourses produce identity" argument can replicate some of the blind spots of socialisation theories which locate the subject as a passive, malleable and "acted upon" recipient of social messages (McLeod 1993). Wendy Hollway has observed that some poststructuralist accounts, despite often promising more, run "the danger of reducing the psychological subject to a series of positions in discourses, not only socially determined but unavoidably fragmented" (Hollway 1994, p.542). This makes it not much better than the socialisation account and risks instituting a fairly crude discourse determinism. Finally, despite the considerable body of research on gender identity in educational settings, studies of the formation of gender identity over time have generally not been well developed, and are particularly uncommon in poststructuralist studies (Bjerrum Nielsen & Davies n.d.). This has been a striking absence, especially given arguments that identity is dynamic, not fixed and in flux. Understanding how identities take shape over time is, then, a central concern of our longitudinal study.

The current attention to discourses and identities suggests one explanation for the popularity of research interviews. Interviews seem to offer unmediated access to the thoughts and feelings of the participants. The text of the interview thus holds many possibilities for analysing discourses, and can be seen as a quintessential or paradigmatic form of evidence for researching the (discursive) construction of identity.

Discovering identity through interviews

Interviewing has become a popular strategy in many research projects and methodologies – narrative inquiry, discourse analysis, action research, life history, oral history, case study, ethnography, or drawn upon as a supplement to "flesh out" or "bring to life" other forms of inquiry. Here, some questions are raised in relation to interpreting the interview as evidence for understanding identity. In researching identity, interviewing claims a certain self-evident appeal, promising to give us a glimpse into the "real", to the authenticity of lived experience and to the processes of subjectivity. The growing popularity of the research interview is thus linked as well to the broader cultural interest in biography and autobiography.

In this flurry of interviewing, however, what kind of knowledge and identities are actually being produced in the encounter between researcher and participant? There are numerous books offering guides to how to conduct the research interview, outlining ethical, technical and research protocols (Minichiello et al. 1995; Kvale 1996; Gillham 2000). But the interview itself is also a forum for the production and re-presentation of identity. Identity is not simply revealed in clear moments of truth, despite the aura of the interview as a kind of a secular confession. Much has already been written on how truth is constructed in the interaction between researcher and researched, that "power relations" can constrain and incite particular responses, and that any insight is always going to be partial (McLeod & Yates 1997), or, in Modjeska's terms, "contingent" and "prismatic". Such contingency is not properly understood as a "limitation" specific to the interview. What research approach can, in fact, give us a complete and full account of the subject? But it does mean that any findings drawn from interviews must be interpreted cautiously, reflexively and in relation to other interviews and research. Simply presenting the "voice" of the participants by describing what they have said (no matter how intrinsically interesting that might be), or quoting large slabs of transcribed "data" does not remove the hermeneutic task of making sense of it all, of bringing together different angles and perspectives, of interpreting one comment against another, or of comparing individual experiences with broader social patterns and cultural practices and with debates in the relevant research literature, and so on.

In this respect, longitudinal studies can offer a more substantial body of evidence for interpreting processes of identity formation and identity practices than single interviews or interviews conducted over a relatively short period of time. This is not to say that such interviews do not offer rich material or suggest insights into an individual's experiences, attitudes, memories and so on. But they offer limited insight into the *ongoing process* of the formation of (gender) identity. Analysing interviews conducted over time can illuminate, confirm or unsettle initial and tentative interpretations, alert us to recurring motifs and tropes in participants' narratives as well as to shifts and changes, suggest continuities or disruptions in emotional investments, in desires and in dispositions, and provide a strong sense of how particular identities are taking shape and developing. This allows identity to be analysed as a process and not simply as a repository of one-off opinions or quotations.

One common criticism of interview-based research and other related forms of qualitative inquiry is that participants' responses are too much shaped by how they were feeling on that day and at the time when they were interviewed: it therefore can be regarded as problematic and unreliable evidence. It is the case that what is reported in interviews is contextual, partial and most likely to be differently inflected depending on how the person is feeling at the time. And in single interviews, there is an additional risk that the significance of a particular response can be either inflated or simply not noticed, lost in the rich detail of the transcript. But, conducting interviews longitudinally, comparing transcripts, addressing a similar group of questions each time, provides some check against over- or misreading particular remarks. It also means that the interpretative process is constantly subject to review and revision, with some initial ideas confirmed, others unsettled.

Interview questions for the 12 to 18 Project range over many topics to do with self, school and future, for example: self description; earliest memories; memories of starting school or of Year 7; social and political attitudes, e.g. to unemployment or racism; relationships with friends and family; favourite and least favourite school subjects; prevalence of bullying at school; daydreaming about the future as well as imagining self in future work or as an adult. In some interviews, one set of questions is emphasised more than the others – for example, at the end of Year 9 questions focused more on the self – and in other rounds, questions are asked about school that are similar to ones asked in earlier rounds, such as comparing answers to what they thought about school subjects at Year 7 and then at Year 10. One aim in such questioning has been to see how students respond at different stages, and whether there are changes in how they describe themselves, or in their judgments of how things are going at school. By asking students a variety of questions about themselves – such as remembering key events, or describing themselves when younger as well as in the present, comparing them-selves at different stages in their growing up or imagining themselves in the future – we are accumulating observations of how they represent themselves over time.

When conducting interviews to investigate (gendered) subjectivity, a number of approaches to reading the interview text should be clarified. First, the transcript can be read as if the interviewee is a register, an embodiment or distillation of key cultural discourses, with the purpose being to find traces or inscriptions of these discourses in the accumulation of responses. This applies to "literal" readings of explicit responses as well as to subtle readings of metaphors, or of the "non-said", of the repressed, for example. The desire in both kinds of reading is to uncover the discourse, to find out more about the wider culture and society in which the subject lives: in some ways, the subject is thus researched as a "vehicle" for the discourse. Second, interview transcripts can be read to find out more about the particular subject – their attitudes, the idiosyncratic ways in which they conduct their lives, how their particular biography or life history takes shape, and the particular technologies of the self that fashion their identity (Rose 1998). The 12 to 18 Project attempts to develop both kinds of readings – and to read back and forth between the two, between the particular individual and the effects of schooling and contemporary social relations.

Third, and in relation to this kind of "double reading", the difference between reading an interview "psychologically" and "sociologically" needs to be acknowledged. The social science research interview, is *not* the same as clinical psychotherapy, despite any intended or unin-tended therapeutic effects, and despite issues of transference being common to both. The clinical interview has different purposes, requires different forms of disciplinary training, involves a distinct ethical client/counsellor relation and consequently produces different kinds of (self) knowledge (see McLeod & Yates 1997; McLeod 2000). Nevertheless, if the purpose of the interview is to do more than catalogue the dominant discourses that position and construct subjects, then it should take account of psychological effects and the powerful vagaries of individual life histories (Donald 1991; Walkerdine 1990, 1997; Hollway 1995). For example, psychological and unconscious processes – desires, fears, anxieties, defences – shape the way participants' speak about themselves. The repetition of certain phrases, patterns and tropes in responses, recurring themes, are clues, signifying aspects of the representation and constitution of identity. We are not primarily concerned with concentrating exclusively on psychological processes or psychodynamic relations, or on developing an elaborated psychological theory of the self. But the effects of psychological processes are acknowledged insofar as they help us to understand the interaction between individual biographies and schooling over time. And, in relation to this, we need to be able to account for both continuity and change in the way in which young people represent themselves in interviews.

The self as a magic writing pad

How can subjectivity be represented and theorised as both (relatively) stable and changing? Is it possible to work with both psychological and sociological accounts of the self?[4] One suggestive way for conceptualising the self has been developed by Harriet Bjerrum Nielsen in an interview-based study of women across three generations. In order to develop a way of understanding gender identity, Bjerrum Nielsen extends Freud's metaphor of "psychic apparatuses" as a "magic writing pad" in which the subject is understood as a kind of palimpsest. "The magic writing pad consists of two layers: a soft wax slate and over it a thin, transparent leaf of paper". This magic writing-pad "all the time receives new inscriptions upon it without having the old ones erased", even though the older ones may not always be immediately apparent and may need to be read and deciphered under special lighting" (Bjerrum Nielsen 1996, p.7).

> With this picture Freud shows us that permanence and change do not rule out the other: the mental apparatus is of such a kind that it is receptive in unlimited way(s) to other new perceptions and yet creates permanent – even if not unalterable – traces of recollection of them (ibid).

The usefulness of this metaphor is that it "makes it possible to maintain a certain developmental perspective on subjectivity, without ending up in either determinism or universalism" (ibid). In other words, it avoids the laws, norms and "general stages" of developmentalism as well as the sense that subjectivity is simplistically determined by either psychological or sociological or discursive imperatives.

The metaphor of the self as a magic writing pad locates the formation of gender identity as a recursive process, one in which identity is neither "randomly constituted", nor determined by an inexorable "linear advancing and logic" (ibid). It offers a way of thinking about the intersections between life histories, narratives of the self, social practices, institutional effects and so on, and the relative impact of these "inscriptions" at different ages and stages. While still analysing subjectivity as produced and discourses as constitutive, it suggests a way of understanding how sociological and cultural practices, in conjunction with psychological and emotional processes, shape the formation of subjectivity over time. In this formulation, we can see how at different times some discursive traces are more pronounced than at other times, that their influence is not neatly predictable but that their markings are never completely erased.

For a longitudinal study, the magic writing pad is a very appealing metaphor. It allows us to simultaneously represent change and the unexpected, and continuity and stability. Though derived from quite different theoretical traditions, it complements our attention to the formation of "habitus", which is partly also a metaphor for describing how subjects are formed, but with a focus on the interaction of social rather than psychological processes.

Bourdieu describes habitus as:

> *the strategy-generating principle enabling agents to cope with unforeseen and ever-changing situations ... a system of lasting and transposable dispositions which, integrating past experiences, functions at every moment as a matrix of perceptions, appreciations and actions and makes possible the achievement of infinitely diversified tasks* (quoted in Bourdieu & Wacquant 1992, p.18).

In the following section, I reflect on some recurring themes in one young woman's interviews, emphasising patterns of change and continuity, and the inscription of "lasting and transposable dispositions" which also allow for a degree of inventiveness.

Representing identity retrospectively

In the final year of the interviews (2000), participants in the 12 to 18 Project were each given a "compilation video" of excerpts from all their video-taped interviews. In a follow-up interview, they were asked for their impressions of the video and encouraged to reflect on themselves and their schooling. We too watched the compilation videos, listening again to them in Grade 6 or Year 8 or Year 11, seeing them describe themselves, or talk about their future or discuss school and friendship. The process of retrospective reflection has underlined recurring patterns in the ways in which individuals represent themselves, their dispositions and their orientation to school and to the world beyond. And it has also highlighted incidents, decisions, shifts in attitude that have produced change.

Sue lives with her mother and four sisters in a small country town and attends an ex-technical school in a working-class part of a nearby provincial city. She works hard at home, especially since her father left, and even as a young girl, took on many household responsibilities – cooking, looking after animals, stacking wood. She often unselfconsciously refers to all the work she does around the house, seeing this as something that just has to be done. Sue successfully completed Year 12, is enrolled locally in a one-year TAFE nursing course, and is planning to move into a flat on her own to be close to work and study. Sue had mixed experiences of schooling, and she and her family are proud of her completing school. At the end of primary school, she was enthusiastic and happy, but in the junior and middle years of secondary, she was miserable, experiencing bullying and teasing, losing interest in school work and lacking confidence in her ability. In Grade 6, she imagines that in the future, she'll "be through university and college and I'll go through there so I can try and find a job" (1993 interview). But secondary school is a disappointment: she does not like much about it all, except "the caf" and she starts to find the work hard. At the end of Year 7, Sue wants to become a chef: "I've always wanted to be a chef. Cause I love cooking" (1994b interview).

By the end of Year 9, Sue is feeling less confident about her capacity to become a chef, doubts she can "manage it". She decides that she will aim for child-care instead, another occupation that draws on her existing domestic responsibilities and one for which she would not need to do much, if any, post-school study. In Year 10, when she imagines herself working in the future, she cannot see herself "in a big, big, place, me own building me own office, I see myself working, but not that kind of work ... Just a small business, don't know what kind, but just a small one" (1997b interview). The kind of future that would make her really happy is one characterised by both conventional fantasies of wealth and by very modest expectations: "If I get the job I want, I win Tattslotto, basically just to have a good life ... Well, I don't want to be a millionaire, but good wealth, a house, a car that runs." (1997b interview). At the end of school, a happy future for Sue would be a "stable one", "not too rich, just comfortable" (2000a interview). In just about all her interviews when asked what she thinks about the future, Sue replies in matter-of-fact way: "just take it as it comes".

At one level, this summary can be interpreted as another story about the reproduction of class and gender identities – nursing for a country working-class girl, alienation from the culture of the school, a modest and circumscribed view of future possibilities and a constrained sense of agency and capacity to act on the world. In terms of "habitus", it could suggest that certain dispositions and orientations to the world have been firmly established, and that class and gender relations remain relatively unchanged. But changes are taking place in relation to gender and class identities, for Sue and for young women like her, and other interpretations are also possible. I want to comment briefly here on two recurring and inter-related themes in Sue's interviews: her relationship with her mother; and her perception of work.

Over many interviews with Sue, "cooking" is revealed as a heavily coded occupation, connected to her relation to her mother and to the imagination of her own future. Sue's mother manages a holiday camp and is responsible for cooking meals for the visitors: Sue is also learning this role. "At the camp, when I help Mum cook, mum lets me cook, like to help me start. Like easier than getting a job" (1994b interview). When asked whether she thought her life would be very different from her parents, she "reckon[s] it will be the same":

Cause you've got like cooking, you gotta do cooking, but the only difference is, right, it's a camp you'll be cooking. You'll be cooking for camps not like for, in a restaurant or something, 'cause you'll be cooking totally different food, but you're still cooking food, so it'll sort of be the same. (1994b interview).

Here, the inevitability of cooking conveys a sense of ever-present responsibilities and hard work, of a future characterised by predictable domestic duties. These comments are not said to us, however, in a "sorry for myself" way: rather they are conveyed as a mundane observation about the way the world is. The repeated phrase, "just take it as it comes", similarly suggests resignation. But, in fact, Sue does not simply "just take things as they come": she also effects changes, plans strategically, envisages and is working towards an independent future, outside immediate familial responsibilities.[5] I am suggesting here that Sue is shaped by (and represents herself in terms of) both fairly traditional, country, working-class expectations for girls, and a newer set of discourses and possibilities afforded by, for example, the expansion in school retention, by the growth of tertiary education (especially the TAFE sector), and by feminism and its legacy of greater possibilities for the economic and emotional independence of women. These are important factors for both Sue and her mother.

Sue has a very close relationship with her mother, and in her description of the family dynamics, appears to have a strong identification with the organisational responsibilities of the "mother". In other ways too, her activities and plans develop in relation to her mother's work and study. During Year 9, the family move away from the camp and her mother returns to part-time study in a welfare course at the local TAFE. As a single parent, her mother manages to care for five children, study and work part-time, and do some voluntary work. Sue sees her mother finish a course and get a job in a social welfare agency. In Sue's Year 12, her mother again returns to do further study to upgrade her qualifications. From Year 11 onwards, Sue starts to focus more on school and study and shows a strong determination to complete school. During this period she also begins voluntary work at an agency providing food and housing assistance. In Year 12, she decides she wants to do nursing, and we hear then that her mother is very happy about this decision as she too had initially trained as a nurse.

Sue's path through school is negotiated in dialogue with her mother's life. Her choices and plans are not simply the result of conscious imitation, but they do suggest the complexity of that psychodynamic relation, one which, at least from what we can see, has had positive effects for Sue. For both, going to school, staying at school, finishing and returning to school, are recurring themes. So, too, is managing the demands of family and domestic responsibilities and working at building a life away from that sphere. Both Sue and her mother experience success at school and both engage in a range of activities – housework and physical labour, voluntary work, paid work, study, family life.

Recent work on girls, class and schooling has examined the production of clever middle-class girls, their busy lives, their anxiety about success, and the pressures they face living up to the feminist expectation that girls can (and should) do everything (Walkerdine, Lucey & Melody forthcoming; Wyn 2000; McLeod 2000). Walkerdine, Lucey and Melody argue that the production of the hyper-busy, success-oriented, middle-class girl is linked to the creation of the rational bourgeois subject as feminine (forthcoming). But, what other issues about "success" and "busyness" might be at play in understanding the lives of young women like Sue? Sue does not represent herself or her imagined future in the language of "success" and "achievement", despite the fact that she has fulfilled her ambitions, exceeded her family expectations and is managing to combine a complicated array of duties. What vocabulary is available for writing about achievements such as Sue's that does not sound patronising? What do the achievements of working-class girls signify? Sue's pathway through school and on to further study is neither a story about working-class escape through university education and the professions, and nor is it simply about failure and thwarted ambition.

Sue's goals and achievements are cut across by another view of her future in which there "will always be cooking" and she will "just take things as they come", phrases which encapsulate a particular habitus, and way of situating oneself in the world. Such expressions of resignation, of "not getting too above yourself" are not contradicted for her by her experience of success and evidence of strategic planning and hard work. These two orientations co-exist and point to patterns of continuity and change in Sue's gender and class identity. Their form and effects cannot be explained by reference to either simply "dominant discourses" or to developmental patterns and crises in growing up. Nor does it seem entirely adequate to describe them as evidence of identity as comprised of "multiple", shifting subject positions. This view, as Hollway (1995) notes, is unable to account for why some positions are more strongly invested in than others, and why the development of particular identities proceeds neither as a "linear advancing" nor as "randomly constituted" (Bjerrum Nielsen 1996). I have attempted to illustrate the formation of identity as "in-process", rather than identity as a completed project that is enacted through static discourses or as a result of inexorable sociological or psychological factors. Reading Sue's interviews retrospectively, we see traces of the psychodynamic relation (between her mother and herself), the formation and performance of habitus, and the effects of specific cultural and historical changes: the interview does not simply reveal self-evident discourses or complete identities. Returning to the metaphor of the magic writing pad, certain inscriptions persist, new ones also appear but they do not completely erase the old. Sue's self-representation in interviews illustrates this double, recursive process. It also challenges us to consider whether habitus as, "the strategy-generating principle enabling agents to cope with unforeseen and ever-changing situations" (Bourdieu & Wacquant 1992, p.18) can, indeed, sufficiently account for continuity and change in contemporary gender and class identities.

Conclusion

I began with Modjeska's idea of the self as "fractured, prismatic, contingent" (2000, p7.) and observed that a fascination with the self and subjectivity is also evident in contemporary social science, especially in feminist and poststructuralist research. The popularity of the research interview is linked to this focus on the self, and I have suggested that the interview itself offers a partial perspective on to the self. It too is "prismatic", reflecting and refracting glimpses of the self from different angles. One of the methodological dilemmas explored in the 12 to 18 Project is how, in the context of the partiality of the interview, the elusiveness of subjectivity, and an array of theoretical possibilities, to interpret the representation of identity. In discussing some of the lenses and metaphors we have found helpful, I have argued that we need to attend to the different form and effects of change and continuity in young people's gender and class identities today.

References

Barrett, M. 1999, *Imagination in Theory: Essays on writing and culture*, Polity Press, Cambridge.

Bjerrum Nielsen, H. 1996, 'The magic writing pad – on gender and identity', *Young: Journal of Nordic Youth Research,* v.4, n.3, pp.2-18.

Bjerrum Nielsen, H. & Davies, B. (n.d.), The construction of gendered identity through classroom talk, unpublished manuscript, Centre for Women's Research, University of Oslo, Norway.

Bjerrum Nielsen, H. & Rudberg, M. 1994, *Psychological Gender and Modernity*, Scandinavian University Press, Oslo.

—— 1995, 'Gender recipes among young girls', *Young: Journal of Nordic Youth Research,* v.3, n.2, pp.71-88.

Bourdieu, P. 1998, *Practical Reason: On the theory of action*, Stanford University Press, Stanford.

Bourdieu P. & Wacquant, L.J.D. 1992, *An Invitation to Reflexive Sociology*, University of Chicago Press, Chicago.

Davies, B. 1989, *Frogs and Snails and Feminist Tales: Pre-school children and gender*, Allen & Unwin, Sydney.

—— 1993, *Shards of Glass: Children reading and writing beyond gendered subject positions*, Allen & Unwin, Sydney.

Donald, J. 1991, 'On the threshold: Psychoanalysis and cultural studies', in *Psychoanalysis and Cultural Theory: Thresholds*, ed. J. Donald, Macmillan, London.

Foucault, M. 1988, 'Technologies of the self', in *Technologies of the Self: A seminar with Michel Foucault*, eds L.H. Martin, H. Gutman & P.H. Hutton, Tavistock Publications, London.

Gilbert, P. & Taylor, S. 1989, *Fashioning the Feminine: Girls, popular culture and schooling*, Allen & Unwin, Sydney.

Gillham B. 2000, *The Research Interview*, Continuum, London.

Golden, J. 1996, 'Critical imagination: Serious play with narrative and gender', *Gender and Education*, v.8, n.3, pp.323-35.

Hey, V. 1997, *The Company She Keeps: An ethnography of girls' friendship*, Open University Press, Buckingham.

Hollway, W. 1989, *Subjectivity and Method in Psychology: Gender, meaning and science*, Sage Publications, London.

—— 1994, 'Beyond sex differences: A project for feminist psychology', *Feminism & Psychology*, v.4, n.4, pp.538-46.

—— 1995, 'Feminist discourse and women's heterosexual desire', in *Feminism and Discourse: Psychological perspectives*, eds S. Wilkinson & C. Kitzinger, Sage Publications, London.

Jones, L. 1996, 'Young girls' notions of "femininity"', *Gender and Education*, v.8, n.3, pp.311-21.

Kamler, B., McLean, R., Reid, J.A. & Simpson, A. 1994, *Shaping Up Nicely: The formation of schoolgirls and schoolboys in the first month of school*, a Report to the Gender Equity and Curriculum Reform Project, Department of Employment, Education and Training, AGPS, Canberra.

Kenway, J. 1997, 'Having a postmodern turn or postmodernist angst: A disorder experienced by an author who is not yet dead or even close to it', in *Education: Culture, economy and society*, eds A.H. Halsey, H. Lauder, P. Brown & A. Stuart Wells, Oxford University Press, Oxford, pp.131-43.

Kenway, J., Willis, S., Blackmore, J. & Rennie, L. 1993, 'Learning from girls: What can girls teach feminist teachers?', *Melbourne Studies in Education*, special issue *Feminism and Education*, pp.63-77.

Kuhn, A. 1995, *Family Secrets: Acts of memory and imagination*, Verso, London.

Kvale, S. 1996, *Interviews: An introduction to qualitative research interviewing*, Sage, Thousand Oaks, CA.

Mansfield, N. 2000, *Subjectivity: Theories of the self from Freud to Haraway*, Allen & Unwin, Sydney.

McLeod, J. 1993, 'Impossible fictions: Utopian visions and feminist educational research', *Melbourne Studies in Education*, special issue *Feminism and Education*, pp.107-18.

—— 1998a, Friendship, schooling and gender identity work, paper presented at the annual conference of the Australian Association for Research in Education, University of Adelaide, December.

—— 1998b, 'Studying young people today: Patterns and points of difference', *Changing Education*, Journal of the Deakin Centre for Education and Change, pp.1-5.

—— 2000, 'Subjectivity and schooling in a longitudinal study of secondary school students', *British Journal of Sociology of Education*, v.21, n.4.

McLeod, J. & Yates, L. 1997, 'Can we find out about girls and boys today or must we settle for talking about ourselves? Dilemmas of a feminist, qualitative, longitudinal project', *Australian Educational Researcher*, v.24, n.3, pp.23-42.

—— 1998, 'How young people think about self, work and futures', *Family Matters*, n.49, pp.28-33.

Minichiello, V., Aroni, R., Timewell, E. & Alexander, L. 1995, *In-depth Interviewing: Principles, techniques, analysis*, 2nd edn, Longman, Melbourne.

Modjeska, D. 2000, 'A writ served', *The Australian's Review of Books*, v.5, n.6, pp.6-7.

Rose, N. 1998, *Inventing Ourselves: Psychology, power and personhood*, Cambridge University Press, Cambridge.

Thorne, B. 1993, *Gender Play: Girls and boys in school*, Open University Press, Buckingham.

Walkerdine, V. 1990, *Schoolgirl Fictions*, Verso, London.

—— 1997, *Daddy's Girl: Young girls and popular culture*, Macmillan, London.

Walkerdine, V., Lucey, H. & Melody, J. (forthcoming), *Growing up girl: Gender and class in the 21st century*, Macmillan, London.

Weedon, C. 1999, *Feminism, Theory and the Politics of Difference*, Blackwell Publishers, Oxford.

Wyn, J. 2000, 'The post-modern girl: Education, "success" and the construction of girls' identities', (this volume).

Wyn, J. & White, R. 1998, 'Young people, social problems and Australian youth studies', *Journal of Youth Studies*, v.1, n.1, pp.23-38.

Yates, L. 1997, 'Constructing and deconstructing "girls" as a category of concern', in *Education into the 21st Century: Dangerous terrain for women?*, eds A. MacKinnon, I. Elgvist-Saltzman & A. Prentice, Falmer Press, London.

—— 1998, Dreams of the future in an era of change: Longitudinal qualitative research speaks back to policy studies, paper presented to the American Educational Research Association annual conference, San Diego, April.

—— 1999, 'How should we tell stories about class and gender and schooling today?' in *Ansvar og Protest: kjonn, klasse og utdanning I senmoderniteten*, eds G.E. Birkelund, A.-K. Broch-Due & A. Nilsen, University of Bergen Press, Bergen.

—— 2000, 'Representing "class" in qualitative research', (this volume).

Yates, L. & McLeod, J. 1996, '"And how would you describe yourself?" Researchers and researched in the first stages of a qualitative, longitudinal research project', *Australian Journal of Education*, v.40, n.1, pp.88-103.

Notes

[1]   The Project began at the end of 1993 with interviews with students in Grade 6, and in 2000 most of the students had either finished or left school. We have interviewed 26 main students twice each year throughout this period, as well as having additional interviews with their selected friends. We have over 350 interviews with 26 main students. The Project has been supported by funding from the Australian Research Council, La Trobe University, Deakin University and the University of Technology Sydney.

[2]   In Australia, Bronwyn Davies' (1989, 1993) ethnographic and poststructuralist studies of pre- and primary school children have been highly influential in establishing the significance of daily interactions between young children in securing the hegemony of sexual binaries and the gender order. Barrie Thorne's (1993) ethnography of North American primary school girls and boys examines the patterns of separation and integration between and among groups of girls and boys. She examines the "dynamics of different social institutions and situations" in order to gain insight into "the fluctuating significance of gender in the ongoing scenes of social life" (Thorne 1993, p.61). A related argument is made by Barbara Kamler et al. (1994) in their rich observational study of the first month of primary school for preparatory students in an Australian provincial city. This study analyses the ways in which, inside and outside of the classroom, discursive practices and regimes discipline the formation of schoolgirls and schoolboys.

[3]   The influence, and the limitations, of "discourse" approaches in the general field of Australian youth studies is usefully discussed in a recent article by Wyn and White (1998, especially pp.28, 32-33).

4   Of course, attempting to bring together psychological and sociological understandings is fraught and problematic: both represent different, even contradictory, perspectives and are often opposed in caricatured form. It is not possible to engage properly with this debate here, but I do want to acknowledge James Donald's comments on the desire to have a "full theory" of the subject by adding psychoanalysis to the social sciences. Donald warns against a common attitude to psychoanalysis which he characterises as the "polyfilla model". In this model, psychoanalysis "fills the gap" in Marxist or cultural studies or sociology ... by apparently offering the possibility of a fuller, complete "Theory of the Subject" (Donald 1991, p.4). The "add psychoanalysis and mix" approach also presumes that it is possible and indeed desirable to integrate psychoanalytic and sociological accounts. Donald argues, however, that: "Any such attempt to merge the two bodies of theory blunts their specific insights and ignores their incompatibilities and contradictions. What seems potentially more fruitful is the dialogue in which although the two discourses remain distinct – they are always in some sense talking past each other – the questions untranslatably specific to each can provoke new thinking and insights in the other" (Donald 1991, p.3).

5   In contrast to the boys at the school Sue attended, the girls displayed a much greater degree of planning, organisation and sense of purpose in the world. But that is the subject of another discussion.

chapter 5

The postmodern girl: Education, "success" and the construction of girls' identities

THE increasing participation of girls in secondary education has tended to be uncritically accepted as a "good thing" for girls. Over the last decade, girls have gradually increased their level of participation compared to boys, from a situation in 1984, where 34% of boys and 37% of girls completed secondary school, to 1998 where 71% of boys and 81% of girls completed secondary school (Marks & Fleming 2000). This overall pattern of gender-based differences in school participation has existed for the past 25 years (Yates 1997). However, the strong exam performance by some girls in traditionally male-dominated subjects, such as physics and mathematics, has been regarded as an indicator of the success of 20 years of anti-sexist educational programs and strategies.

In this context, the education of girls is now seldom problematised and questions of educational disadvantage have shifted focus from girls to address "the boys question" with many authors claiming that boys are the new disadvantaged, educationally (e.g. West 1995). In this chapter, I move the discussion of gender and education away from questions of "advantage" and "disadvantage" to explore instead the ways in which different groups of girls construct identities in relation to education.

The discussion takes as a starting point, questions posed by Johnson (1993) in her book *The Modern Girl*. Johnson's study of the intersections of education and youth in the 1950s reveals how educational discourses were shaped by contemporary understandings of youth. She demonstrates how girls were expected to make very different uses of education from boys. For example, Johnson shows how schools in the 1950s ensured that girls learned the domestic sciences of cooking and sewing; skills regarded as essential for their main occupations as adults. The transformation of the "girl" into the "young woman" is illustrated through the image of the "school girl" in her bulky school uniform in contrast to the (same) elegant, fashion-conscious "young woman" in the figure-accentuating dress which she has sewed for herself in sewing classes (Johnson 1993, p.80). Today there is no comparable, visible, transformation role that schools play. Yet, schooling is a significant site for the construction of girls' and young women's identities, with "success" carrying a new meaning for girls and their families, particularly middle-class girls. This chapter focuses particularly on the construction of educational success and its impact on young women's subjectivities.

In previous work (Wyn & Dwyer, 1999) I have suggested that young people of the post-1970 generation are entering adulthood incrementally, in stages, earlier than the "baby boomer" generation. The traditional, linear concept of transition to adulthood, from school to work is increasingly out of step with the realities of young people's lives. I have also raised the possibility that young people's life patterns may provide evidence of a "new adulthood", which is different in key aspects from that of the pre-1970s generations; in other words, the meaning of adulthood is changing. Engaging with new workplace practices that involve flexible practices, short-term and insecure employment, contesting sexualities, balancing work, leisure, study: young people are embracing an adulthood which differs in significant ways from that which was experienced by the baby boomer generation. What role does schooling play in the constitution of feminine identities which are associated with a "new adulthood"?

In this chapter I explore what current research and writing can reveal about the way in which schooling and education constitute young women's identities, and suggest some directions for future research into the relationship between education, youth and society. I begin with a summary of the main arguments put forward by Johnson. I identify some key themes in the relationship between education and contemporary feminine identities and provide a discussion of what this might mean for future research agendas.

The postmodern girl

What kinds of ideals of individuality and personhood does education offer young women today? How are girls' identities constructed in relation to education in the 2000s? These questions draw on Lesley Johnson's analysis of the relationship between girls, identity and education (Johnson 1993). Her work provides a useful reference point from which to pose questions about the relationship between girlhood and education in the 2000s.

Johnson explores the historical relationship of women to the cultural ideals of personhood and individuality through an account of the social definitions of girlhood and growing up in Australia in the 1950s and early 1960s. Johnson essentially looks at the problems faced and possibilities opened up for young women in Australia during that period as they encountered modern ideals of individuality and personhood – and especially the idea of the "unitary self" – in the institutional setting of the school.

There are two elements of Johnson's work that are of particular interest. She links the personal and the institutional, demonstrating how individual identities and institutional processes "fitted" together through the 1950s and 1960s. Her insistence on historical specificity means that, in analysing these social processes, she avoids essentialising girls and women as a category. Second, she reveals how certain elements of "youth" were problematised and in particular, how "the problem of youth" focused in large part around concerns about masculinity and the future of manhood in Australia. Both of these elements are of direct relevance to contemporary youth and education research agendas.

One of the explicit roles of education in the 1950s was to prepare young people for their place in the "modern world" (Johnson 1993, p.35). Youth was constructed as a period during which one "became" someone, identity was constructed and the individual was established as an independent entity. Adulthood (or marriage for women) was a destination, a point of arrival and the end point of the period of youth. Education, as an integral phase of the passage into adulthood, was one of the events of youth, located by the science of developmental psychology within a linear process of development, propelled towards the achievement of maturity. The significance of the processes of youth development, of which education was a part, lay only in their leading to a marked ending. The modernist notion of youth, according to Johnson, was one in which youth was a time of experimentation and self exploration, which ended when one became adult and learned how one belonged in a stable society – as opposed to the possibility of directing one's own life to one's own risk and danger. The notions of individuality and of personhood that dominated educational thinking in the 1950s and 1960s were that growing up entailed making a closure, becoming an adult was the end of the process of education (Johnson 1993, p.150).

Yet, as Johnson reveals, there were tensions between the realities of young people's lives then, and the dominant discourses which stressed the role of education in ensuring the social integration of youth. For example, a number of texts in the 1950s claimed that with the consumer society, young people were faced with the possibility of reinventing one's self, and with the prospect that youth need not come to an end (Johnson 1993, p.38). Fears were expressed that young people would not be able to form stable selves under these conditions, and that this would undermine notions of community and order. These were texts which constructed youth as a social problem and which provided a rationale for the intervention of professionals in young people's lives in order to ensure correct developmental processes (see Wyn & White 1997).

Central to the concerns that emerged in the Australian texts on youth development and education in the 1950s, were fears which were related to changes to manhood. Johnson's study reveals the deep-seated anxiety about ensuring the correct conditions for the continuity and social order. This concern was focused largely on young men and in particular on the emerging participation of working-class young men in new patterns of consumption and in new "subcultural" practices of expression, which were particularly noted in the UK literature (Hall & Jefferson 1976; Wyn & White 1997).

These ideas provide a useful framework for questioning the relationship between education and girlhood in the 2000s. The contemporary "what about the boys" issue, for example, has certain continuities with the earlier concerns about the future of manhood. Concern about working-class youth, which dominated thinking about youth in the 1950s and 1960s, is replaced in the 2000s with fears about the futures of middle-class boys. As Yates (1997) and Teese (1998) have pointed out, it is this group of boys whose outcomes are threatened by the educational success of middle-class girls.

Another continuity with the older discourses is the way in which schooling is implicated in the "project" of the construction of the rational, unitary subject, or self. Walkerdine (2000) suggests that the phenomenon of high-performing, middle-class girls represents a continuation of this project. She argues that this project has emerged in a new form, as the constitution of high-aspiring, career-minded middle-class professional women, who have the capacity to engage with new, flexible, work practices and the increasing contingencies of life. Walkerdine's descriptions of educationally successful middle-class girls in the UK suggests that the phenomenon of "clever girls" is a cultural construct, taken up by many girls who enact endless performances of excellence.

In other respects, the changes associated with "late modernity" have meant discontinuity with older educational discourses. The possibility of closure to the period of youth is, by 2000, a questionable concept. The role of education in the development of "mature" identities, which formed a significant part of the discourses surrounding the emergence of mass education in the 1950s, is no longer feasible. Yet, education continues to be implicated in the processes of identity formation.

Rattansi and Phoenix (1997) suggest that the period of change, which is characterised as late modernity has significant implications for the construction of young people's identities. The transition from industrial to post-industrial production, they argue, is creating new hierarchies in the labour force and class structure. They see evidence of the emergence in the UK of an "underclass" of insecure, part-time, peripheral workers, and "core workers" who straddle the older manual/non-manual divide (Rattansi & Phoenix 1997, p.123). The rise of new service and financial sectors is associated with the creation of new groups of highly paid workers. For individuals, Rattansi and Phoenix argue, the impact of these changes is to increase the complexity of their lives, and to create a context of flux rather than of certainty. They suggest that under these conditions, identities become "disembedded" and "de-stabilised" and at the same time, opportunities are opened up for the "invention and re-invention of identities" – loosening earlier class-based identifications (Rattansi & Phoenix 1997, p.123). A significant element in the de-stabilising of identities, they suggest, is the potential for gendered identities to be "transformed" with the increased participation of women's employment and the increase in male unemployment. These changes and their significance for identity formation have been noted by many social theorists, including Beck (1992) and Giddens (1991) and by youth researchers (for example, Wyn & Dwyer 1999; Walkerdine 1996; Furlong & Cartmel 1997).

The implications of these changes for the relationship between young people and education have not yet been widely explored. It is clear though, that rather than aiming for closure, certainty and completeness, education for the new economies of late modernity is implicated in the construction of very different subjectivities. Although much educational literature remains locked into the 1950s linear thinking about *the* transition to adulthood, there is a growing literature and research base which demonstrates the multifaceted, complex and nonlinear nature of the process of "growing up" (Wyn & Dwyer 1999). Many authors have commented on the difficulty even of ascertaining when the end point of youth has been reached and adulthood has been achieved. Far from finding one's "authentic self", young people have engaged with the "postmodern" reality that people possess multiple selves, just as they inhabit multiple sites and are involved in many different kinds of relationships. For example, a young person may be employed part-time as a section manager of a supermarket and also be a student in senior secondary school. Such a young person is positioned very differently in each institution and to the people within them, having adult responsibility and authority in the workplace and childlike constraints in school. In the following section, I explore some of the implications of these changes for education and the formation of young women's identities.

Education and the formation of identities

In this discussion of recent thinking about education, the construction of gendered identities and subjectivity I explore three, connected themes, which are relevant to the formation of femininities: girls and educational success, the relationship between feminism and femininity and education, work and risk.

Clever girls

"Clever girls" is a highly "classed" concept. It refers to a particular kind of "success" and performance (which is, at the same time, being regarded as a problem for middle-class boys). Mostly, "girls' performance" and being "clever" is code for achievement as measured by examination results, and more generally, gaining entrance to prestigious tertiary courses and institutions. Who are these "clever girls"? Australian research on school performance confirms that class remains a significant element in predicting outcomes. Yates and McLeod's seven-year qualitative, longitudinal study of young people and schooling provides up-to-date evidence of the continued significance of social class to young people's experiences of and outcomes from schooling – and of the continued importance of class for schools themselves (Yates 2000). Other research programs also provide conclusive evidence of the influence of class on educational outcomes and on young people's post-school trajectories (Teese 1998; Dwyer 2000; Lamb 1998). Carrington has suggested that working-class and Aboriginal girls are circumscribed by schooling as sexual(ised) and delinquent and argues that schooling channels working-class girls into a future of domesticity (1993, pp.58-59). This research inevitably raises questions about the extent to which the concept of "class" can be used today, and how it should be used (see Yates 2000 and in this volume). However, for the purpose of the question of education and girls which is under consideration here, I want to bracket this question and focus instead on the point that however "class" is defined, girls' educational success is not about *all* girls – it is about middle- and upper-class girls. As Lucey comments (in relation to education and girls in the UK):

> *How, within current models, can we understand the middle-class girls' lives as anything but the unproblematically "successful" norm to be aimed for, and the working-class girls' lives as full of anything but failure, disappointment, under-achievement and loss of potential?* (Lucey 1996, p.2).

In Australia and the UK, researchers have begun to question "current models" of education and success, especially with regard to girls. The work of Lucey (1996) and Walkerdine (2000) in the UK and Yates and McLeod (Yates 2000) in Australia in particular, have drawn attention to the ways in which middle-class girls have become "positioned" by education, as significant subjects within new class formations. Each of these researchers has begun to problematise the notion of "clever girls". Walkerdine is interested in the psychosocial mechanisms which are associated with the reinvention of the self and which allow young women to "bear the burdens of liberty" of modernity (Walkerdine 2000). She suggests that new subjectivities are being generated, which produce subjects who can imagine themselves as free to make choices about their lives, and who see themselves as autonomous subjects who will willingly reinvent themselves.

Central to the construction of these identities is the capacity for self-regulation of emotions and anxiety about performance. Walkerdine emphasises that in her study, "clever girls", who were performing at the highest levels, paradoxically, regarded themselves as being "not good enough". She suggests that an important part of the high-achieving academic performance of middle-class girls is the constant anxiety that they will fail according to almost impossibly high standards. This is linked, Walkerdine argues, to broader, class-based anxieties about securing class positioning for middle-class girls, who can no longer rely on a man and his job to ensure a high standard of living. While these class-based anxieties have not been noted in the same way in the Australian context, there are nonetheless similarities in the ways in which successful girls are "performing". Yates writes:

> *From the earliest interviews, we were struck by the highly self-reflexive and self-monitoring mode of the middle-class girls. Even at age 12, they would frequently comment ironically on something they had just said; or monitor and adjust their stance with an eye to our imputed reaction* (Yates 2000, p.13).

In other words, the higher rates of school retention of middle-class girls, and the educational success of this social group, can be seen as one of the effects of education in shaping new subjectivities. It is suggested that in one sense they are developing "new identities", which allow these young people to engage positively with new, flexible workplaces and complex economies. The girls in Yates and McLeod's study are part of a generation of young women from middle-class backgrounds who are "doing extremely well in school", and

> *school is asking more and more for sensitive and positioned readings in the curriculum and these girls can produce this. In the work force too, "people skills" are in high demand* (Yates 2000, p.14).

The "psychosocial mechanisms" that are being described by Walkerdine may well be a part of the explanation for the paradox of the "optimistic" approach that appears to characterise educated youth of the post-1970 generation (Furlong & Cartmel 1997). Their objective circumstances in the labour market would not at first seem to warrant optimism, but they nonetheless have confidence that they will negotiate a future on their own terms, demonstrating a proactive and pragmatic approach to life (Wyn & Dwyer 1999; Evans 2000).

Yet, despite the apparent optimism and positive engagement that many young women exhibit, it is commonly noted that there are also costs that are borne by young people. Elsewhere I have drawn attention to a possible link between "autonomous subjects who willingly reinvent themselves" and high rates of mental illness among young people (Wyn & Dwyer 2000). Walkerdine also comments on the high levels of anxiety apparent in the lives of the high achieving middle-class girls in the UK. Her research on young women found that for middle-class girls, "failure is unthinkable" as they progress through their anxiety-ridden schooling, following "straitjacketed career trajectories" (Walkerdine 1996, p.357). High levels of anxiety have also been reported among girls in post-compulsory education in Finland (Anttila et al. 2000).

These studies problematise "successful girls", link educational success with class struggles and raise questions about the costs of "success" as measured in terms of examination results. They challenge the notion of the "mainstream" as undifferentiated and unproblematic and question a narrow notion of academic success as a healthy norm which should be aimed for.

Feminism and the Wonderbra

A rationale for encouraging girls to become "clever" has its basis in second wave feminism. The slogan "girls can do anything", for example, can be seen as a direct outcome of the "anti-sexist" programs of the 1970s and 1980s. What is the relationship between feminism and the kinds of feminine identities that are being shaped today? In the 2000s, the feminist project of gender equality sits in an awkward relationship to the bold assertion of femininity that is epitomised by the popular media (e.g. the Spice Girls). "Girl Power" and the celebration of femininity and of young women's bodies can also be seen as a form of compulsory performativity. Young women, especially young middle-class women, have to do "success" in more ways than just in exams. Young women's bodies are also performed, managed reflexively by young women themselves and measured against standards that, like academic success, will ensure feelings of failure and of never being good enough.

Yet the research on the meaning of consumption reveals enormous complexity. Some research on young women's patterns of and styles of consumption stress that, far from placing them at risk of being "lured away from traditional values of the culture", the capacity to own and to display fashionable items boosts young women's self confidence (Rattansi & Phoenix 1997). It is also claimed that production is increasingly significant to young women's identity:

> *The growth of unemployment among young working-class men has meant that young women, for whom more jobs are still available, and continue to be created, have evolved cultures of greater independence and self-confidence* (Rattansi & Phoenix 1997, p.139).

While education is a significant site for identity formation and the performance of "the self", education can no longer be treated in isolation. Work (production) and leisure (consumption) are also significant spheres of identity formation alongside that of education. Hence, it is not surprising that there is now interest in exploring the different identities that young women learn, construct and express while at school. Schultz, referring to young urban women of colour in the US, comments that the young women bring "shifting identities" to school, that they distinguish themselves from "the mainstream" and that:

> *The identities these young women adopted were contingent; they were connected to numerous external and internal realities as well as the contingencies of their everyday lives. Any assumptions about these students based on their eleventh-grade performance would have been wrong* (Schultz 1999, p.97).

Hence, as well as bringing multiple identities to education, young women's identities are represented, expressed and shaped through consumption and through production. Young women's changing relationship to schooling and to educational performance, their relationship to new patterns of consumption and their contribution to the production of new cultural styles (through the media) and through their engagement with the work force all need to be taken into account in developing understandings of the "the postmodern girl".

This means that one of the significant differences between this project and that of analysing the "modern girl" and girlhood in the 1950s, is that education now clearly is only one of the sites where identity is constructed. Given that mixing school and work is now normative for boys and girls, young women's identity formation cannot be understood without reference to both areas, and to the relationship between the two. Similarly, consumption is a highly significant cultural practice, which interfaces with work and education. While some feminist researchers have begun to analyse these complexities, this remains a relatively unexplored dimension of youth research (McRobbie 1997; Griffin 1997).

The picture which emerges from the research on girls and education then, is not necessarily consistent with the feminist concepts of girls who can do anything. The continued significance of social class in patterning girls' outcomes means that girls from working-class backgrounds are not likely to gain the benefits that education can bestow, in terms of securing jobs at the relatively more secure end of the labour market. New research on the previously unexamined "mainstream" of successful girls suggests that their educational success is also a form of "straitjacket", often a product of anxiety about individual performance and carrying the weight of concern by middle-class families about securing middle-class futures for their daughters. While the media construction of "girl power" does offer a sense of celebration of the power of femininity, at the same time its celebration of girls' bodies creates standards of performance that many young women cannot reach. Hence, the visibility, "power" and success of girls needs to be explored and analysed critically – and this analysis made available to girls through their schooling, so that they can gain a more critical perspective on girlhood, work, consumption and education.

Risk

The concept of risk is a central element in any discussion of girls and education. The idea of risk in education is frequently expressed in the terms of students "at risk". This concept is based on the idea of a "mainstream" from which a small proportion of students are either predicted to deviate in the future or from which they have already strayed (Wyn & White 1997). The recent research on girls and education referred to here, challenges the usefulness of this term, because of its tendency to "normalise" certain kinds of behaviour and performance and "pathologise" others. As Walkerdine and Lucey make very clear, educational success, for girls, may come at an emotional, social and psychological cost, and should not necessarily be held up as a standard or norm against which others students are measured.

In the Australian educational literature there is a strong interest in students "at risk" of not achieving educational success (Withers & Russell 1998). At the centre of most of this literature is the conviction that the main problem is that young people are at risk of not conforming to the prevailing models of educational success. While much of the literature focuses on lack of conformity among boys, pregnancy and young motherhood continues to be regarded as a prime "risk factor" for educational success for girls – by young women as well as by professionals. Walkerdine (1996) makes a strong case for arguing that, in the UK context, middle-class girls would regard pregnancy as the worst form of failure. Lucey (1996) makes the point that some middle-class girls in her study opted out of having sexual relations altogether, because all their energy went into education, and they could not bear to negotiate the risks of pregnancy.

Yet, other research suggests that straying from the (mythical) mainstream is not necessarily a sentence to failure for young women. Probert and Macdonald (1999) found that young mothers did not see their motherhood as excluding them from taking up further education options, and many were managing to be economically independent. Researchers in the US also point out that young motherhood does not necessarily doom young women to the margins of educational success – on the contrary, becoming a parent is seen to motivate young women to stay in school, find a job and think more seriously about a career (Schultz 1999, p.89). It may be that, despite the anxieties created by credentialism, the reality is that the contingency and flexibility of jobs also offer a wider range of options for individuals. This is especially the case as educational institutions begin to respond with more a more flexible delivery mode.

Linking education with questions of risk has other dimensions which are relevant to the construction of educational success. Taking a different angle on the concept of risk (as in risk and the stock market), education is often referred to as an "investment" in the production of individual "cultural capital". The notion of education as a private investment in the individual, as opposed to a public investment in society, is written into Australian educational policy – as providing an element of certainty and advantage in an uncertain world (Marginson 1993). The investment is often an intergenerational one, as families face the uncertainties of the labour market and lack of predictable career jobs and the pressures of educational achievement. The findings of the Youth Research Centre's Life Patterns project confirm this point:

> *Those who have now completed their studies leave us in no doubt that they are aware of those uncertainties and realities. The fact that the investment has been made, that it has been an investment in knowledge and personal growth, and that it has been inter-generational is now leading them to question their original expectations and to reassess for themselves their pre-formed priorities in life* (Wyn & Dwyer 2000).

The kind of involvement by families in education in the UK, which is noted by Lucey, would be relevant also to many Australian families, in which:

> *homework is treated as a "family project". The economic investment in such an education by the parents is not a hidden one and is paralleled by normative expectations of obligation from the children* (Lucey 1996, p.8).

Under these circumstances, education becomes a kind of "bargain" between parents and their children, and failure means not just personal failure, but letting the family down. But there is no guarantee that educational success will yield subsequent success, security or certainty. In other words, the educational investment itself is very "risky" because outcomes from education (the "pay-off") are far from certain. There is not a direct link between educational credentials and employment. The new "flexible" work practices mean that even for the credentialled, employment is contingent and insecure.

Despite the apparent educational success of some girls, compared with the traditionally high achieving groups of boys, the work force remains remarkably impervious to change along gender lines. The great majority of women in Australia are still employed within five main industries and two occupational groups and it has been noted that gender segregation has increased both industry-wide and within specific occupations (Kenway & Willis 1995, p.5). New industries reinvent gender segregation (Probert & Wilson 1993) and research shows that despite apparent improvements in women's educational levels over the past two decades, women's earnings are consistently less than those of their male counterparts. In a discussion of the outcomes of higher education, Marginson comments that:

> *If the position of women in the work force is better than it was, gender power still works against women. In a review of human capital theory in Australia, Preston (1997, pp.51-78) finds that there is a "raw" gender gap of 19.9 per cent between male and female earnings* (Marginson 1999).

The Youth Research Centre's Life Patterns project has found that "vocational integration", or the extent of fit between sphere of study and area of employment is sufficiently poor for education to be regarded as at best a risky form of investment (Dwyer, Harwood & Tyler 1999).

Conclusion

One of the most revealing aspects of Johnson's *The Modern Girl*, is the discussion of the discourses which framed the process of growing up in the 1950s and 1960s. These discourses were based on the idea that it was possible to arrive at an identified and recognisable point in life, beyond youth, called adulthood, and that a fundamental part of this process was the construction of a prescribed, unitary, integrated "self". Schooling was strongly implicated in the social construction of gendered identities that conformed to this understanding. The very organisation of schooling which was established in the immediate postwar years was premised on the idea that certain developmental "tasks" would proceed in a linear fashion, in defined "stages", with the school years mirroring the period of youth and, on leaving school, being employed (for boys) or becoming married (for girls) would mark the achievement of adulthood.

In the contemporary context, education is still implicated strongly in the discourses which frame the process of growing up. While many educationalists would argue that many dimensions of Australian life have changed significantly from the 1950s, few have considered what has changed about the relationship between education and the construction of identities. For young people today, secondary schooling is experienced simultaneously with (not prior to) almost all elements of adult life. Young identities are formed in relation to the relationships young people have with consumption, leisure, family and work, as well as education, *while they are still at school*. This positions education and schooling very differently in young people's lives from the way in which mass schooling was conceived in the early 1950s.

This chapter has focused especially on the way in which education, and specifically the idea of "educational success" for girls is based on the construction of particular identities in the late 1990s and into the 2000s. The apparently untroubled, conforming, educational "mainstream", against which others (students at risk) are judged, is held up to scrutiny. The focus has been on the phenomenon of "clever girls" as a product of uncertain times, in which older sources of stability and privilege are eroding and families are investing on an unprecedented scale in educational credentials as a means of security. While both men and women face the same circumstances, informal processes still contribute significantly to the production of unequal employment outcomes for men and women (Preston 1997) and women still rely more heavily on formal credentials to establish themselves.

In order to more fully understand what is happening for girls in education today, this preliminary analysis suggests that the following areas are fundamental.

Understandings about education and gender need to move beyond categorical notions of gender – neither "men" nor "women" are useful analytical categories. The analysis of the construction of success in education and its relationship to particular notions of girlhood ("clever girls") reinforces the need for analyses to focus more critically on the ways in which educational discourses shape our understandings of gender. More work needs to be done on how identities are produced in specific situations.

The dichotomy of "disadvantage – advantage" obstructs rather more than it elucidates for our understanding of the processes that contribute to young people's educational outcomes. This discussion has suggested that rather than seeing one group as being advantaged (at the expense of other groups), it is important to see how educational discourses of risk and the mainstream can blind us to the complex, multidimensional relationships and processes that contribute to young people's outcomes. This discussion has explored the way in which the apparent success of some groups of girls has been largely taken for granted by educationalists, as a "natural" phenomenon and as a "good thing".

The relationship of education to wider processes of social change needs to be more fully acknowledged and explored. While the fundamental organisation of educational institutions has changed little over the last quarter of a century, it is young people themselves who are engaging with new work practices and coming to terms with new uses of education and educational credentials.

A critical, complex and compassionate understanding of the needs of different groups of young people must inform the re-shaping of education that will take place in the near future. Their active engagement with many elements of the "new adulthood" makes them valuable partners in the development of the "new education".

References

Anttila, T., Poikolainen, K., Uutela, A. & Linnqvist, J. 2000, 'Structure and determinants of worrying among adolescent girls', *Journal of Youth Studies*, v.3, n.1. pp.49-60.

Beck, A. 1992, *The Risk Society: Towards a new modernity*, Sage, London.

Carrington, K. 1993, *Offending Girls, Sex, Youth and Social Justice*, Allen & Unwin, Sydney.

Dwyer, P. 2000, The epistemological fallacy and social background as a determinant in career attainment: A longitudinal study, paper presented at European Research Network: Youth in Transition 2000, Antwerp.

Dwyer, P., Harwood, A. & Tyler, D. 1999, *Seeking the Balance: Risk, choices and life priorities in the Life Patterns Project 1998–1999*, Youth Research Centre, Melbourne.

Evans, K. 2000, Agency and young adult transitions in England and New Germany, paper presented at American Educational Research Association Annual Conference Symposium, Reinventing Youth at the Turn of the Century, New Orleans, 24–28 April.

Giddens, A. 1991, *Modernity and Self Identity*, Polity, Cambridge.

Furlong, A. & Cartmel, F. 1997, *Young People and Social Change: Individualisation and risk in late modernity*, Open University Press, Buckingham.

Griffin, C. 1997, 'Troubled teens: Managing disorders of transition and consumption', *Feminist Review*, v.55, pp.4-21.

Hall, S. & Jefferson, T. (eds) 1976, *Resistance Through Rituals: Youth subcultures in post-war Britain*, Hutchinson, London.

Johnson, L. 1993, *The Modern Girl: Girlhood and growing up*, Allen & Unwin, Sydney.

Kenway, J. & Willis, S. 1995, *Critical Visions: Rewriting the future of work, schooling and gender*, Department of Employment, Education and Training, Canberra.

Lamb, S. 1998, 'Completing school in Australia', *Australian Journal of Education*, v.42, n.1, pp.5-31.

Lucey, H. 1996, Transitions to womanhood: Constructions of success and failure for middle and working class young women, paper presented at British Youth Research: The new agenda, Glasgow University, Jan.

Marginson, S. 1993, *Education and Public Policy in Australia*, Cambridge University Press, Cambridge.

—— 1999, 'Young adults in higher education', in *Australia's Young Adults: The deepening divide*, Sydney, Dusseldorp Skills Forum, Sydney.

Marks, G. & Fleming, N. 2000, *Longitudinal Survey of Australian Youth Report No. 17, 'Year 12 completion in Australia'*, Australian Council for Educational Research, Melbourne.

McRobbie, A. 1997, 'Bridging the gap: Feminism, fashion and consumption', *Feminist Review*, v.55, pp.73-89.

Preston, B. 1997, 'Where are we now with human capital theory in Australia?', *The Economic Record*, v.73, n.220, pp.51-78.

Probert, B. & Macdonald, F. 1999, 'Young women: Poles of experience in work and parenting', in *Australia's Young Adults: The deepening divide*, Dusseldorp Skills Forum, Sydney.

Probert, B. & Wilson, B. 1993, 'Gendered work', in *Pink Collar Blues: Work, gender and technology*, eds B. Probert & B. Wilson, Melbourne University Press, Melbourne.

Rattansi, A. & Phoenix, A. 1997, 'Rethinking youth identities: Modernist and postmodernist frameworks', in *Youth, Citizenship and Social Change in a European Context*, eds J. Bynner, L. Chisholm & A. Furlong, Ashgate, Aldershot..

Schultz, K. 1999, 'Identity narratives: Stories from the lives of urban adolescent females', *The Urban Review*, v.31, n.1, pp.79-107.

Teese, R. 1998, 'Curriculum hierarchy, private schooling and the segmentation of Australian secondary education 1947–1985', *British Journal of Sociology of Education* v.19, n.3, pp.291-304.

Walkerdine, V. 1996, 'Subjectivity and social class: New directions for feminist psychology', *Feminism and Psychology*, v.6, n.3, pp.355-60.

—— 2000, Feminist and critical perspectives on educational psychology, invited address, Committee on the Role and Status of Women, American Educational Research Association.

West, P. 1995, Giving boys a ray of hope: Masculinity and education, unpublished paper.

Withers, G. & Russell, J. 1998, *Educating for Resilience, Prevention and intervention strategies for young people at risk*, Catholic Education Office, Melbourne.

Wyn, J. & Dwyer, P. 1999, 'New directions in research on youth in transition', *Journal of Youth Studies*, v.2, n.1, pp.5-21.

—— 2000, 'New patterns of youth transition in education', *International Social Science Journal*, v.164, pp.148-59.

Wyn, J. & White, R. 1997, *Rethinking Youth*, Allen & Unwin, Sydney.

Yates, L. 1997, 'Gender equity and the boys debate: What sort of challenge is it?', *British Journal of Sociology of Education*, v.18, n.3, pp.337-47.

—— 2000, In what sense is "class" still a useful concept?, paper presented at American Educational Research Association Annual Conference Symposium, Reinventing Youth at the Turn of the Century, New Orleans, 23–28 April.

Georgina Tsolidis

Diasporic youth: Moving beyond the academic versus the popular in school cultures

It all depends on the way that you have been brought up. It comes from the pressure you get from your parents. Bill's parents are more Greek. My father is more assimilated. I slack off, I think that it won't help. Greek students who still have their ethnic parents work harder. Their parents are stricter and make sure that they take school seriously.

(Year 10 Melbourne school boy)

This statement captures poignantly the knotted relations, which are of interest here – those between home and school, educational aspirations and experience, and the ways these converge with processes of ethnic identification. This paper explores the relationship between processes of ethnic identification and educational aspiration, attainment and experience through a school-based study undertaken in Brisbane and Melbourne. Particular attention is given to the dichotomy established by secondary students between academic and social success. The argument is made that it may be students from communities with a historic experience of diasporic existence who are best placed to challenge this dichotomy because of the presence, within their communities, of a wider range of cultural choices, including those which value education and are acceptable in terms of popular youth culture.

For the Year 10 student quoted above, being "more" Greek in opposition to being assimilated is understood as good for academic achievement. Assimilation is elided with being "slack", and hard work and strictness are associated with being "ethnic". This is not an uncommon association and much has been written about the relationship between ethnic minority immigrants and their educational aspirations as a means of explaining their relatively high achievement rates (Taft 1975). However, what is of interest here are attitudes to education in relation to processes of ethnic identification rather than the relationship between educational aspirations and migration. The Year 10 boy quoted above was born in Australia, as were his peers. In his comments we recognise the association between being "ethnic" and academically successful, and being assimilated and "slack". Why is there this sense that being "ethnic", like taking exercise and eating the right food, may be good for you but is not much fun? For the students who were interviewed for the study drawn on here, "good for you" was interpreted in relation to academic achievement; "fun" was interpreted in relation to social success. Their comments cemented a dichotomy between fashionable youth, the students most often described as "cool", and academic achievers, those described by one group of girls as the "nerds, dags and geeks". Yet through these interviews, there also appeared glimpses of a third space, somewhere where there was a possibility of being comfortably academic and fashionable, of being "ethnic" and having fun. It is this space I am most interested to explore here. What possibilities are available to minority students within the institutional practices and discourses of their school cultures to create such spaces and how do they understand the relation of such spaces to their home cultures?

Much of the literature concerned with academic achievement and ethnicity has tended to consider birthplace, either that of the immigrant student or that of the immigrant parents, as the critical descriptor. In both cases, and most particularly with reference to the so-called "second-generation", that is children born to immigrant parents, this results in a failure to engage with the fluidity and complexity within and between ethnic categories. As a major descriptor, place of birth cannot provide subtle insights into evolving cultural identifications and their relationships to education which are of interest here. The Year 10 student quoted above was born in Australia and his parents were born in Greece, this was also the case for his peers, yet his statement alerts us to differences within this category. These differences exist within all birthplace categories and are increasingly complex and interesting as a result of immigration, multiple migration, rapidly diversifying source countries, intermarriage and evolving understandings of ethnic identity, including notions of Australianness. The intention here is to explore the relationship between ethnicity and education within frameworks which construct ethnic identifications as fluid, contingent, and evolving and recognise this to be the case irrespective of place of birth. It is my belief that through such frameworks educationists may gain insights into students' academic experiences by engaging their cultural aspirations. Similarly, insights related to education may increase our understandings of processes of ethnic identification.

Academic achievement

In relation to Australian ethnic minorities, educational attainment has been debated passionately for many years (Birrell & Seitz 1986; Jakubowicz & Castles 1986). The notion that those from ethnic minority communities are over-represented in the tertiary sector, relative to others from comparable socioeconomic groupings, has been argued and attributed to a range of factors, including the high aspirations which are part of the immigration process, and a work ethic, as this is attributed to particular communities. It is no coincidence that this debate has an interface with debates about immigration more generally and, more specifically, with the need or otherwise for educational equal opportunity and affirmative action strategies within the tertiary setting.

Traditionally, this has been highlighted in relation to the children of post-war European immigrants. In more recent years, the debate about educational attainments has shifted away from the European groups to the so-called Asians, with some commentators claiming these groups are now over-represented in tertiary education. Attention has also been given to those groups which in the past have been considered well-represented but, it is now argued, are slipping, for example the grand-children of Greek immigrants (Birrell & Khoo 1995).

This debate is not straightforward. A range of issues underpins it, including notions of disadvantage relative to discrimination, the construction of minority groups implicit in the use of databases, racism, and the quality of educational participation as well as its outcomes. Moreover, it is increasingly difficult to move beyond the educational attainments of immigrant students into studies of the so-called "second generation" because of the increasingly fluid and ambiguous nature of ethnicity.

While the debate about ethnicity and migrancy in relation to educational attainment has proceeded, another debate has emerged related to gender. Recently, there has been a questioning of whether, in fact, women and girls are educationally disadvantaged. In relation to schooling it is now argued that girls' retention rates are outstripping those of boys, and with regard to higher education, that women are entering universities in equal to or higher numbers than men (Birrell et al. 1995).

These debates related to the educational attainment of ethnic minorities and women and girls need to be considered in relation to each other. While much Australian educational research has tended to view ethnicity and gender as stand alone issues, an exploration of how these issues articulate is imperative, particularly in the context of such recent debates and their policy implications (DEET/NBEET 1990).

For students, the lived experience of schooling and the understandings of what constitutes "cool" for example, integrate both gender and ethnicity. A Chinese boy will be recognised within a different set of criteria to that applied to a Turkish girl. Commonsense understandings exist related to who does well at school and who enters universities and furthermore what type of courses various groups prefer. It is not unusual to hear teachers and tertiary educators make statements exposing beliefs about ethnic groups and their academic preferences, aspirations and achievements. "Asian" students prefer business courses. Turkish girls are not interested in (or not allowed to contemplate) tertiary education. Jewish students or Greek students or Chinese students are over-represented at universities, particularly within law and medical faculties. Maltese and Lebanese boys have low academic aspirations and relate more readily to the world of small business. These are familiar, if not empirically-based, understandings of what goes on within ethnic minority communities, and it must be considered that such judgments inform practices, particularly within schools, and this could determine the range of options such students can avail themselves of in the future.

The study

These commonsense understandings and their consequences were some of the issues at the heart of a study established by the Bureau of Population, Immigration and Multicultural Research. The intention was to provide some empirically-based insights related to ethnic educational attainment as a means of engaging with an emerging policy debate related to real or imagined educational disadvantage.

In broad terms, the intention of the study was to explore commonsense understandings of which groups do well and not so well educationally. A range of issues such as fields of study, course type, place of birth, ethnic background and gender were explored. The study had both quantitative and qualitative components. The quantitative element used Department of Education, Employment, Training and Youth Affairs (DEETYA) and Australian Bureau of Statistics (ABS) data to provide a national mapping of tertiary (mainly university) attainment, paying particular attention to gender, ethnicity and migrancy. On the basis of this mapping, a number of key groups of students were isolated for the qualitative phase of the study. Students from these groups were interviewed in a variety of schools in order to understand factors which contributed to their success or otherwise in accessing and participating in university education. In this way, it was intended that both the presences and the absences would be read and a picture formed as to which school-based factors help or hinder educational attainment of this kind.

Levels of attainment were established using census and DEETYA data premised on the mechanisms used by government bodies to determine ethnicity, most commonly birthplace and language/s spoken. This was clearly problematic, particularly for minority students born in Australia. For this group of students, data related to language/s spoken at home can become an indication of varying rates of mother-tongue maintenance among ethnic groups, rather than ethnic background. Alternatively, for groups such as Spanish speakers, such data fails to tell us whether their ethnic identification relates to Spain or one of a wide range of countries in Latin America, for example. The qualitative phase of the study was premised on the ethnic self-attributions of the students involved. It should be noted that the intention of the study was not to link the two sets of data in any strict way, but instead to use the quantitative data to determine which groups were worthy of consideration at the school level. Most significance is attached here to the school-based material.

The communities selected represent exemplars of a range of relevant factors with the particular aim of investigating the educational experiences within communities associated with both high and low educational attainment. The groups included in the study were Russian, Italian, Greek, British, South African, Polish, Vietnamese, El Salvadorean, Turkish and Chinese.

The qualitative aspect of the study, included approximately 200 students from various schools in both Brisbane and Melbourne. Interviews with these students were undertaken in single-sex, ethno-specific groups based on students' self-identifications. Students were asked to complete a questionnaire which explored a range of issues, including educational and career aspirations, understandings of what constituted a good education, an estimation of whether their current schooling met their expectations, which groups of students succeeded at school and their understandings of their parents' opinions on related topics. Students were then asked to discuss these issues as a group. The schools drawn on included single-sex schools and schools from the state, independent and Catholic systems. Included also were language centres where newly arrived students were interviewed through interpreters.

Within the study, the notion of ethnicity was explored in a framework which conceptualises it, along with factors such as gender, as part of a process of identification which is shifting in response to context (de Lauretis 1990). A major intention was to understand the processes students used to determine for themselves (and others) ethnic and gender identifications and how these processes interrelated with academic aspiration, experience and achievement.

Researchers asked teachers to invite students, regardless of place of birth, to self-select as from particular ethnic groups for the interviews. Students indicated no misgivings about labelling themselves as Turkish, Greek, Chinese or Polish, for example. In all schools, single-sex groups of students from specific ethnic groups were established with relatively little reticence or difficulty on the part of teachers or students. Most awkwardness surrounded the formation of the UK groupings in schools. Being British, even for those born overseas, was not the same brand of Other as being "ethnic", even if the "ethnic" is Australian-born. The link between "Britishness" and "Australianness" became evident in the fluidity of identification between these groups.

In itself, this process provided an exemplar of the continuing importance of processes of ethnic identification as these operate within Australian society. The challenge is to reflect on these in relation to our role as educators. What understandings of our students do we teach to when we are faced by a group of students who are labelled Russian Jewish boys, or newly-arrived Poles or Turkish girls? What is the relationship between their aspirations, expectations of schooling and ours as these are reflected back to us through our commonsense under-standings of who the students are and what they and their parents want from life in Australia?

Such work creates for the researcher the task of problematising what is presented as unproblematic and "out there"; that is, the straightforward use of ethnic categorisations through self-identification. On the one hand, I have argued that ethnicity is fluid, shifting and contingent and yet, on the other hand, I have recognised that within schools it seems far from this. Students own ethnic labels as much as teachers use them. Students would self-select as Chinese, for example, yet within group discussions these "Chinese" students would reveal much difference – different birthplaces, different languages, different religions and different experiences of migration. Yet, there were also many similarities, including the wish to self-identify as Chinese. Of most interest here are similarities between such students linked to academic aspirations and expectations of schooling. Following Spivak's (1993) notion of strategic essentialism, I am interested to explore the strategic significance of ethnic labels in the context of schooling: how do students mobilise under such identities in ways which assist or detract from their academic achievements?

Identity and schooling

How we understand education and its role in processes of identification is increasingly respon-sive to globalisation. Understandings of ethnicity, definitions of "Australian", who accesses education and to what ends, are all issues which must be examined as they emerge out of a global market, culture and communication system. With mass movements of peoples across the globe, notions such as ethnicity become increasingly problematic. What is the basis on which we judge ethnicity and what is its relevance in relation to national boundaries and understandings of citizenship? These issues are particularly pronounced in a country like Australia where a history of migration has made terms such as "Australian" contentious in themselves. More so than ever before, the possibility of a crisply delineated "Australian" category is under scrutiny. This situation is exacerbated with time. There are the children and grandchildren of immigrants, the children of mixed marriages, there are multiple migrations, remigration and the conscious decision made by many to live between two countries. The reality of globalisation means that national boundaries and the ethnic groupings which exist within these are constantly reinterpreted, not only by migration but, related to this, also by global economic structures and communications and a global popular culture. While globali-sation, with its increasingly fluid national and cultural boundaries, at one level homogenises, at another level it also makes differences more familiar. "Australian" no longer exists as a category associated with a British heritage, interrupted by the familiar post-war immigrant groups. Instead Australia, along with many nations, faces the challenge of interpreting citi-zenship through the fluidity and hybridity which is the result of globalisation.

Ethnicity has been traditionally conceived of as linked to inclusion and exclusion within collectivities established through a common feature associated with birthright. Factors such as birthplace, language/s spoken, religion, customs and values have been highlighted in this regard (Anthias & Yuval-Davis 1993). Increasingly, such definitions have been problematised. How do we judge the ethnicity of someone who was born in Australia to parents whose parents were born in Italy? How do we judge the ethnicity of someone who was born in Australia to parents who migrated respectively from two different countries? How do we judge the ethnicity of someone who was born in Russia to Jewish parents from the Ukraine who now live in Australia? Or how do we judge the ethnicity of someone whose family actively chooses to live between Australia and Hong Kong?

The familiarity of difference brings into sharper focus many of the issues surrounding notions of citizenship and nationhood (Castles 1997). In this context, ethnicity can only be linked to a form of identification which is voluntary and shifting. Whether the intention is to include or exclude, it is problematic to link ethnicity and nation. For an Australian raised within a Greek cultural framework, being labelled Australian can be as oppressive as being labelled Greek. The term "Australian" can imply forms of assimilation just as the term "Greek" can imply forms of rejection. The context for such labelling is of paramount significance and determines the power relations, which underpin the exercise, and the ease with which an individual can accept, reject or reinterpret the labels.

Schooling is a context within which labelling takes place. Through formal and informal processes, students are understood and come to understand themselves as having particular identities. These processes are underpinned by institutional power relations which reflect what goes on in the wider society; for example, what is taught and how it is taught and assessed, give strong messages about socially valuable knowledge. Additionally, there is the playing out of power relations through the minutiae of interpersonal relations, particularly those between students.

Processes of identification are interpreted and reinterpreted through institutional practices and discourses associated with schooling. How students see themselves is as much a reaction to their cultural backgrounds, their families, the processes of migration, as it is to the ways in which they are seen by friends and teachers. Schools represent a powerful interpretation of "Australian" through the formal and informal relationships they mediate between people and their cultures as these are represented through discourses related to ways of understanding and ways of doing. In the context of schools, students learn what it is to be Australian, who it is who is allowed to claim this label and whether or not they wish to challenge or accept mainstream understandings of these issues.

In similar ways, the institutional practices and discourses of schooling frame understandings of femininity and masculinity. These mediate the ways in which students confirm, deny or reinterpret gender representations through formal and informal curriculum, peer cultures and mainstream cultures. Students' capacity to create gender identifications respond to the power underpinnings of the many social interactions they experience. Critical among these in Australia are those concerned with ethnicity. For boys and girls from all ethnic backgrounds, self-identification processes reflect the articulation of their gender and ethnicity as these are expressed through the power relations mediated by schooling. In this study, significance is given to educational aspirations, experiences and attainments as already discussed. It is not unusual for teachers and students to understand these aspirations in ways which are both gendered and ethnicised. There exist strong commonsense understandings, for example, of the aspirations Chinese boys bring with them to school and the reasons for these. These are understandings which exist as a reading of what it means to be a male within Chinese culture, as this is interpreted within mainstream Australian culture. The argument being developed here is that processes of ethnic identification, particularly as these are gendered, interact with academic aspiration, experience and achievement; and that these processes of identification also intersect with cultural interpretations produced through globalisation.

The cultures of academic versus social success

It became clear through this study that there were marked differences between groups of students related to the significance attributed to education. In attempting to understand these differences, it would appear from this study, that ethnic identifications provided more of an explanation for this patterning, than gender, place of birth, reasons for migration or class as these may be interpreted through the interviews. So, for example, a student who identified as Vietnamese, regardless of gender, place of birth, length of Australian residency or type of schooling experience, expressed very similar understandings of what constituted "good" schooling and what should be the outcomes of schooling and the reasons for this. Related to this, was the fact that students tended to create a stark distinction between academic compe-tence and being "cool", that is, successfully interpreting popular youth culture. Of most interest here, is the fact that students in the study drew a clear distinction between "good" students and "cool" students. Furthermore, they associated particular ethnic groups with academic success and by implication, with being "daggy" in contradistinction to "cool". In this way, being and not being "cool" was ethnicised in particular and significant ways.

During discussions with students, they were asked to describe the students who did well at school. The following student comments provide some insights into their responses.

"Those who are nerds – people who spend all night working."
"Students who are more about their work than their social life."
"Students who believe that an academic life is better than a social life – nerds, dags and geeks."
(Group of South African girls from a private Jewish school in Melbourne)

"There are some Australian kids who do very well."
"There are no nations who only do well or badly."
"Australian parents don't care what their children do."
"They must be the best parents. 'Really cool.'"
"European parents care. It comes down to the attitudes of the parents. Our parents will support us."
(A group of Polish boys from a Melbourne state school)

"The Chinese have a high work ethic and stricter parents."
"It depends on which group you associate with – there are groups who are doing better or not. Students from Eastern countries have parents who are very strict. The harder you work the more money you will get. The Asian parents say if you are working hard you are getting something done."
"In a couple of generations it will be there. We will have the same expectations for our children. It is a matter of what kind of people you are."
(A group of Chinese boys at a Melbourne state school)

"Students from Taiwan, Hong Kong and China may do better because they have a good moral training."

(A Chinese boy at a Brisbane language centre)

"Students whose parents push them, who don't have many friends and who don't have many distractions."
"They don't talk – are not popular."
"They are boring with no sense of humour."
"Anyone who is daggy."

(A group of Greek boys at a Melbourne state school)

"More boys do well than girls. Parents are scared for girls. They don't want them to get boyfriends. If a girl gets a boyfriend then they get boy mad at school and they don't concentrate as well."

(A Greek boy attending a Melbourne state school)

"Many of the Asian kids do very well, not all of them, however."
"They put more effort into their studies. They don't socialise."
"They are committed to their studies in their country. Their learning system is very hard. Also, many of them are very poor and they want to do better."

(A group of Polish boys at a Melbourne state school)

Comments made by students during this study indicated that a strong dichotomy existed within the cultures of their schools between the academic and the fashionable. The Chinese and Vietnamese students, for example, situated themselves and were situated by others on the academic side of this divide. What the Chinese and Vietnamese students saw as the need to work in order to achieve and the support of their families for this endeavour, other students characterised as either the product of their repressive family situations or their inability to socialise and have fun in ways understandable within school-based renditions of mainstream popular culture. Another illustration of this same dichotomy was furnished by one group of El Salvadorean students who situated themselves on the social and fashionable side of the divide. These students described themselves as underachieving academically because they preferred to go out, have fun and be fashionable.

It becomes clearer to understand why academic achievement is a risky business for students who describe the educationally competent in such negative terms. No sense of humour, lack of friends, not wishing to get involved with boyfriends and being "daggy" are all associated with academic success. If this is juxtaposed with the images in popular culture of young people as sexually attractive and active, fashionable and immersed in labyrinthine personal and social relations, one is not surprised that so many students faced with a dichotomy between the "daggy" (academic) and the "cool", opt for the "cool" (non-academic).

Diaspora – a "third space" between the academic and popular

The groups interviewed for this study were diverse and included groups with various lengths of residency in Australia. Similarly, their attitudes to education were varied and there existed no clear pattern linking factors such as length of residency with attitudes towards education.

The Vietnamese and El Salvadorean students, for example, shared similar migration experiences and yet expressed markedly different attitudes to education. There seemed to exist, however, a similarity between students from what could be described as "diasporic communities" with regard to the significance they attached to education.

It is important to distinguish between diasporic and immigrant communities although the two may coincide. The notion of diaspora has existed for a long time and is associated with communities which live outside their natal territories, imagined or otherwise, and have maintained an "... inescapable link with their past migration history and a sense of co-ethnicity with others of a similar background" (Cohen 1997, p.ix). The term has been used commonly with reference to banished or exiled groups such as Jews, Palestinians and Armenians, but also with reference to migration and colonisation (Cohen 1997).

Rather than understand such diasporic communities as pure or authentic cultural outposts existing outside their homelands, I would like to explore the proposition that, instead, their lived experience captures a range of cultural negotiations, which exemplify Hall's notion of diasporisation. The notion of diaspora has taken on new and significant meanings associated with cultural studies. Hall, for example, uses "diasporisation" to refer to identities which are produced through interlocking histories and cultures in ways which make this inseparable. He explores this in relation to the impact of globalisation (Hall 1996). Here I am interested to constitute diasporic communities in relation to such understandings, but also in relation to more foundational understandings of diasporic communities. I would argue that these are not only compatible but interrogate each other in ways, which provide valuable insights.

There is a pronounced tension within diasporic communities between sameness and difference. This is a product of relations between ethnic majorities and minorities, as these are commonly constituted in societies such as Australia. This tension also exists with regard to the country of origin, for example, the differences and similarities between Greek-Australians and Greeks. Importantly also, this tension is pronounced in relation to co-ethnicity, for example, similarities and differences between those who identify as Chinese from Hong Kong or Taiwan or Malaysia. Most profoundly, however, I would argue that these differences and similarities are constituted across national boundaries in ways which influence each other in two-way flows. As I have argued elsewhere in relation to Greeks, what happens in Australia is changing definitions of Greekness in Greece as much as the other way around (Tsolidis forthcoming). It is the notion of co-ethnicity as much as it is the impact of globalisation which is contributing to the cultural fluidity which characterises such communities. Cohen provides nine characteristics of diasporic groups as follows:

(1) dispersal from an original homeland, often traumatically; (2) alternatively, the expansion from a homeland in search of work, in pursuit of trade or to further colonial ambitions; (3) a collective memory and myth about the homeland; (4) an idealisation of the supposed ancestral home; (5) a return movement; (6) a strong ethnic group consciousness sustained over time; (7) a troubled relationship with host societies; (8) a sense of solidarity with co-ethnic members in other countries; and (9) the possibility of a distinctive creative, enriching life in tolerant host countries (Cohen 1997, p.180).

Of the 10 groups involved in the study being discussed here, the Greeks, Jews and Chinese are commonly associated with diasporic experience in Cohen's sense of the term. In the case of the Greek students, all were born in Australia to parents who had been born here or immigrated at a young age. The overwhelming majority of Jewish students were born in either

South Africa or Russia and had been in Australia for between two and five years. The Chinese students represented more diversity, with some recently arrived from places such as Hong Kong, Taiwan, China or Vietnam and others having been born in Australia. Both within and between these categories there was a vast range of difference. Encapsulated in the Chinese, Jewish and Greek students in this study are differences arising out of gender, class, ethnicity, language, birthplace, reasons for migration, within, as well as between the categories. Yet, there were also clear commonalities through a range of the characteristics outlined by Cohen above. One of the key considerations here, is the relationship between diasporic experience and education. Cohen comments that within diasporic communities there exists a passion for knowledge "… usually reflected in a desire for education or, to be more specific, a passion for certification" (Cohen 1997, p.172). From this can it be argued that attitudes to education form a critical component in processes of ethnic identification within such communities and that these assist students to create "third spaces" between the "daggy" and the "cool"?

The Jewish students from South Africa and Russia, the Chinese and the Greek students who participated in this study, despite the significant variation which existed within each group, had in common strong, ethno-religious, community-based, cultural identifications. Students within these groups described, in straightforward ways, their identification with their respective communities. There does not exist the scope here to go into details about the variations between and within these groups. And in the case of the Jewish students these were particularly interesting given the significant differences between the South Africans and the Russians. Similarly, the differences between the Chinese students were also very interesting given the variety of reasons for migration; for example, those who had left the People's Republic of China relative to the daughters and sons of Hong Kong business people. Nonetheless, these students remained, in their terms, Jewish, Chinese or Greek. They attached to each of these terms, a range of cultural practices, a language, Hebrew in the case of the often-multilingual Jewish students, a religion and a community. They described a social life intrinsic to that community within which they and their friends were happy to participate. The situations, in which they socialised, were not always ones formally attached to community-based organisations. In the case of one group of Greek students, for example, they described a neighbourhood tavern which had become a meeting place for them. What they enjoyed was the Greek music, way of socialising and the fact that they could share this with friends who understood the "way we do things". In relation to their schooling, the overwhelming majority of the Russian and South African students involved in the study, attended Jewish schools and stated this was their preferred option. The Greek students, on the other hand, attended state schools. In the case of students at one of these schools where there was a significant proportion of Greek students and a Greek language program, they stated that this was a clear advantage for them. Similarly, the Chinese students attended state schools, but as with so many of the Greeks, many of them also attended community-based after hours schools. In the case of the Greek after-hour schools, students learnt language and aspects of Greek culture including dance, religion and history. In the case of Chinese students, some attended after-hour schools, where they were given assistance with subjects such as maths in Chinese. These students also attached, as markers of their cultural identification, attitudes to education. In the case of these students, being Greek, Chinese or Jewish, meant having "serious" attitudes towards education. Interviews with these students indicated that most were proud of the academic expectations they understood as part of their cultures.

While this "serious" attitude to education is often attributed to immigrants, the argument being made here is that in the case of diasporic groups this attitude is part of their ethnic self-identification. It is in this context that the work with Greek students in this study is perhaps most relevant. While most of the Chinese students and an overwhelming majority of the Jewish students interviewed were born overseas, the Greek students were born in Australia and, in most cases, their parents were also born here or immigrated at a very young age.

For the Greek students, their strong cultural identification with "Greekness" existed regardless of their or their parents' place of birth. However, relative to the Jewish and Chinese students, there existed more variation among them, as to their optimism of attaining university places and professional careers. For example, while it was common for these Jewish students, particularly those from South Africa, to aspire to medicine, and anticipate achieving this, the Greek students were less uniform in this regard. Some included trades or running small businesses among their anticipated vocations, reflecting their stated pessimism of achieving high status professions requiring university qualifications. In this way, the high aspirations so often associated with immigrants, became less significant. Within this community also, the relatively high levels of attainment commonly associated with migration seem to have dipped (Birrell & Khoo 1995). Yet as the quotation at the beginning of this paper indicates, a serious attitude to education remained a defining characteristic of Greekness, that is: "Greek students who still have their ethnic parents work harder. Their parents are stricter and make sure that they take school seriously."

It was striking through the interviews, how students from these communities had a clear sense of who they were and the relationship between this and their academic aspirations. To various extents, what was particularly noteworthy in this context, were these students' descriptions of alternative forms of youth culture, which were embedded within their minority cultures. This was particularly striking with the Greek and Jewish students. In the case of the Greeks, this type of youth culture is evident in the weekly Greek newspapers, some of which include an English language supplement. Evident in these is an array of social venues and activities earmarked for youth, as well as a range of national and transnational organisations intended as diasporic youth forums. It is worth considering this historic diasporic experience as a means of challenging the dichotomy between academic and peer-based social success.

Perhaps it is the existence of this diasporic youth culture which allows students from these groups to create a third space (Bhaba 1983) between academic and mainstream popular cultures, particularly at a moment when the popular in Australia is defined in such narrow, culturally-hegemonic terms. We have tended to consolidate constructions of minority cultures in deficit terms, even when the aim has been to draw attention to racism. The fact that mainstream Australian culture takes little account of what is familiar to minorities may not be the only story to tell. The tension between similarity and difference can be creative and productive. For diasporic youth, there may be an added element of choice in the cultural repertoires which resource their ethnic identifications if they can draw on the global networks and understandings which surround who they are and who they want to be in their adult futures. It seems that attitudes to education are seriously implicated in these repertoires and the task for educators is to understand the positive potential implicit in these attitudes.

References

Anthias, F. & Yuval-Davis, N. 1993, *Radicalised Boundaries – Race, nation, gender, colour and class and the anti-racist struggle*, Routledge, London/New York.

Bhaba H., 1983, 'The other question: The stereotype and colonial discourse', *Screen*, v.24, n.6, pp.18-36.

Birrell, B., Dobson, I., Rapson, V. & Smith, T.F. 1995, 'Female achievement in higher education and the professions', *People and Place*, v.3, n.1.

Birrell, B. & Khoo, S. 1995, *The Second Generation in Australia – Educational and occupational characteristics*, BIMPR/AGPS, Canberra.

Birrell, B. & Seitz, A. 1986, 'The myth of ethnic inequality in Australian education', *Journal of the Australian Population Association*, v.3, n.1, pp.52-74.

Castles, S. 1997, 'Multicultural citizenship: A response to the dilemma of globalisation and national identity?', *Journal of Intercultural Studies*, v.18, n.1, pp.5-22.

Cohen, R. 1997, *Global Diasporas – an introduction*, University of Washington Press, Seattle.

DEET/NBEET 1990, *A Fair Chance For All – National and institutional planning for equity in higher education, a discussion paper*, AGPS, Canberra.

de Lauretis, T. 1990, 'Upping the anti (sic) in feminist theory' in *Conflicts in Feminism*, eds M. Hirsch & E. Fox Keller, Routledge, New York.

Hall, S. 1996, 'The meaning of new times', in *Stuart Hall – Critical dialogues in cultural studies*, eds D. Morely & K. Chen, Routledge, New York/London.

Jakubowicz, A. & Castles, S. 1986, The inherent subjectivity of the apparently objective in research on ethnicity and class, paper presented at SAANZ Conference, July.

Spivak, G. 1993, *Outside in the Teaching Machine*, Routledge, New York/London.

Taft, R. 1975, *The Career Aspirations of Immigrant School Children in Victoria*, La Trobe Sociology Paper n.12, La Trobe University, Bundoora.

Tsolidis, G. (forthcoming) 'The role of the maternal in diasporic cultural reproduction – Australia, Canada and Greece', *Social Semiotics*.

Peter Kelly

chapter 7

Youth as an artefact of expertise

My last point will be this: The emergence of social science cannot, as you see, be isolated from the rise of this new political rationality and from this new political technology. Everybody knows that ethnology arose from the process of colonisation (which does not mean that it is an imperialistic science). I think in the same way that, if man – if we as living, speaking, working beings – became an object for several different sciences, the reason has to be sought not in ideology but in the existence of this political technology which we have formed in our own societies (Foucault 1988, p.162).

This chapter is not so much about young people – in the unruly, embodied, flesh and blood sense. Rather, my concerns here are with the ways in which unruly young minds and bodies provoke anxieties in the intellectual and policy spaces of adults in such a way as to energise diverse surveillance and management practices and projects. Adult anxieties about young people are not new phenomena. During the past 150 years, official and popular concerns with the behaviours and attitudes of certain groups of young people have emerged periodically and structured a variety of policy and community responses to the "youth question" (Bessant & Watts 1998; Hebdige 1997). Youth has historically occupied the "wild zones" in society's imagination. In these "zones", certain groups of young people have been perceived as "ungovernable" and as lacking in "self regulation". These representations of "abnormality" have always been fundamentally shaped by race, class and gender and situated in relation to conceptions of "normal" youth (Kelly 1998; Tait 1995).

During the last half of the 20th century, the liberal democracies, including Australia, have been characterised by profound social, economic and cultural transformations. In these settings community and policy discourse has been marked by widespread adult concerns about today's young people. These concerns relate to how young people should be schooled, policed, housed, employed, or prevented from becoming involved in any number of so called "risky" practices – sexual, eating, drug use or peer cultural. Indeed, in Australia, commentators such as Richard Eckersley (1988, 1992) and Hugh Mackay (1993) have argued that there exists a contemporary "crisis of youth".

In these settings of uncertainty and "crisis", adult anxieties about the public and private behaviours and dispositions of young people mean that Youth looms large and threateningly in community perceptions, in academic and policy areas such as juvenile justice, youth work, education, health promotion, adolescent mental health, family and social work. Powerful narratives of risk, fear and uncertainty structure a variety of emergent processes and practices aimed at regulating the actions and thoughts of young people. These practices include:

- an increasingly widespread use of electronic surveillance technologies (video, audio) in spaces such as shopping malls, streets and schools;
- the proposed and actual introduction of state and local government laws and by-laws allowing night curfews, zero tolerance policing and electronic tagging of young offenders; and
- by-laws which set limits on the number of young people who may gather in certain public spaces, and which allow police (public and private) to move young people on if they cause others anxiety (White 1998).

In association with these more direct policing practices, increased levels of anxiety and uncertainty provoke new forms of adult interventions into young people's lives on the basis of professional concerns about young people's welfare. These practices include:

- the involvement of youth, community and health workers in street work with young people on projects which attempt to regulate antisocial practices;
- various education programs which target the risky sexual, eating and drug practices of young people, or the nature of their transitions to adulthood; and
- a general concern for any youth activity which gives the appearance of being beyond the management or surveillance capacities of various agencies (Youth Research Centre 1998).

These concerns are evidenced in the countless research projects and reports that seek to better understand all aspects of youth (see, for example, the papers in this collection). This constantly growing research literature promises to develop more sophisticated ways of identifying and differentiating populations of young people with regard to various community, intellectual and policy concerns – about transitions, about sexuality, about identity. Cultural and policy contexts that are framed by uncertainty, fear and anxiety provoke "dangerous" (Foucault 1983) possibilities in the regulation and surveillance of young people. In such contexts, the promise of certainty, which frames many of these surveillance and management practices, can only be delivered within the domain marked out by the intersection of Youth Studies and the government of Youth, via more "sophisticated" techniques of identification and intervention (White 1993).

It is against this backdrop that I want to argue that representations of Youth in the institutional domain of Youth Studies can be conceived as the products or artefacts (constructed truths) of various forms of expertise. In this chapter, I direct my attention to the institutionalised processes of abstraction which construct these truths, and the roles played by these processes of abstraction in the restless problematisation of Youth as the object of countless competing and complementary governmental programs (Rose & Miller 1992). I will argue that any rethinking or reassessment of the modes of representing Youth (Wyn & White 1997, 1998) ought to take some account of the institutional and abstract nature of these processes of representation, and of the implication of these processes in the regulation of populations of young people. More so when we acknowledge that Youth is only rendered knowable, in all its similarity, difference and complexity, through these processes of representation.

Governmentality and the regulation of populations

Maybe what is really important for our modernity – that is, for our present – is not so much the etatisation of society, as the governmentalisation of the state (Foucault 1991, p.103).

The mode of analysis developed in this chapter is indebted to Michel Foucault's problematisations of Power (and its effects), and of the Subject. A principal concern in Foucault's (1991) investigations of the forms and effects of modern "governmentality" was to foreground the emergence of the idea of *population*. Foucault's investigations were grounded in the proposition that, from the 16th century through to the early 19th century, there was a transformation in the ways in which European government was conceived. This transformation involved a movement from a concern with the nature of the relation between the Prince and his subjects (an issue of sovereignty), to a concern with the nature of the relations between the state and the government of its populations (a concern with the art of government). Foucault's interest in the practices of government is evident in his studies of early modern government which addressed such questions as: "How to govern oneself, how to be governed, by whom the people will accept being governed, how to become the best possible governor" (Foucault 1991, p.87). In conceiving of government in this manner, Foucault constructed government as the "conduct of conduct". Government, in this sense, "is a form of activity aiming to shape, guide or affect the conduct of some person or persons" (Gordon 1991, p.2).

Foucault argued that the "discovery of populations", or more correctly, the discursive construction of populations, and of populations within populations, became central to the art of European government from the 16th century onwards. Foucault traced the production of regimes of truth in a variety of domains. He argued that these discourses – on madness on punishment, on pedagogy, on sexuality – worked to define the field in which true and false statements could be made: about these particular fields and the interconnections between these discourses, practices and the various sites and populations which they sought to define and govern. For Foucault, the art of liberal government is made possible by coming to *know better* the diverse persons, groups and populations which are the objects of these various rationalities and technologies.

What is important in terms of the present discussion is the ways in which power relations, conceived in terms of actions upon actions, have, in the space of the modern liberal democratic nation state, become "governmentalised". Foucault (1983) argued that the forms of the "government of men by one another in any society are multiple". These power relations, these actions upon actions, can be "superimposed, they cross, impose their own limits, sometimes cancel one another out, sometimes reinforce one another" (p.224). However, with regard to the particular forms of power in the Liberal Democracies, "the state is not simply one of the forms or specific situations of the exercise of power – even if it the most important – but that in a certain way all other forms of power relation must refer to it" (p.224). Here, Foucault's argument rests not on the notion that these other specific relations of power are derived from the state. Instead there is a sense in which other forms of power relations – in schools, in the justice system, in families, in economic relations – are increasingly regulated by the state. These diverse relations and settings, these various fields of actions upon actions, have become "governmentalised, that is to say, elaborated, rationalised and centralised in the form of, under the auspices of, state institutions" (Foucault 1983, p.224). The governmentality litera-ture that has emerged in the past 20 years has emphasised the ways in which a vast array of quasi autonomous non government organisations (QUANGOs and NGOs) assume various responsibilities for regulating the "free" conduct of individuals, families, communities and populations – conduct that ranges across all possibilities of human behaviour and action (for a useful recent overview of these processes see Rose 1999). As Rose and Miller (1992) argue, government in this mode of analysis can be conceived as being:

> *intrinsically linked to the activities of expertise, whose role is not one of meaning an all pervasive web of "social control", but of enacting assorted attempts at the calculated admin-istration of diverse aspects of conduct through countless, often competing, local tactics of education, persuasion, inducement, management, incitement, motivation and encouragement* (Rose & Miller 1992, p.175).

Populations of youth: artefacts of the activities of expertise

> *[I]n societies such as ours, youth is present only when its presence is a problem, or rather when its presence is regarded as a problem. The category "youth" only gets activated, is only mobilised in official documentary discourse in the form of editorials, magazine articles, in the supposedly disinterested tracts on "deviance", "cognitive dissonance", and "maladjustment" emanating from the social sciences, when young people make their presence felt ...* (Hebdige 1997, p.402).

In *Governing the Soul,* Nikolas Rose (1990) examines the "powers that have come to bear upon the subjective existence of people and their relations one with another: political power, economic power, institutional power, expert power, technical power, cognitive power" (p.ix). Central to his project is an examination of the ways in which the government of human behaviour "has become bound up with innovations and developments in a number of scien-tific discourses that have rendered knowable the normal and pathological functioning of humans" (p.ix). Institutionalised disciplines such as the "psy" sciences, criminology, sociology, cultural studies, critical pedagogy, feminism, bio-genetics, emerge from and produce processes that have:

> *taken up and transformed problems offered by political, economic, and moral strategies and concerns, and ... have made these problems thinkable in new ways and governable with new techniques. In the course of these events these ways of knowing have profoundly and irre-versibly transformed political rationalities, institutional life, moral discourse and personal life itself* (Rose 1990, p.ix).

Thinking of Youth in terms of population enables an engagement with processes of expert knowledge that have a long history of producing the truths of Youth (Hebdige 1997). In this section I argue that this form of engagement suggests that Youth can be understood as an artefact of various forms of expertise – a product that is produced via institutionalised processes of truth production. My concern in this chapter is with problematising these processes of truth production, a problematisation that is fundamental to thinking differently about the nature and effects of attempts to represent and regulate populations of Youth in contexts of uncertainty and insecurity.

A point of entry into this discussion is provided by a debate begun in the pages of *Youth Studies Australia* in 1992, which took as its object the theoretical means available for "telling the truth about Youth". This particular debate is useful for a number of reasons. In the first instance, it introduces Foucault's problematisations of Power and of the Subject into the intellectual domain of Youth Studies. In the second instance, this debate foregrounds the contestation between particular intellectual traditions as forms of truth telling in relation to Youth. In what follows I will demonstrate that this debate is indicative of the processes of colonisation, and constitution of Youth (as population, as discourse) by diverse forms of expertise. These processes work at a number of levels: via the construction of a concept of Youth, a concept rendered knowable in particular ways; through the emergence of an institutionalised intellectual domain named as Youth Studies; and through the contestation within this domain between the expertise of psychologists, sociologists, Youth Work professionals and cultural studies academics over claims to tell the truth about Youth. Rob White (1993), then a research associate at Melbourne University's Youth Research Centre, highlighted, in an edited collection that brought together contributions to this debate, the increasingly "sophisticated", institutionalised processes of expert knowledge production which take as their object the truths of Youth:

> As "youth studies" has emerged as a distinct field of inquiry, with identifiable writers and its own youth-specific institutions (such as the Youth Research Centre at the University of Melbourne), so too discussion in the field has become more sophisticated, and the scope of analysis has likewise broadened. It is in this framework of rekindled intellectual interest and vigour that we are now seeing concerted efforts to stretch conceptual boundaries, to more readily engage in considered argument about relevant empirical and theoretical matters, and to think more seriously about the politics of research and analysis (White 1993, p.vii).

White also foregrounds the processes of differentiation which mark a field such as Youth Studies. Thus, locations within different intellectual *disciplines* (sociology, psychology, education, criminology, cultural studies); different objects of intellectual abstraction (Youth as unemployed, students, homeless, juvenile offenders, adolescents, young men and women); different methods, forms and levels of analysis; and different interpretive frameworks – all these processes work to constitute the discursive terrain of Youth.

This particular debate about how to "tell the truth of Youth", emerged as a response to an article by Gordon Tait (1992, 1993a) which sought to introduce Foucault's discussions about knowledge/power, regimes of truth and government into the domain of Youth Studies. Tait's purpose was to argue that Youth, as constituted by various experts in diverse centres of expertise could be conceived as an "artefact of government", constructed at the "intersection of a wide range of governmental strategies"; an intersection marked by expert problematisations of crime, education, the family, the media, popular culture, (un)employment, training and risk. Tait's strategy in arguing for the efficacy of a Foucauldian analysis of Youth rested on positioning this form of analysis in relation to the intellectual legacy of youth subcultural theory that emerged from the Birmingham Centre for Contemporary Cultural Studies (CCCS). Tait (1992) argued that the legacy of CCCS analyses of Youth subcultures had resulted in "contemporary discourses on youth" taking on a "rather familiar" appearance (p.12). The unproblematic reiteration of constructs and concepts derived from this legacy posed the danger, argued Tait, of youth research continuing to produce "work which is, at best, unaware of its own origins, or, at worst, outdated and anachronistic" (p.17).

In response to this argument, Howard Sercombe (1992, 1993) suggested that Tait's critique was a "welcome and refreshing contribution to theoretical debates in Youth Studies". Youth Studies, as an institutionalised intellectual domain tended, Sercombe (1993) argued, to be dominated by empirical, "descriptive studies" at the expense of any "serious, critical" debate about categories such as transitions, adolescence, school leaver or Youth (p.7). Yet, Sercombe also argued that Tait's critique of the CCCS legacy tended to *freeze* subcultural theory in the late 1970s, with its focus on *Resistance through Rituals* and *Learning to Labour*. He further argued that Tait's focus on spectacular Youth subcultures as somehow defining the field of cultural studies of Youth failed to acknowledge that: "Spectacular youth subcultures are a titillating but marginal phenomenon in work around youth, involving a tiny minority of young people" (p.7). For Sercombe (1993) there is a sense that what Tait's critique is *really* about is the "contest for the general theoretical ownership of the youth phenomenon ... His argument is that the CCCS approach is no good, and that Foucault's approach is" (pp.7-8).

At this level, the debate here is about the practices of intellectual knowledge production, practices whose motive forces include not only varied attempts to tell the truth of Youth, but also to tell the truth about how these truths can be produced. In the institutional spaces in which these various forms of expertise produce constantly expanding knowledge about Youth there is also contestation about the efficacy, the utility, the value and the conse- quences of particular forms of truth production. In these settings the truth of Youth emerges as only one concern in the contest between various forms of practice capable of producing these truths. So, while Sercombe (1993) may be correct in arguing that Tait's (1992) *scholarly* critique is limited, or flawed, or that in *fact* its purpose is to stake a claim for the "theoretical ownership of the youth phenomenon", his critique supports Tait's (1993b) argument that Youth "exists as a governmental object at the intersection of a variety of diverse problemati- sations" (p.10):

> For example, youth has been constructed and operationalised as a category through the different mechanisms and knowledge associated with law enforcement – primarily within terrains such as drug abuse, prostitution, petty theft and gang related crimes. The policing of youth itself has drawn upon rationales of behaviour and discourses circulating within a variety of other terrains, from jurisprudence to career guidance, from psychology to medicine, from sociology to welfare and from demographics to marketing (Tait 1992, p.16).

Indeed, what Sercombe (1992, 1993) and White (1993) both fail to acknowledge is that this increasingly "sophisticated" process of institutionalised intellectual knowledge produc- tion about Youth is fundamentally implicated in the formation of populations of Youth "at the intersection of a variety of diverse problematisations".

Expertise and the nature of uncertainty

It can be useful to think of these debates about processes of expert knowledge production, including the observation by Tait (1992) that the CCCS legacy in Youth Studies is the product of "critique" and "recuperation", as instances of the "institutional reflexivity" of "abstract systems" under the conditions of "reflexive modernisation" (Giddens 1994b; Beck, Giddens & Lash 1994). Giddens' (1994b) thesis foregrounds the institutional dimensions and reflexivity of modernity, and the facilitation of this reflexivity via the activities, practices and institu- tional location of diverse forms of expertise.

Processes of reflexive modernisation are characterised by the thoroughgoing penetration of the *natural* and the *social* by systems of expertise and the knowledges they produce. Giddens (1990), for example, argues that the conditions of "radicalised modernity" are marked by processes of reflexivity in which claims to certainty in knowledge production – the very bedrock of Enlightenment thinking – become intensely problematic. So much so that the intensification and globalisation of reflexively produced knowledge results in a "runaway world", of "dislocation" and "uncertainty" (Giddens 1994a, p.3). Giddens (1994a) argues that human existence is not necessarily more risky under contemporary social conditions but that the origins of risk and uncertainty have changed; "manufactured risk is the result *of* human intervention into the conditions of social life and into nature" (p.4, original emphasis). Moreover, "what was supposed to create greater and greater certainty – the advance of human knowledge and "controlled intervention" into society and nature – is actually deeply involved with this unpredictability" (p.3).

In relation to Youth, I have suggested that this reflexivity is characterised by the monitoring of both the processes of truth production about Youth, and the truths produced by these processes. This "institutional reflexivity" is characteristic of processes of reflexive modernisation, processes which structure the institutional spaces and practices which are fundamental to enabling Youth to function as a series of truths, and the mobilisation of these truths in various attempts to govern the behaviours and attitudes of young people.

Characterising processes of reflexive modernisation in this manner points to a *phase* in the historical *development* of these expert systems which makes it increasingly difficult to think of Youth other than as an artefact of expertise. Liberal government is always an incomplete project and reflexive expertise is involved in constant attempts to know better the truths of Youth and the ways to produce these truths, as youthful bodies, motivations, behaviours and dispositions (however these are understood) *elude* and *escape* the frames and categories which attempt to order them. Yet, it is only within representational frameworks that these truths come to mean *anything*. It is the domination of these representational frameworks by systems of expertise that characterises processes of reflexive modernisation, and hence, makes it possible, historically, to conceive of Youth as an artefact of expertise.

Foucauldian genealogies of government point to the processes of individualisation and normalisation at work in the practices of modern government. Increasingly, these practices take as their objects the *unconscious*, the *soul*, *desire*, *aesthetics*, the *body*, as well as the rational cognitive *mind* of the individuals and the populations they attempt to govern. Here the *"why"* aspects of human behaviours and dispositions appear, increasingly, as the objects of expertise impelled by concerns for certainty, mastery and order. With respect to Youth, these processes have a special significance. In the quest for certainty in relation to youthful behaviours and dispositions, young people's motivations and desires, their *embodied*, *desiring*, *partial* and *provisional* subjectivities, and their *identity work* emerge as the object of varied forms of expertise. "Psy" scientists, social and youth workers, health professionals, cultural commentators, journalists, the police and juvenile justice experts, teachers, feminist poststructuralists, postmodern cultural theorists, critical theorists and Foucauldian genealogists are all implicated in institutionalised processes restlessly producing vast amounts of "intellectually grounded" (Watts 1993/94) knowledge about the past, present and future lifeworlds and life chances of populations of young people. Moreover, where the conditions of reflexive modernisation subject claims to mastery and certainty to the principle of radical doubt, they also impel expert systems to further processes of knowledge production. These processes are fundamental to various programs that seek to know and govern Youth in more sophisticated ways.

Some conclusions: the dangers of uncertainty

If it is true that young people are the nation's most precious resource, then the nation needs better means of measuring the overall effectiveness of the socialisation process. Systematic efforts are needed to assess the adolescent population over time. Such efforts will require multi-faceted measures that examine a range of adolescent attributes, including perceptions, behaviors and accomplishments. Data collection must be organized to produce findings according to age, gender, race, ethnicity, and socio-economic status (Panel on High-Risk Youth 1993, pp.255-56).

In contemporary settings of uncertainty, processes that construct the truths of Youth can be understood as "dangerous" (Foucault 1983). These processes are dangerous in the sense that the construction of these truths emerge from the promise of increasingly sophisticated processes of surveillance, identification and intervention. These processes target particular populations of young people in various attempts by experts and centres of expertise to know and manage the uncertain in the name of certainty – processes that are particularly evident in the above quotation from a report of one such gathering of experts.

Zygmunt Bauman (1990), writing from a position better able to judge than many of us, is particularly wary of modernity's attempts to "exterminate ambivalence", and the dangers (even horrors) of the means mobilised to achieve this *end* (of uncertainty, of history). Bauman (1990) identifies in histories of the Holocaust a number of strategies that work to construct this genocide as either a *"one-off historical episode"* which was the "culmination of the long history of Judeophobia"; or as a *"German* affair" (p.19, original emphasis), which was the culmination of a particular set of historical contingencies centred on the German Nation State, or as a "singular eruption of pre-modern (barbaric, irrational) forces as yet insufficiently tamed or ineffectively suppressed by (presumably weak or faulty) German modernisation" (p.19). These histories fail to recognise that in modernity's war on ambivalence (made so murderously concrete in the practices of National Socialism), there has been a profound convergence between the "practical tasks posited by the modern state", and the "legislative reason of modern philosophy and of the modern scientific mentality in general" (p.26). As Bauman (1990) argues: "Modern rulers and modern philosophers were first and foremost *legis-lators*; they found chaos and set out to tame it and replace it with order" (p.24, original emphasis). The modern project of the Enlightenment was, argues Bauman (1990), motivated "by the dream of a masterful humanity", a humanity which was *"collectively* free from constraints" and thus able to "respect" and "preserve" human "dignity" (p.26, original emphasis). The realisation of this dream was to be facilitated via the elevation of "Reason to the office of supreme legislator" (p.26). Notwithstanding this attachment to the narrative of human sovereignty, there was, Bauman (1990) suggests, a certain "elective affinity" between the "strategy of legislative reason and the practice of state power bent on imposition of designed order upon obstreperous reality" (p.26).

These, and similar lessons from history ought to force us to confront "the end of innocence" (Flax 1993) with respect to the uncertain consequences (the *dangerousness*) associated with the production and appropriation of intellectually grounded knowledge about Youth, knowledge which secures legitimacy through its scholarly characteristics. Historical analyses such as Bauman's ought also to alert us to the dangerousness of the mobilisation of scholarly work in modernity's attempts to "exterminate ambivalence". Indeed, in the activities and dreams and ambitions of intellectuals and the "educated classes" can be found traces of the promise of Order to be delivered by interventionist and transformative logics and practices. Such logics promise perfectibility in human interactions, behaviours and dispositions if only we could produce *more* and *better* knowledge of these processes. This promise of the practice of social engineering is:

> *perfectly reflected in the imagery of the social ideal standing ahead of social reality and pulling it forward; in the vision of society as pliable raw material to be moulded and brought into proper shape by architects armed with a proper design; in the image of society incapable, if left to its own course, of either improving itself or even comprehending what the improvement would look like; in the concept of knowledge as power, reason as the judge of reality and an authority entitled to dictate and enforce the ought over the is* (Bauman 1990, p.37).

Bauman's critique is not unique. Postmodern and feminist critiques of modern "legislative reason" rehearse similar arguments (see, for example, Flax 1990, 1993). Bauman's (1990) contribution, however, foregrounds the dangerousness of holding out the promise of redemptive progress if only we knew *more*, or *better* the things which provoke uncertainty and anxiety, in this instance, the *unruly* young minds and bodies which escape the ordering processes of our (limited) understandings. *More* understanding, *better* truths could structure the mobilisation of progressive, enlightened, emancipatory processes of social engineering with regard to Youth, processes which promise a better, less dangerous, more certain world. As Bauman (1990) argues, the promise of legislated reason, a promise to be delivered via the activities and practices of expertise, is not the sole province of the "Police States of history". The same hopes and ambitions structure the identification of future research objects in the reports produced by youth research centres; panels on high-risk youth; departments of education, training and youth affairs; faculties of education; and the many other centres of expertise so characteristic of Liberal Democracies at the start of the 21st century. In such reports can be found the "normative, engineering ambitions that are inherent in all scientific enterprise ... and that may lend themselves easily and joyously to political uses – *anytime* and *everywhere*" (Bauman 1990, pp.40-41, original emphasis).

In uncertain times, in times when Youth looms large and threateningly in community and policy spaces, there exists a need to problematise the processes of intellectuality which tell the truths of Youth. These truths, as I have argued, promise, within various governmental projects, to exterminate uncertainty with regard to the behaviours and dispositions of certain expertly identified populations of young people. In "rethinking youth", in thinking about how we "represent youth", it might be useful to also ask questions of a more fundamental level. Such questions might include: What is it that we do as producers of intellectually grounded knowledge when we take Youth as our objects? What might be the consequences, intended or otherwise, of these institutionalised processes of knowledge production for the regulation of the young people who are the objects of these processes?

The institutionalised reflexivity which characterises the conditions that continually problematise the truths of Youth, and the means available to produce these truths, preclude any quest for some *final solution* to these questions. Further, the promise of an emancipatory project for Youth Studies (Wyn & White 1998) is problematised if we acknowledge that Youth Studies exists as an institutionalised, intellectual domain that secures legitimacy via its promise that it can produce "sophisticated" knowledge about Youth. One task that might follow such a problematisation could be to "rethink youth studies", rather than to continue "rethinking youth".

Acknowledgments

I would like to thank Lyn Harrison for her comments on an earlier draft of this chapter.

References

Bauman, Z. 1990, *Modernity and Ambivalence*, Polity Press, Cambridge.

Beck, U., Giddens, A. & Lash, S. 1994, 'Preface' in *Reflexive Modernisation: Politics, tradition and aesthetics in the modern social order*, eds U. Beck, A. Giddens & S. Lash, Polity Press, Cambridge.

Bessant, J. & Watts, R. 1998, 'History, myth making and young people in a time of change', *Family Matters*, n.49, pp.5-10.

Eckersley, R. 1988, *Casualties of Change: The predicament of youth in Australia*, Australia's Commission for the Future, Carlton South.

—— 1992, *Youth and the Challenge to Change*, Australia's Commission for the Future, Carlton South.

Flax, J. 1990, *Thinking Fragments*, University of California Press, Berkeley.

—— 1993, *Disputed Subjects*, Routledge, New York.

Foucault, M. 1983, 'The subject and power', in *Michel Foucault: Beyond structuralism and hermeneutics,* eds H.L. Dreyfus & P. Robinow, University of Chicago Press, Chicago.

—— 1988, 'The political technology of individuals', in *Technologies of the Self: A seminar with Michel Foucault,* eds L. Martin, H. Gutman & P. Hutton, The University of Massachusetts Press, USA.

—— 1991, 'Governmentality', in *The Foucault Effect: Studies in governmental rationality*, eds G. Burchell, C. Gordon & P. Miller, Harvester Wheatsheaf, Hemel Hempstead.

Giddens, A. 1990, *The Consequences of Modernity*, Stanford University Press, Stanford.

—— 1994a, *Beyond Left and Right*, Polity Press, Cambridge.

—— 1994b, 'Living in a post-traditional society', in *Reflexive Modernisation: Politics, tradition and aesthetics in the modern social order,* eds U. Beck, A. Giddens & S. Lash, Polity Press, Cambridge.

Gordon, C. 1991, 'Governmental rationality: An introduction', in *The Foucault Effect: Studies in governmental rationality*, eds G. Burchell, C. Gordon & P. Miller, Harvester Wheatsheaf, Hemel Hempstead.

Hebdige, D. 1997, 'Posing ... threats, striking ... poses: Youth, surveillance, and display', in *The Subcultures Reader*, eds K. Gelder & S. Thornton, Routledge, London.

Kelly, P. 1998, Risk and the regulation of youth(ful) identities in an age of manufactured uncertainty, unpublished PhD thesis, Deakin University, Geelong.

Mackay, H. 1993, *Reinventing Australia: The mind and mood of Australia in the 90s*, Angus & Robertson, Pymble.

Panel on High-Risk Youth, Commission on Behavioral and Social Sciences and Education,

National Research Council 1993, *Losing Generations: Adolescents in high-risk settings*, National Academy Press, Washington, DC.

Rose, N. 1990, *Governing the Soul*, Routledge, London.

—— 1999, *Powers of Freedom: Reframing political thought*, Cambridge University Press, Cambridge.

Rose, N. & Miller, P. 1992, 'Political power beyond the state: Problematics of government', *British Journal of Sociology*, v.43, n.2, pp.173-205.

Sercombe, H. 1992, 'Youth theory: Marx or Foucault', *Youth Studies Australia*, v.11, n.3, pp.51-56.

—— 1993, 'Youth theory: Marx or Foucault?', in *Youth Subcultures: Theory, history and the Australian experience,* ed. R. White, National Clearinghouse for Youth Studies, Hobart.

Tait, G. 1992, 'Reassessing street kids: A critique of subculture theory', *Youth Studies Australia*, v.11, n.2, pp.12-16.

——1993a, 'Reassessing street kids: A critique of subculture theory', in *Youth Subcultures: Theory, history and the Australian experience,* ed. R. White, National Clearinghouse for Youth Studies, Hobart.

—— 1993b, 'Foucault, sex and youth policy', paper presented at the Rethinking Policies for Young People Conference, April, Melbourne.

—— 1995, 'Shaping the "at-risk youth": Risk, governmentality and the Finn Report', *Discourse*, v.16, n.1, pp.123-34.

Watts, R. 1993/1994, 'Government and modernity: An essay in thinking governmentality', *Arena Journal*, n.2, pp.103-58.

White, R. 1993, 'Youth studies: Debate and diversity' in *Youth Subcultures: Theory, history and the Australian experience,* ed. R. White, National Clearinghouse for Youth Studies, Hobart.

—— 1998, *Public Spaces for Young People*, Australian Youth Foundation & National Campaign Against Violence and Crime, Sydney.

Wyn, J. & White, R. 1997, *Rethinking Youth*, Allen & Unwin, St. Leonards.

—— 1998, 'Young people, social problems and Australian youth studies', *Journal of Youth Studies*, v.1, n.1, pp.23-38.

Youth Research Centre 1998, *Annual Report*, University of Melbourne, Melbourne.

chapter 8

Researching VET pathways with disengaged and disadvantaged young people

My friends said why do a course? There aren't any jobs.

Steve

I do nothing. I can't even read.

Aaron

WITHIN the post-compulsory sector of education, the past few years have been a time of continued change and cutbacks, followed by grand plans for new schemes for vocational education and training (VET). At the same time, the unemployment rate among young people remains at disturbingly high levels. In some areas, such as Geelong, where signs of "economic recovery" have not yet been seen, young people who had been early school leavers, remain disengaged from VET or employment. Increasing numbers of young people are becoming early school leavers and later finding themselves long-term unemployed (Dwyer 1998). With the virtual disappearance of the youth labour market, employment prospects for these most disadvantaged young people do not seem to be improving. So the problem remains; young people who have been early school leavers often are unable to access current provision of VET and thus remain with limited scope for employment. Programs have been developed which achieve successful outcomes for educationally disadvantaged young people, when outcomes are measured more broadly than simply finding a job. But these programs remain on the margins of VET provision, as indeed do the young people who might access them. The research project described here was recently undertaken in Geelong with young people and providers of VET programs. The research aimed to gain perspectives from young people and from those working with them, as to what they saw as barriers to their vocational education and employment, and to discuss the implications of the findings for further provision of VET for disadvantaged young people. This paper reflects on the possibilities for reflexivity in research which attempted to engage young people themselves in discussions about their own Vocational Education and Training (VET) needs, through a series of community-based projects.

According to the dominant policies constructing the field of post-compulsory education and training, and in particular VET, all students should complete Year 12, but currently school retention rates are dropping in Victoria, from 76% to 71% (Kirby 2000.) The key policies from the early 1990s, which influenced the formation of current VET provision, aimed to have all 19-year-olds in work or VET (Finn 1991; Carmichael 1992). In 1998, when the research was undertaken, 27% of young people nationally were unemployed, and in Geelong, 41.5% of young people were unemployed.

Many industrialised cities across Australia, such as Geelong and Adelaide, have suffered prolonged economic downturn, which in turn has further reduced work opportunities for young people. The rapid expansion of the manufacturing sector in the 1960s and 1970s, particularly in the car industry, resulted in thriving regional cities, with ample job and vocational education and training opportunities for young people when they left school, prior to completion of Year 12. But by the 1990s the situation for young people had changed markedly. The youth labour market has now virtually disappeared, to be replaced by expansion in part-time work, but not in full-time work or in career opportunities for young people (Sweet 1998). Recent reports on changes in the Australian labour market show that there are certain "sink" areas in the labour market, that is areas with continued high rates of unemployment and no new job opportunities opening up (ANTA 1994).

For many young people the transitional pathways out of school into work or VET are not clear in theory, and are extremely complicated in practice. The sector is neither institutionally bound, as are schools, TAFE institutes and universities, nor directly funded. The sector is made up of a complex mix of public and private provision, standards and accreditation systems of diverse locations, courses, teachers and status. VET programs are located in universities and TAFE institutes, as degree or diploma courses of several years duration, apprenticeships and traineeships, to short courses of four to six weeks offering an industry accredited certificate. It is within this context that we undertook the ANTARAC funded research project, Paths to Pathways: Vocational Education and Training (VET) for educationally disadvantaged groups of young people.[1]

In investigating the transition and pathways young people make between school, work, VET or unemployment, one aim was to make visible, within the research context, the lived experiences of disadvantaged young people who are excluded from the current dominant discourses in the field of vocational education and training.

> Since I was eight I can remember her going off at night to work. I would cook my own tea. I got kicked out at 14. I live in West Geelong with a friend. My Mum lives with her boyfriend.
>
> Aaron

A further important focus was to examine how young people are constructed in the VET policies and the discordant reality of young people's lives. Along the way, major shifts in the research design and approach eventuated as government policy, funding and providers were all restructured, adding new complexities to the already most complex field of educational provision.

Given research perspectives in other sectors of education, VET policy discourses appear fixed in an earlier modernist framework (Anderson 1995). VET discourses totalise the field, attempting to construct an appearance of unity of identity, where different contexts and individual difference with regard to skills are denied. Second, and more problematically for young people, VET policy discourses render the young people themselves invisible. Again, concerning young people as VET students, the policy discourses ignore differences in gender, ethnicity, socioeconomic context and, most importantly for this research, assume successful completion of Year 12 with a high level of general skill. Life issues of homelessness, risk behaviours and low levels of basic skills, all of which impact on young people's decisions to remain in school, or continue on into VET, are nowhere addressed. As one trainer noted, "If they drop out of school it's ludicrous to think they can get a job without assistance". The totalising policy discourses of the ideal student, present a young person who is capable of staying in school, achieving high levels of skills in all areas of the curriculum, as well as social skills to make them work ready. We wanted to work with young people who had been early school leavers, to explore the ways in which their life circumstances mediated their decision to leave school and their post school choices. We aimed to research the ways in which such policies and programs, enable, or failed to enable certain groups of disadvantaged young people to continue in VET and successfully find their ways into employment.

> We have a lot of young people here who don't live with their parents. They certainly don't have any contact with a parent.
>
> Community worker

> Many students leave school at Year 11 but don't have a clue how to access a pathway into VET. They think the Gordon (TAFE) is unobtainable.
>
> Community worker

Young people who do not complete secondary school are presented as failures, while the difficult reality of their lives is silenced within schools and policy formation. Yet, as Fine (1992) argues:

> *… it is the very naturalness of not naming, of shutting down or marginalising conversations for the "sake of getting on with learning" that demands educators attention, particularly so for low income youths highly ambivalent about the worth of a diploma, desperately desirous of and at the same time discouraged from its achievement* (Fine 1992, p.149).

Within the totalising research and policy discourses which dominate VET, is it possible to present the voices of disengaged and educationally disadvantaged young people? Would this research project, yet again, reproduce a deficit view of early school leavers, and continue to marginalise young people or deny their lives and subcultures (Hebdige 1988)?

Initial research design

> Young people are very tentative, even about accessing some of the services, particularly the bureaucratic ones.
>
> Job and Course Preparation tutor

The research approach began with the intention of working through participatory action research and case studies of successful programs for young people, engaging young people themselves in the research design and activities. The intention was to work with a group of people who would join in a participatory action research project and work through a number of cycles of investigation, reflection, negotiation and identification of issues of concern and possibilities of developing change. The plan was to engage an ongoing team of stakeholders, employing young people in this research process. It was hoped that the young people's experiences in school, employment and unemployment and subsequent vocational courses, could be presented along side those of trainers, providers and welfare workers.

The research activities therefore were planned in several distinct phases. The first involved mapping the field of provision and the dilemmas that were facing the providers of services and programs for young people who had been early school leavers through a series of community meetings. The next stage involved engaging young people to work with the research team to undertake interviews with a range of young people, from different backgrounds and experiences of school, work and VET. And the final stage was to undertake a case study of a successful VET program, one that young people and support agents found to be successful with early school leavers. This had been the initial research design as put forward to the funding agency. As we attempted to work with young people and providers to gain understandings of how the complex array of welfare services, agencies and VET programs worked with and for these young people, a number of issues began to arise which resulted in these plans being redesigned several times.

Dilemmas in the research process

The research began by mapping the field through a series of community meetings from which we had hoped to draw a group of people who would become involved in the participatory research project. An open invitation was issued though youth support networks to anyone providing services to young people to participate. The response was amazing, with a large group of service providers attending a series of meetings. The participants included representatives from schools, VET, TAFE, Migrant Resource Services, disability services, Juvenile Justice, housing, health and welfare support, case management, CES and employment services. A number of young people also attended, both those in school and those who had already left school. The responses revealed an extensive network of agencies all working for young people, thriving in a climate of competitive tendering for funding. Competitive tendering policies attempted to set one provider against another, seeking the limited resources available, discouraging collaboration. The providers' responses showed a high level of resistance to these policies of privatisation and marketisation in this sector of education and welfare provision. Hutton argues that:

> The vitality of the welfare state is a badge of a healthy society; it is a symbol of our capacity to act together morally, to share and to recognise the mutuality of rights and obligations that underpins all human association. It is an expression of social citizenship (Hutton 1996, p.306).

While marketisation won out over quality VET program provision at policy level, on the ground many providers continued to work collaboratively for the benefit of young people (Anderson 1997; Marginson 1997). Soon after the introduction of the competitive tendering policy, a sense of extreme paranoia developed among providers, as those who had previously seen themselves as working collegially in order to provide the best options for their students, found themselves constructed as and constructing "competitors" (Blackmore & Angwin 1997). This resulted in widespread job loss for teachers and experienced program managers working in the field. In the past, before the introduction of compulsory competitive tendering, these network meetings were a regular part of most out-of-school education programs, whether specifically TAFE, ACFE, or AMES. However, the impact of competition on these network meetings has been disastrous. "It's tearing the heart out of the sector," stated one of the SkillShare Providers interviewed.

We had hoped to gain input for the future directions of the research project from the groups of people working in some way with young people. A number of important issues and dilemmas for the project emerged from these meetings. First, while we had outlined that the focus of our research project would be on young people aged 16 and over, as these young people had reached school leaving age, the major concern at that time was the growing number of very young early school leavers, that is those aged between 12 and 15. One welfare teacher reported that "more and more 12- and 13-year-olds are falling out of the school system. They don't cope". A welfare worker observed: "There are no truant officers any more. Young people can move from school to school and the authorities just say the student finished here and say they've gone there. No-one particularly cares. They drop out."

There are so many different regulations for the very young early school leavers in relation to which programs different young people are eligible for. Those working with young people identified significant gaps and difficulties in finding appropriate VET provision, both in terms of eligibility and appropriate pedagogy for very young students. "It's difficult to get training for younger age students. They are not long enough out of school, therefore there's not a lot for these very young people," said one welfare teacher. Far too often the young people have to spend several months without any program or support, after which time it is even more difficult to get them back into school or a course, and at that age, employment is not an option. Thus many involved in the community meetings wanted the research project framed to focus on these youngest school leavers. However, as the research funding was from ANTA, and addressed 16- to 20-year-olds, this shift in focus was not possible.

Other major concerns raised at the community meetings which impacted on the research, were the planned changes to the CES and the closure of the Youth Access Centres, following the election of a new federal government. "We have a great relationship with the Youth Access Centre at the CES. But I don't know what's going to happen now," stated one of the Job and Course Preparation tutors.

These centres were the key pathways for disengaged young people back into VET and a pathway into the work force. Providers had no idea as to how the changes to the CES would impact on their work with young people. They believed, and indeed it proved to be the case, that access to Case Management would be further restricted with the privatisation and break-up of the CES. There was widespread concern as to how these young people would fare under the new funding arrangements – arrangements where long-term unemployed early school leavers find it almost impossible to find work without undertaking some VET program. Under Working Nation policy, an appropriate outcome was seen to be undertaking VET or moving into work. Within this new policy structure, outcomes could only be measured in terms of employment, which meant that the most disadvantaged young people would once again be seen as failures, if they did not succeed in finding a job after a four-week course.

This major change in direction of policy concerning programs for young unemployed people further impacted on the research, as many providers were uncertain as to how they would be able to maintain their programs and their staff. As one of the VET providers commented: "How can we hope to keep committed people when this sword of Damacles is always hanging over their heads, never knowing if their job will survive the next round of funding".

Those working in the field with the young people live in a constant state of uncertainty as to how they would be able to continue their programs and for the teachers and trainers, whether they would actually have a job over the next few months. For tutors, it can be especially concerning: "We are uncertain about our future funding. We've put in for future funding. We'd like to continue the programs as they are, simply because they work."

And those working with young people have shown that a range of alternative programs can make a difference to these young people's lives.

> The LEAP programs were successful because the young people wanted to do them.
>
> Case manager

> It's much better than we thought it would be. Let's do it for six or eight weeks.
>
> Steve

> Most courses have a 30% successful outcome. We have between 60–70%.
>
> Job and Course Preparation tutor

There was difficulty in engaging some of the stakeholders in the research projects. While we had a wide-ranging response from all sorts of agencies working with young people, it was interesting to note that two groups did not respond to numerous invitations to attend meetings or requests for interviews. Throughout the project the group which remained the most difficult to gain information from remained the private providers of VET courses.[2] One such trainer observed: "With the young people we are talking about, you can't make any money training them on this arrangement, and you can't be certain that they will stay in a job three months. So business is not good."

Despite numerous contacts, invitations to meetings and seminars and requests for interviews, most of these providers refused to participate in the formal research process. Informally, we were able to interview a number of providers and teachers and trainers who requested that neither they nor the organisation for whom they worked would be named. Competitive tendering seems to have resulted in a level of paranoia as to what competitive edge another group might gain by working collaboratively in research.

> Their whole approach is about brochures. Always working on a new strategy. They seem more worried about image than what's in the picture. They used to be running computer courses for small businesses, now they run retail skills.
>
> Trainer

A second group which was difficult to engage with were employers. Although at the outset of the project a number of local employers expressed interest in participating in the project, when meetings were held, very few employers participated. In interviews, some of these employers questioned their role in assisting these young people, who appear to have few skills and were not job ready. Given the incredible growth of the private sector in providing VET and the recent reports raising concerns as to the quality of the training provided, this absence from the project was disturbing, although similar to others' experiences researching in this sector (Schofield 2000).

Another tension for our initial research plan was the difficulty in maintaining an ongoing action research group from the community, even though good numbers of service providers were keen to attend community meetings and keep in touch with the project. As major changes were being flagged to their sector they found it impossible to find the time to spend in ongoing processes. A second stage of the research involved a series of interviews conducted by the research team and several different groups of young people. From the meetings we had identified various groups within the community who could offer differing perspectives on post-school pathways for early school leavers. These included teachers in the school sector, providers of VET and other community services, such as Case Managers, the Brotherhood of St Laurence, Salvation Army and family agencies, to ascertain their views on the particular difficulties and possibilities for increasing participation in training in this area. Further interviews were conducted with local school staff, including career, welfare teachers and coordinators.

At the same time a number of young people were engaged to conduct interviews with early school leavers in their communities. The first interviews were conducted by a group of senior secondary students, with young people in the target groups of early school leavers. Many of the school students had friends in the local area who had left school and had not participated in any courses available to early school leavers. Several other young people, who had been early school leavers and experienced long-term unemployment, undertook a series of interviews with young people and school teachers to gain their perspectives on early school leaving and the pathways young people were making between school, VET work and unemployment. The first group were young people of both English- and non-English-speaking background who had left school before the completion of Year 12. Some younger students from Adult Multicultural Education Services (AMES) interviewed recently-arrived young immigrants concerning their attitudes towards undertaking further VET courses after finishing their English program.

An interesting but disturbing finding from these interviews conducted by young people, both those who were seen to be successful at school and those who had been early school leavers, was the consistent reporting of young people's negative experiences in the school system.

> I found school to be like ... they think that you are the student so you've got no brains. They say that if you don't understand something, then its too bad.
>
> James

> I wasn't difficult. It was if they decided they didn't like me, what could I do? If I hadn't left, then I would have been pushed out.
>
> Chet

> If I'd stayed they'd have kicked me out. They didn't like the type of person that I am.
>
> Darren

> They should have more practical stuff instead of sitting writing all the time. The teachers are like zombies most of the time. They just say "sit there, do that" and hand you a piece of paper.
>
> Zeke

At first we were concerned that none of the interviews seemed to report positive experiences of school, but listening to the students' tapes, we too were overwhelmed with the high levels of alienation that young people had developed during their time at school. These findings have been confirmed by recent studies of post-compulsory education, in a widespread manner (Kirby 2000; Dwyer et al. 1998; Teese 2000). This proved to be a major barrier to young people feeling confident that they will be able to succeed in a post-school VET program.

> I couldn't read and write but they just kept passing me every year.
>
> James

> Most kids I've worked with have found that school did not work for them. Most have learning difficulties which haven't been identified.
>
> Tutor

The final stage of the research project became the case study of a Job and Course Preparation Program run at BAYSA.[3] Interviews were undertaken with young people who were participating in JPET. In an attempt to work with the young people undertaking the Job Preparation course, it was decided that only one member of the research team would work closely with them. From the outset she explained her role in the research project to the young people. She attended some sessions each week, spending time talking on an informal basis with each participant. A key engagement with the young people involved joining the outdoor activities program one day a week. Thus each week she participated in the day's activity, from rock climbing to swimming with the seals, and hours chatting on the bus! As time passed, she became an integral member of their program and the young people sought her out and disclosed information about their lives and concerns.

Researching in VET with disadvantaged young people

> We do follow up work with the young people, but its impossible to give them the support that they actually need to make a transition into something else. I usually ring or get a call about six months after they leave. They've usually not finished the course or been kicked out of employment. If they were given additional support maybe that wouldn't have happened.
>
> Migrant welfare worker

There were a number of dilemmas we encountered when working with the young people which made us reflect on how we were to continue working with them. The first involved surveillance: how would the information that they might choose to disclose be used in the future. As earlier research has shown, almost all groups of young people are at some stage involved in illegal activities to a greater or lesser extent (Watts 1995). A number were involved in a range of activities which placed them and their friends at some risk. Therefore in what contexts were they likely to disclose aspects of their lives with outsiders, who they did not know well, nor understand why they were interested in them in the first place. Already some young people felt that they were being forced to attend a course and had little confidence that they would gain anything from their participation.

> I wanted a job. I thought when I left the Gordon that it would be easy. But there "are no jobs". That's why I had to do another course.
>
> Lynne

> I've applied for about 400 jobs but I haven't got anything.
>
> Brett

> We get them job ready but there are no jobs to go into.
>
> Community worker

A second concern was the enormous need that some of these young people had to try to get their lives together with the very limited support that is provided to them. Among those professionals working in this area, there is tremendous burnout and job change. They are constantly juggling the very limited resources to try to assist someone in real need. They also know that inevitably, without ongoing support, many of these young people will be most unlikely to find employment or further VET, and without being able to earn a viable income in order to establish themselves in a more independent life. As one trainer reflected, "No-one's ever taught these kids how to get a job".

Transient nature of people and programs

> I live at home now, but I haven't been living there [long].
>
> Peter

The youth workers stated that one of the difficulties of working with this group of young people is the transitory nature of their lives. Many of these young people have moved out of home, some experience periods of homelessness, many move from house to house. Throughout the research project it was extremely difficult to find and maintain contact with a cohort of young people to work with, as many of the young people in these programs have left home and move around a great deal.

> I've lived in a caravan park in Belmont, since last June. I got kicked out of a house I shared with two other girls who go to Deakin Uni. One Friday night they put my things on the porch and I was on the streets. I stayed in shelter for a few weeks. I found out that the tenancy laws don't protect you. I used to pay $53.00 a week and expenses, now I have to pay $80.00 and electricity. They've tried to get me out of the Caravan Park because my friends got into a fight and I got blamed. It wasn't my fault. I'm a decent person, and I pay my rent. I get $331.16, which includes rent assistance.
>
> Cathy

While all this reorganisation was under way, many young people dropped out of the networks which were formerly working with them. "They move around a lot and it is easy to lose contact", commented one of the local welfare workers.

Through the interviews it became apparent that for many young people who have been early school leavers, accommodation issues remain a barrier to finding secure pathways into work or VET. Many of them talked about having to move out of home during their school years, and often this move is associated with leaving school. Many of the young people moved several times during this period, making it difficult for agencies to keep contact with them, unless the young person maintains contact.

> Some come from transient families which is why they often end up here because they've been at different schools every four months. Getting into a new social network and keeping up with school just doesn't happen.
>
> Welfare manager

Some young people interviewed had been living on the streets, several were now living in caravans; one had spent some time in a clothing bin.

> If a kid's having trouble with accommodation, we won't attempt to place them in employment or get the case manager to, because accommodation is a bigger barrier than substance abuse.
>
> Youth worker

Trying to survive without the support of any adults who might be working therefore becomes a real issue for these young people.

> No, I got kicked out. I live with a friend, and we split the rent in half. I get $230.00 a fortnight from the dole and it costs $185.00 a fortnight for rent, gas and electricity. So that only leaves you with $45.00 a fortnight to spend.
>
> Aaron

And, at the same time, those working with young people also moved from program to program as they lost their jobs with funding cuts and unsuccessful tendering. An ongoing difficulty faced in undertaking research in the sector has been the enormous complexities of policy, provision, and funding arrangements. Venues for courses change frequently, and with an increasingly casualised VET work force, identifying background knowledge and experience of teachers and trainers has become difficult to monitor. One ongoing difficulty we experienced in the research process was the constant turnover of staff within most of these organisations. Almost all of the groups contacted were uncertain as to their ongoing funding arrangements and the effect that this would have on the maintenance and future provision of their programs. Time after time an earlier contact would be followed up only to find that the particular person or that program was no longer with or provided by that organisation because of loss of funding. At the same time, those working in the sector were moving on themselves: there was the pressure to constantly be on the lookout for another job which might offer some security of employment.

This was not simply an issue for the researchers, but is also one for the field in general. With short-term funding of programs, youth workers, teachers and trainers move from job to job. Young people find it extremely difficult when their worker, the person who has built a relationship with them, has left the program or the program has closed. When they find that their local centre has closed or is being restructured and the person they trusted has lost their job, further alienation is experienced.

Long-term disengagement among early school leavers

> You need a reason to get out of bed, that's where we have to start.
>
> Youth worker

> I haven't been on a course before. I left school at 13. I was kicked out of C Secondary then I went to St A's for eight months. Then to another Secondary. Only stayed there a term. Then nothing. I live at home now, but I haven't been living there [long].
>
> Peter

> I'm 16, 17 in May – unemployed for four years. I left school in 1994 at 13. I haven't been on any other program.
>
> Louise

One of the hidden factors in working with this group of young people is that, despite their young ages, many of them have already been out of school and unemployed for some time. There is clear evidence that the longer a person is out of the work force and the social networks that this entails, the more difficult it is for them to re-enter the work force and maintain that lifestyle.

The young people living in Geelong are surrounded by networks of unemployed people. They are surrounded by intergenerational unemployment. Many of the young people said that their friends and family were not working. These patterns of everyday life set up barriers to actually getting back into work-ready habits.

> I do go out each day. At 3.00 p.m. I meet a few people at the bus stop outside Matthew Flinders. The guy I share with doesn't even do that. He does absolutely nothing. I do nothing, I can't even read.
>
> Aaron

> Adam is a bit jealous of me doing this course. I think he's used to having me to himself for the past two years. If I talk about what we've been doing he gets all upset. I love him deeply, but I don't want him telling me that I shouldn't do anything with my life.
>
> Donna

Given these factors, there remains a disturbingly high number of young people who are leaving school without the necessary levels of skill to be successful in the type of VET programs which are available to them.

> I'm 17 now and I feel stupid.
>
> Shona

> I couldn't read and write but they just kept passing me every year. I was okay at Maths and no good at English. I never learnt to read and write. The teachers only helped the kids who could do it. So I lost interest in school and fell behind. I should have stayed.
>
> Shane

Young people who have experienced school failure are unlikely to want to return to a learning situation, which they may perceive to be a "school", where they recently had so many difficulties. Given their negative attitude towards teachers, it is unlikely that they will be willing to work with a series of adults from different agencies in order to find the best pathway for them into VET or work. At the individual level, a typical pattern saw young people whose attainment's in literacy and numeracy were low, unable to be supported adequately within school due to the lack of specialised resources as well as market-driven diversion of existing resources.

> Many students leave at Level 3 (similar to Year 10) which is considered to [have provided] adequate skills to cope with the workplace. Now that the school census is complete, the schools allow students easy options to leave school. We have many 15-year-olds in these certificate level courses. Fifteen and 17-year-olds are the norm.
>
> TAFE teacher

> And they have a famous threat: "We don't need you: If you do that, you're out."
>
> Doug

Young people's motivation to undertake training and work

> I came on the course because of my case manager. I made the choice to come. I think I made a good choice.
>
> Louise

Despite the difficulties that these young people are experiencing in their lives, health and accommodation issues, once they found a course where they believed they were able to succeed and that the tutors were really intent on helping them, the turnaround in their attitudes and expectations was impressive. Most of the young people undertaking the Job and Course Preparation Program (the focus for the participant observation stage of the research) had initially been sent to the provider by a case manager or welfare worker. Their motivation increased as, perhaps more importantly, did their self-esteem.

> When they talk about confidence and liking yourself ... you do things you think you wouldn't do. Even coming on the course, I didn't think I would come back. I went and saw my case manager and asked if I could enrol myself into a course. The one I was going to do was a retail skills course. I went to the info session on BAYSA, the types of courses, then decided to change.
>
> Jann

> Rob's going to fix me up with an interview at the Gordon. I feel quite positive to take up the challenge. I may need to do some preliminary certificate first. This course is good for me, gets me out of my comfort zone.
>
> Chet

A key factor in the young people's perceptions of the course was the rapport that was established at the outset. They had known the staff a relatively short time yet they felt that they were sincere in their endeavours to help them.

> Because they want to help us, they get joy out of helping us. It makes them feel good. They treat you like you are equal.
>
> Darren

> Here at BAYSA if you don't understand something and you ask, they are willing to tell you what they're on about.
>
> James

The students were most impressed by the ambience and camaraderie of the BAYSA staff who helped them to feel they were given a real opportunity to identify the life skills they needed to manage their lives. This is not to say that the young people did not genuinely find other aspects of the course and techniques for job interviews useful. Seeing the students a week after the course, and then two weeks after the course, confirmed their need to explore new avenues to self-discovery through communicating ideas and information with the course coordinators. Each participant expressed some degree of support for learning how to go about getting themselves work at the end of the course.

> ... an excellent course. It was really good. I'd recommend it. But also I'd tell them what the opportunities are, and what you get out of the course. You learn new experiences, about things you've never been taught before, such as interview techniques, letter writing skills, plus they have a non-stress situation where they take you out to do activities.
>
> Brett

> It really gets you thinking on what you can do. And not what other people say you can't do, like school teachers, parents.
>
> Shane

It became apparent in the research that one of the strengths of VET provision in the Geelong region is the coordinated level of support that is available in some sectors. The networks which those working at BAYSA had established with the community in order to assist the young people make the transition out of their courses into further VET or work, were most extensive and impressive. No matter what the interests or needs of the young person, the Job and Course Preparation Program tutors were able to direct them to a viable pathway. This extensive networking into the local community is a key feature in the success of this course and a model, which could be established elsewhere.

Implications for VET policy

VET policy appears to be designed around young people who have already achieved a strong educational foundation through their compulsory schooling. If you achieve a high score in your school certificate, opportunities for university, TAFE, traineeships are there. However, increasing numbers of young people are not following this path and are falling out of the policy agenda. There is an endless rhetoric as to the effectiveness of VET in schools, traineeships in industry, dual pathways to the completion of VCE. However, two recent reports into post-compulsory education and vocational education and training bring these claims into question (Kirby 2000; Schofield 2000).

In reality, there has developed a huge gulf between VET provided for young people who are able to achieve within the policy framework and the young people who fall outside these discourses and become unemployed. Once a young person has been unemployed for six months, the VET opportunities available to them are quite different and of a markedly different quality than those provided for young people within mainstream VET provision or workplace-based VET. There is a major distinction between the provision of VET for employed young people or those who have gained access to TAFE courses and the unwaged, unemployed young people (Hunt & Jackson 1992).

Over the past few years there has been a marked turning away from public funding of education, in a process of redefining education itself. Arising out of the late 1980s with *Australia Reconstructed* (ACTU/TDC 1987) followed by the Finn (1991), Mayer (1992) and Carmichael (1992) reports, there was an attempt to redefine education away from the traditional social good to being an instrumental good in terms of work outcomes (Marginson 1993). At many levels there has been an attempt to lay the required economic reconstruction at the feet of school education, while ignoring the effects of globalisation on the erosion of the labour market and in particular the disappearance of the youth labour market.

For those working in VET programs with early school leavers, there is seen to be a need to develop a far more integrated approach to both general and VET education within the VET programs. Those currently working in VET programs report difficulties in working with young people with little academic achievement and consequent poor self-esteem, who fall into the youngest age group. There is a decontextualised aspect of training in the sector that runs counter to learning theories in VET, which suggest that learning needs to be situated in the community in which the young person is training as well as the community of the workplace (Stevenson 1994; Billett et al. 1997). The poor attendance and high drop-out rates show regular VET programs appear to be unable to cater for their needs. The success of the VET program depends on the development of the young people themselves – through a sustained focus on the development of personal skills, which will enable these young people to find and remain in employment. The focus on "life skills" in a range of VET programs examined to date appear to be far too short-term to really support these young people at this crucial stage of their lives.

Conclusions

Working with disengaged and disaffected young people is not easy. They find it difficult to trust outsiders, particularly those who came from "education". So many have experienced failure and alienation in their recent school experience that they are often extremely wary as to why people want to ask them questions and are concerned about what is going to happen to the information that they might disclose. It takes time to break down these barriers, but for many young people engaged in the research process, time became a barrier for them. At times the situation of the young people, from a broader "academic" perspective and indeed on a personal level, was extremely distressing. Questions of appropriate intervention, as Fine notes, were constantly debated within the research team. Our participant researcher found herself going back to the centre each week after the project had finished, as the young people tended to drop in on a regular basis and she was keen to find out how they were faring.

As with many of the issues identified in research activities, there appears to be a question of "ownership"; whose problem is it any way? The primary school, the junior secondary, senior secondary, post-compulsory or welfare? While "the problem" is pushed from bureaucratic department to department, increasing numbers of young people are continuing to leave school and disengage from the broader educational system. The research has raised many more questions about working with young people and what effects the research experience ultimately has on them, if indeed, any. It seems clear that the difficulties that many young people are experiencing in staying on in school or making successful transition from school are not diminishing. While employment rates might be improving, for some young people the entry requirements remain beyond them under most of the programs they are offered. First, in today's economic climate, with the disappearance of the youth labour market, what is the nature and purpose of the vocational education and training that we should be providing all our young people before they leave school? What are the knowledge, skills and attitudes which will equip them for their own futures, rather than some future described in policies – futures which won't, in reality, exist for them? Further, we need to ask how well do the courses available to young people with few skills assist them to gain the sorts broad life skills which will enable them to become the flexible, technologically rich workers of the post-industrial future (Giddens 1994). A narrow focus on "successful outcomes" as only "jobs", places both tutors and young people in a far too limited system.

Finally, despite, the many difficulties experienced by early school leavers, many of the young people who were at some stage engaged with this research showed an extraordinarily high level of good will and optimism. Even after years of extremely serious problems with their family, risk behaviours and peer group pressures to do nothing, once the young people find a program where the tutors are committed to them as people, who work to support them and improve their self-esteem, they work well to achieve their goals.

> Take surfing. On the boards was like a child learning to stand up. Take going to an interview, that's like learning to crawl. Then when you get the job, that's like learning to walk. On a surfboard it's the same thing. You've got to go through

stages, you've got to get on the board. That's your interview. Then you've got to stand up. Lots of people could stand, lots might not. That's the best learning experience of the day.

Steve

References

ACTU/TDC 1987, *Australia Reconstructed: ACTU/TDC Mission to Western Europe*, AGPS, Canberra.

Anderson, D. 1995, *Blurring the Boundaries: Public and private training colleges in the open training market*, NCVER, Adelaide.

—— 1997, *Competition and Market Reform in the Australian VET Sector*, NCVER, Adelaide.

Angwin, J., Henry, C., Laskey, L., McTaggart, R. & Picken, N. 1998, *Paths to Pathways: Vocational education and training for educationally disadvantaged groups of young people*, Deakin Centre for Education and Change, Geelong.

ANTA (Australian National Training Authority) 1994, *Towards a Skilled Australia*, AGPS, Canberra.

Billett, S., Cooper, M., Hayes, S. & Parker, H. 1997, *VET Policy and Research: Emerging issues and changing relationships*, Office of Training and Further Education, Melbourne.

Blackmore, J. & Angwin, J. 1997 'Educational outworkers: Emerging issues for women educators in the "restructured" post-compulsory educational labour market', *Forum of Education*, v.52, n.2, pp.1-23.

Carmichael, L. 1992, *The Australian Vocational Certificate Training System*, Employment and Skills Formation Council, National Board of Employment, Education and Training, Canberra.

Dwyer, P. et al. 1998, *Negotiating Staying and Returning: Young people's perspectives on schooling and the youth allowance*, Department of Education, Melbourne.

Fine, M. 1992, *Disruptive Voices: The possibilities of feminist research*, University of Michigan Press, Ann Arbor.

Finn, B. 1991, *Young People's Participation in Post Compulsory Training*, Report of the Australian Education Council Review Committee, AGPS, Canberra.

Giddens, A. 1994, 'Living in a post-traditional society', in *Reflexive Modernization: Politics, tradition and aesthetics in modern social order*, Stanford University Press, Stanford.

Hebdige, D. 1988, *Hiding in the Light: On images and things*, Routledge, New York.

Hunt, J. & Jackson, H. 1992, *Vocational Education and the Adult Unwaged: Developing a learning culture*, Kogan Page, London, pp.57-85.

Hutton, W. 1996, *The State to Come*, Virago, London.

Kirby, P. 2000, *Ministerial Review of Post Compulsory Education and Training Pathways in Victoria*, DEET, Melbourne.

Marginson, S. 1993, *Education and Public Policy in Australia*, Cambridge University Press, Cambridge.

—— 1997, *Educating Australia*, Cambridge University Press, Cambridge.

Mayer, E.C. 1992, *Employment Related Key Competencies for Post Compulsory Educational Training: A proposal for consultation*, The Mayer Committee, Melbourne

Schofield, K. 2000, *Delivering Quality: Report of the Independent Review of the Quality of Training in Victoria's Apprenticeship and Traineeship System*, Schofield, Melbourne.

Stevenson, J. 1994, *The Development of Vocational Expertise*, NCVER, Adelaide.

Sweet, R. 1998, 'Youth: The rhetoric and the reality of the 1990s', in *Australia's Youth: Reality and risk*, Dusseldorp Skills Forum, Sydney.

Teese, R. 2000 (unpublished), Young people's participation in VET: Components of growth in Victoria, 1994–1999, student orientations and implications for policy, Educational Outcomes Unit, University of Melbourne.

Watts, R. 1995, 'Education for citizenship and employment in Australia', *Melbourne Studies in Education*, v.36, n.2, pp.83-106.

Notes

[1]   This paper reports in part on an Australian National Training Authority Research Advisory Council Vocational Education and Training Small Project Research Grant undertaken by Jennifer Angwin, Colin Henry, Louise Laskey, Robin McTaggart, Nicola Picken from the Deakin Centre for Education and Change (for the report see Angwin, J., Henry, C. et al. 1998).

[2]   A large number of groups involved in VET have become registered training organisations (RTOs). These include schools, TAFE institutes, welfare agencies such as the Salvation Army, and private companies who see VET principally as a business.

[3]   Barwon Accommodation and Youth Support Agency (BAYSA) has provided a range of support, accommodation and training services to young people for over 30 years. They were keen to support the research and evaluation of their project. One aspect of the project was funding two of the course leaders to prepare and publish a curriculum document from the course, which has been distributed widely.

Catherine Beavis

chapter 9

Youth culture and the texts of the new technologies: Reading the research

Intersections between individual and social identity, literacy, pedagogy and societal change permeate research about young people's engagement with the texts of the new technologies. Digital culture is presented as seductive and persuasive, and as actively productive of identity and cultural relations. It is celebrated as an emergent and innovative form, and as a site for creativity and resistance, and at the same time identified as a part of a global economic machinery which works to commodify and standardise. The texts of digital culture are seen as producing "cultural pedagogies" (Kellner 1995) about "how to become consumers and how to become boys and girls ... [these are] lessons about skills and values, and broad sociocultural and political lessons about gender and social power" (Nixon 1998, p.23). Digital culture is presented somewhat breathlessly as entirely new and unprecedented change (Rushkoff 1994) and as the most recent instance of an ongoing succession of emergent cultural forms, each of which has elicited moral panics in its time. Young people are presented both as the young lions and the unwilling dupes of massive technological change, as autonomous and as having agency, especially with respect to the Internet (Tobin 1998; Rushkoff 1994), and as an uncritical and nonresistant market for global commodities. In a confusing and contradictory set of discourses, as Sefton-Green notes, "Whatever position one takes ... it is clear that digital culture has become a key site for anxiety about the changing nature of community" (Sefton-Green 1998, p.9).

In this chapter, I have taken Nintendo and computer games as my central examples of the texts of the new technologies. I focus on research on young people's engagement with these games, and some of the assumptions, tensions and contradictions that characterise work in this field, with particular reference to constructions of reading and of the young person or child. Implicit in these debates are views of childhood and youth; of community; of reading and textuality; of subjectivity and of the desirability, presence or absence of resistance and critique. Perspectives drawn from fields as diverse as cultural studies, media studies, gender, literacy, history and literature differently explore relationships between constructions of childhood and the new technologies, between computer texts and the formation of personal and cultural identities, relationships which are constructed differently again by research coming out of welfare, social and psychological fields such as the 1998 Parliamentary *Inquiry into the Effects of Television and Multimedia on Children and Families in Victoria* (Victorian Parliamentary Family and Community Development Committee 1998).

Central to most discussions about digital culture are four questions, differently asked and answered:

- what is the nature of digital culture?
- what is the nature of young people's engagement with digital culture texts?
- what are the consequences of their engagement with these texts? – the "effects" debate; and
- what, if anything, should we do?

Two further questions I want to pose are:
- what is the presumed nature of the interaction between readers and texts, and
- how, in these debates, are young people constructed?

Youth and childhood

Research into relationships between young people and the new technology is always grounded in assumptions about the nature of youth and childhood, whether or not these are explicitly addressed. As Sefton-Green notes, "concerns about the changing nature of childhood – or indeed about its apparent 'disappearance' – have become inextricably bound up with wider anxieties about the impact of technological change". "Evidence" for the demise of childhood includes the relocation of play from outdoors into the "safer" space of the home, and the supposed displacement of more traditional forms of play. However, as Opie and Opie noted 40 years ago, "the belief that traditional games are dying out is in itself traditional" (Opie & Opie 1959 in Sanger et al. 1997, p.9). The shift of play from the streets to more supervised and protected spaces has implications also for youth culture (James 1993 & Buchner 1990 cited in McNamee 1998, p.195), both for males and females (McNamee 1998, p.196). Other arguments suggesting connections between the end of childhood and the new technologies posit a loss of innocence consequent upon the sexualisation and commodification of childhood, through the mass media and the creation of the youth market.

Despite Sanger et al.'s reminder (1997), apocalyptic and millenarian views linking technology with the end of childhood are common. The most valuable research into this area seeks to configure the causal connections differently. Walkerdine, for example, locates fears and moral panics concerning boys and computer games within larger anxieties about children and the status of childhood at the end of the 20th century (Walkerdine 1998, p.1) and explores juxtapositions within the present which have produced this anxiety. Underlining the diversity and specificity of the experiences of different groups, Walkerdine explores the ways in which historically established discourses are at work in the construction and regulation of attitudes towards middle- and working-class boys' engagement with computer games. Sefton-Green discusses connections between digital culture and a "new world order" in terms of relationships between modernism and postmodernism, drawing on Giddens (1990) to argue that "the current state of affairs resembles a continuation of the immediate past more than a new beginning" (Sefton-Green 1998, p.5). Like others, Sefton-Green stresses the need not to lose sight of continuities between digital culture and older popular media forms.

A related set of anxieties concerns the effects that new technologies, in particular, texts such as Nintendo and computer games (and interactive screen engagement) have on young people's subjectivity. One fear here is that the new technologies have so profoundly changed young people that we are faced with "aliens in the classroom" (Green & Bigum 1993). An important set of questions at issue here concerns the interrelationships of reading, texts, subjectivity and construction. Arising from this is the issue of the "effects" of computer game content, particularly in respect to violence and aggression, and to representations of masculinity. For researchers working in diverse fields, this is perhaps the most pervasive, complex and troubling dimension of young people's engagement with the texts of the new technologies. I return to this critical question in the concluding section of the chapter.

In considering these issues, it is essential, as Walkerdine (1998) suggests, to distinguish between/among specific groups of young people and children. While many studies make the point that popular fears and assumptions about the "effects" of the new technology reflect more far-reaching views about the nature of childhood, the concept of youth or childhood itself, for the most part, tends to remain undifferentiated. This imposes serious constraints on understanding the nature of young people's interactions with the texts of the new technologies in different instances, the implications of their engagement with such texts for the construction of personal and cultural identities, the ways in which they are positioned within discourses mobilised by their readings, and the social contexts and consequences of their involvement with computer games. As Alloway and Gilbert note, research which treats young people as a homogeneous group, "bypass[es] the interplay of gender, class and ethnicity in the ways in which children take up positions in relation to cultural pursuits; representing children as equally and commonly positioned in cultural meaning making" (Alloway & Gilbert 1998, p.96). In such analyses, they continue:

> a focus on "childhood" at the expense of the social and discursive construction of the child as a gendered, classed and ethnic subject, can blind us to the ways in which participation in children's and youth culture almost always involves participation as a gendered, classed and ethnic subject (Alloway & Gilbert 1998, p.96).

Digital culture: the texts of the new technologies

It is clearly the case that the new technologies have created not just the possibility but the reality of very different types of text compared to those with which we have been familiar – those in print, oral, aural and visual form. The nonlinear nature of "hyperfictions" epitomises the ways in which such texts challenge print-based "commonsense" notions of reading, simultaneously overturning many aspects of traditional literary theory, while being seen literally to embody the new (Douglas 1989, 1992; Snyder 1996, 1997). The ways in which the structures of the new forms, whether hyperfiction or the more widely popular computer games, maintain or reconfigure what we understand by both narrative and reading has been a source of fascination for many (for example, Snyder 1997; Green, Reid & Bigum 1998). In seeking to understand and evaluate the nature of young people's interaction with such texts, revisiting what we understand by "reading" in this context, including its role in the construction of subjectivity, is both necessary and appropriate.

Some studies approach this dimension through a consideration of the structures and characteristics of computer games. Games work within highly diverse but specific generic conventions, drawing on literary, filmic and other references across a range of cultures, utilising familiar structures of variation and repetition. Computer games almost physically enact metaphoric dimensions of literary theory. The text literally only comes into existence when engaged by the reader/player. The reader is an active participant in the joint construction of meaning, with the meaning, or at least the action, created only through the player's physical participation. While each level has a prespecified configuration, and the traps, fights and puzzles are written into the program, it is also true that one never plays quite the same game each time, one never reads the same text twice. Reading/playing moves forward through an interaction between expectations, extra and intratextual knowledge and prediction, and so on, with intertextual and intergeneric knowledge at a premium in making sense of both narrative and symbol. Readers/players are literally invited to take up the subject position offered by the texts, at the keyboard, with the invitation often offered in the form of direct address whereby players are required to merge first, second and third person to move the game forward, simultaneously operating both an omniscient and an entirely partial overview.

Yet, while there are clearly similarities in many respects between playing games and reading fiction (Beavis 1997), there are also obvious disjunctions. "Interactive software" connects, as Friedman notes:

> the oppositions of "reader" and "text", of "reading and writing" together in feedback loops that make it impossible to distinguish precisely where one begins and the other ends. Recognising a reader's changing expectations and reactions as a linear text unfolds is one thing, but how do we talk about textual interactions "in which every response provokes instantaneous changes in the text itself, leading to a new response and so on" (Friedman 1995, p.73).

This intermeshing and confusion make it doubly hard to untangle the nature of young people's engagement with digital texts. This is particularly so in relation to understanding their enmeshment in/distance from the ideologies and pleasures of the games. There are implications here for the formation of subjectivity, in different contexts and for different groups. Similarly, there are also differing positions and possibilities suggested in relation to young people's agency in the world. Pursuing specific features of the structures and demands of computer games has led to useful explorations both of the nature of players' engagement at other levels, and of the literacy learnings – the "new" literacies – they entail. Some of the most interesting work focuses on elements of design (Kress 1997) and space (Johnson-Eilola 1997; Fuller & Jenkins 1995).

For Kress, digital and multimodal texts are part of a changed landscape of semiosis which calls for a new theory of representation, one which takes account of changes in forms of text, uses of language and modes of communication (Kress 1997, p.75). Kress wants to locate users/readers/players as active within the changed context of "electronic, multimodal, multimedia textual production" (Kress 1997, p.77), to see individuals as "the remakers, transformers of sets of representational resources – rather than users of stable systems, in a situation where multiple representational modes are brought into textual compositions" (Kress 1997, p.77). Kress argues that young people need to be conversant with design and with visual forms of representation, as active shapers and makers as well as viewers. This position is consistent with arguments for an enlarged view of literacy which includes the capacity to read and negotiate images and textual representations of all kinds. For Kress, young people are constructed, potentially at least, as complex meaning makers in a variety of forms, with sophisticated literacy capacities fostered by their engagement with the new technologies.

Johnson-Eilola (1997), and Fuller and Jenkins (1995) differently explore the spatial structures of computer games to hypothesise about the kinds of reading practices and sensibilities both taught and required. Computer games are often described as archetypal postmodern texts, concerned with surfaces and pastiche, and free of modernist parameters of simple rules, sequence and linear time. Johnson-Eilola is among those who believe there is indeed a changed consciousness and way of being in the world for young people, as a consequence of their immersion in digital culture and the new technologies – these are ways of being that we, "the occupants of history" could do well to learn from. He argues that, in playing computer games, young people learn "to deal tactically with contingency, multiplicity and uncertainty" (Johnson-Eilola 1997, p.195). Successful game playing requires a postmodernist sensibility, whereby players "are capable of working such chaotic environments from within, moment by moment." In a highly romantic and somewhat wistful evocation he describes his version of the "aliens" young people seem to have become, as evidenced in their playing of these games: "their domain is space rather than time. They exist with time, dancing across it, rather than being subordinated to it" (pp.195-96).

Fuller and Jenkins draw somewhat different conclusions about the implications of the spatial organisation of games. They compare computer games not with literary narratives but with 16th and 17th century New World voyage documents, such as Walter Raleigh's *Discoverie of the large, rich and beautiful empire of Guiana* (1596) or John Smith's *True relation of such occurrences and accidents of noate as hath hapned in Virginia* (1608). They argue that computer games represent a shift from narrativity to geography, with parallels concerning the navigation, mapping and mastery of physical and cyberspace. The pleasures of playing, they argue, lie not so much in narrative action, which tends to be inconclusive and/or deferred, as in the continual opening up of new spaces and screens. Characters, in their view, are "little more than a cursor that mediates the player's relationship to the story world" (Fuller & Jenkins 1995, p.61).

This question of players' relationship to character is of considerable importance in assumptions made about ideology, and the ways in which games work on players' subjectivity, and is especially pertinent to the various debates about masculinity, effects and violence. Fuller and Jenkins suggest that game playing is ideological almost by virtue of its structure, regardless of "content", as content is traditionally conceived. Playing computer games, in an overfamiliar, overcrowded and overly regulated America, they argue, allows the recreation of the Renaissance encounter with America without guilt. "Virtual reality opens up new spaces for exploration, colonisation and exploration, returning to a mythic time when there were worlds without limits and resources beyond imaging" (Fuller & Jenkins 1995, p.58).

What is one to make of this? Where computer games' chief pleasures are seen to lie in the exploration and conquering of space, the lure for players entails both the deeply rooted appeal of the urge to create new worlds, and an outlook whereby exploration and expansion are coterminous with achieving "mastery" – a mastery which amounts to colonisation and conquest in the non-virtual world at least. How the young player is then construed as explorer/coloniser/conqueror becomes a matter of considerable ambivalence and uncertainty. The coupling of admiration for such "virtues" as heroism and intrepid venturing with the uneasy entertainment or suppression of the dimensions of conquest (or more likely its celebration), is, in many, ways emblematic of the contradictory and coexistent discourses about games. Detailed and specific studies are needed to explore the ways in which such texts work polysemically, the ways they engage and position readers, and the ways in which young players in turn are both constructed by and resistant to "the pleasures of the text".

Consumption and youth culture

What these accounts of the possibilities of reading/playing games all share is a view of players as informed, as autonomous, and as "super-rational" (male) beings (Walkerdine 1998). When games are considered in relation to market forces, as big business and part of multimillion dollar multinational enterprises, more compromising and troubling issues arise. Computer games are part of a much wider cultural/industrial, military/entertainment complex (for example, Sheff 1993; Shuker 1996; Wark 1996). As Helen Nixon entitled a recent paper 'Fun and games are serious business' (Nixon 1998). She cites Baudrillard and Lury to explore what this "business" means. For Baudrillard, consumption is "a cultural phenomenon, entering the cycle of symbolic exchange that is contemporary consumer culture" (Baudrillard 1981 in Nixon 1998, p.25). For Lury, such consumption is "to do with meaning, value and communications as much as it is to do with exchange, price and economic relations" (Lury 1996, p.10 in Nixon 1998, p.25). Within this context, young people as a market are heavily researched and targeted, so that the purchase and playing of games is already implicated in much wider discourses and practices to do with identity, privilege and opportunity, and with what is seen to be current and "cool", and so on.

What does the playing/consumption of computer games mean and do for youth culture in the economic context of a heavy emphasis on consumption, the "relentlessly material" nature of society and new patterns of social division – the world Hall describes as "New Times" (Hall 1996a)? How autonomous are players/consumers in this context? The "threats" to local culture from globalisation are well documented (Wark 1994; McNamee 1998). And what of issues of access in relation to gender and class differences? Many argue persuasively that in the nexus between the local and the global, multimedia technologies and digital cultures operate to maintain unequal relations of power, carrying their own "cultural pedagogies" or "pedagogies of everyday life" (Kellner 1995; Luke 1996). These pedagogies, and fears about the ways in which computer games, like other texts, circulate and are embedded within existing discourses of gender, ethnicity, class and power are at the heart of the anxieties and analyses connecting games with violence in the community.

Violence, masculinity and computer games

The question of the relationship between popular culture and levels of violence in society is one of urgent interest to many sectors of the community. Inquiries into such connections are conducted repeatedly, a recent example being the Victorian Parliamentary *Inquiry into the effects of Television and Multimedia on Children and Families in Victoria*. Terms of reference for this inquiry include, among other things, the brief to "assess the likely impact on children and families of new and emerging forms of multimedia technology and [to] consider ways that this technology may enhance the well-being of families" and to "examine the relationship between violence on television and violent behaviours within families". Such connections are explored repeatedly (e.g. Durkin 1995), yet such inquiries consistently fail to establish unequivocally the causal links between image and effect which they seek to find (Alloway & Gilbert 1998).

What interests me here are the overlaps, intersections and collisions in relation to the "effects" debate on the one hand, and poststructuralist positions on the discursive construction of subjectivity on the other. On the face of it, both fields and findings seem quite contradictory. As Sefton-Green notes, "research from the effects tradition either sets out to create anxiety" (see Newsom 1996) or to explain and allay such concern in the context of moral panics (Sefton-Green 1998, p.14; see also Buckingham and Sefton-Green 1997). Effects research encompasses both the insistent search for the pernicious image that might turn society (or the individual) bad, categorising and quantifying violent images and games with an implied link between these and violent behaviour within families, and audience research, that shows readers/viewers to be well aware of distinctions between fact and fantasy and so quite capable of critique. Feminist poststructuralist work on the role of discourse and story in the formation of subjectivity complicates this picture, stressing the role of images and story in popular culture and in constructions of masculinity and violence particularly. Such research comes often with a pressing moral imperative, arguing strongly for intervention and the teaching of critical literacy, to enable games and stories to be read differently, and different stories to be read.

Central but invisible in research of this kind is the figure of the reader, and beliefs and understandings about what reading entails. The conceptual knot I'm working at is one which intertwines, on the one hand, a scepticism about the view of young people as passive and uncritical consumers who are easily led, with, on the other, poststructuralist insights into the discursive construction of subjectivity, and the potent role of stories and representations in shaping power relations and gendered subjectivities, particularly for young people. Part of the answer, in sorting through such apparently contradictory positions, must lie in developing greater specificity and differentiation within studies and research agendas. Similarly, distinctions might usefully be made between different constructions of young people and between different groups. A further element to be untangled concerns the nature of texts themselves, and the fears and apprehensions held about them.

Walkerdine locates current moral panics about digital culture and identity in relation to more longstanding anxieties about the susceptibility of the masses to the negative effects of popular culture. She points to the class differences in readings of young people's engagement with computer games, whereby working-class boys are seen as "proto-violent and addicted" and the middle-class boy as a "super-rational" explorer (Walkerdine 1998, p.6). She concludes with a number of questions pertinent to untangling the effects/subjectivity knot I have described:

- What kinds of subjects and subjectivities are created through game playing and through other popular media?
- What are the ways in which such discourses and practices prepare children for the world beyond the screen?
- How might we begin to explore the situated production of all subjectivities of the world's children as they face the huge differences confronting the new millennium? (Walkerdine 1998, p.26)

Poststructuralist perspectives have a great deal to offer in teasing out the ways in which computer games, like other popular culture texts, are deeply implicated in the formation of youth culture and constructions of masculinity, particularly in relation to overtly violent and misogynist texts, such as many computer games. Alloway and Gilbert (1998) and Gilbert and Gilbert (1998) explore the role of computer games in contributing to constructions of masculinity for young people that are both limiting and "dangerous" (Alloway & Gilbert 1997). Computer games are seen as tapping into, endorsing and recirculating discourses of masculinity that are largely hegemonic and non-reflective, and that legitimate and promote violence, exclusion and domination. Their research takes them back not just to the young person – the player/reader – but also to the text. They distinguish both between different groups of readers (young people), and between different types of games – those which promote versions of masculinity linked unproblematically to violence, and those where the use of violence is also a matter for some reflection on the part of the hero or other characters.

Alloway and Gilbert (1998) foreground the role of text in the process of reading, while also exploring the reading process, and the construction of subjectivity. They argue that young people need to be helped to critique and resist the subject positions and ideologies of computer games. The games themselves may become the focus of critical literacy work undertaken with young people, but such work must go beyond textual analysis. As Gilbert and Gilbert put it:

> Working with boys … does not simply involve identifying the politics of the texts. The issue is about critical and reflective analysis of cultural practice; about enabling students to read the processes wherein they take up personal, relational and cultural meanings; about mobilising boys' desire to do their gender otherwise (Gilbert & Gilbert 1998, p.81).

The question of how to mobilise the "desire to do [one's] gender otherwise" foregrounds the complexity of working with popular culture and intervening to change the direction and nature of engagement, to allow contestation and debate. It's a question that is always problematic, and always central to discussions linking pedagogy, subjectivity and youth culture, where the concern is to make available to young people opportunities for resistance and critique. A recognition of the role of pleasure and desire entailed in engaging with popular culture texts, such as computer games, and of young people's willing complicity in many features of the games' style (Hall 1996b, p.470), if not their ideologies, must be a key feature of any exploration of young people and computer games. Like Luke (1996) and others, Alloway and Gilbert see computer games along with other popular culture texts as "cultural and community pedagogies [which] offer sites for meaning making and pleasure; they market representational politics; and at the same time, they pass as apolitical entertainment." (Alloway & Gilbert 1998, p.100).

Conclusion

Computer games as new texts, digital texts, and texts of youth culture, themselves provoke multiple readings in relation both to their own, reflexive, textual nature, and to their implications for young players. As the positions canvassed in this paper show, constructions of youth, of youth culture and of reading in relation to computer games vary considerably across a range of fields. For some theorists, players/young people are heroic and flexible adventurers with tolerances and literacy abilities far beyond those of the generations researching them. For others, players, particularly boys and young men, are complex but nonreflective subjects, likely to be much influenced by the discourses and ideologies of computer games.

Understandings of the nature of reading, and of the role of digital texts in youth culture and in the construction of subjectivity, have material implications in many spheres. Computer games must be seen in the context of the cultural/industrial, "military-entertainment" complex which produces them, and the multinational socioeconomic context within which they are marketed and sold. Complex understandings of the links between representation and identity, between pleasure and aesthetics, between dominant discourses and hegemonic practices and a recognition of texts' appeal are all important factors in exploring the nature of young peoples' engagement and fascination with computer games, and in helping young people become informed and critical. So too is the exploration of the textual nature of games, of the changing nature of both literacy and narrative, and a recognition of the defining role of youth and popular culture in many young people's lives.

References

Alloway, N. & Gilbert, P. 1997, 'Everything is dangerous: Working with the "boys and literacy" agenda', *English in Australia*, v.119–120, pp.35-45.

—— 1998, 'Video game culture: Playing with masculinity, violence and pleasure', in *Wired-Up: Young people and the electronic media*, ed. S. Howard, UCL Press, London.

Beavis, C. 1997, 'Computer games, culture and curriculum', in *Page to Screen: Taking literacy into the electronic era*, ed. I. Snyder, Allan & Unwin, Sydney.

Buckingham, D. & Sefton-Green, J. 1997, 'From regulation to education', *The English and Media Magazine*, n.36, pp.28-32.

Douglas, J.Y. 1989, 'Wandering through the labyrinth: Encountering interactive fiction', *Computers and Composition*, v.6, n.3, pp.93-101.

—— 1992, 'What hypertexts can do that print narratives cannot', *Reader*, v.28, pp.1-22.

Durkin, K. 1995, *Computer Games Their Effects on Young People: A review*, Office of Film and Literature Classification, Sydney.

Friedman, T. 1995, 'Making sense of software: Computer games', in *Cybersociety: Computer-mediated communication and community*, ed. S.G. Jones, Sage, Thousand Oaks, CA.

Fuller, M. & Jenkins, H. 1995, 'Nintendo and New World travel writing: A dialogue', in *Cybersociety: Computer-mediated communication and community*, ed. S.G. Jones, Sage, Thousand Oaks, CA.

Giddens, A. 1990, *The Consequences of Modernity*, Polity Press, Cambridge.

Gilbert, R. & Gilbert, P. 1998, *Masculinity Goes to School*, Allen & Unwin, Sydney.

Green, B. & Bigum, C. 1993, 'Aliens in the classroom', *Australian Journal of Education*, v.37, n.2, pp.119-41.

Green, B., Reid, J.-A. & Bigum, C. 1998, 'Teaching the Nintendo generation? Children, computer culture and popular technologies', in *Wired-Up: Young People and the Electronic Media*, ed. S. Howard, UCL Press, London.

Hall, S. 1996a, 'The meaning of New Times', in *Stuart Hall: Critical dialogues in cultural studies*, eds D. Morley & K.-H. Chen, Routledge, London & New York.

—— 1996b, 'What is this "black" in black popular culture?' in *Stuart Hall: Critical dialogues in cultural studies*, eds D. Morley & K.-H. Chen, Routledge, London & New York.

Johnson-Eilola, J. 1997, 'Living on the surface: Learning in the age of global communication networks' in *Page to Screen: Taking literacy into the electronic era*, ed. I. Snyder, Allan & Unwin, Sydney.

Kellner, D. 1995, *Media Culture: Cultural studies, identity and politics between the modern and post-modern*, Routledge, London.

Kress, G. 1997, 'Visual and verbal modes of representation in electronically mediated communication: The potentials of new forms of text', in *Page to Screen: Taking literacy into the electronic era*, ed. I. Snyder, Allan & Unwin, Sydney.

Luke, C. (ed.) 1996, *Feminisms and Pedagogies of Everyday Life*, State University of New York Press, Albany, NY.

McNamee, S. 1998, 'Youth, gender and video games: Power and control in the home', in *Cool Places: Geographies of youth cultures*, eds T. Skelton & G. Valentine, Routledge, London & New York.

Newsom, E. 1996, 'Video, violence and the protection of children', in *Electronic Children: How children are responding to the information revolution*, ed. T. Gill, National Children's Bureau, London.

Nixon, H. 1998, 'Fun and games are serious business', in *Digital Diversions: Youth culture in the age of multimedia*, ed. J. Sefton-Green, UCL Press, London.

Opie, I. & Opie, P. 1959, *The Lore and Language of Primary School Children*, Clarendon Press, Oxford.

Rushkoff, D. 1994, *Cyberia: Life in the trenches of hyperspace*, Harper Collins, London.

Sanger, J. with Wilson, J., Davies, B. & Whittaker, R. 1997, *Young Children, Videos and Computer Games: Issues for teachers and parents*, Taylor & Francis, London.

Sefton-Green, J. 1998, 'Introduction: Being young in the digital age', in *Digital Diversions: Youth culture in the age of multimedia*, ed. J. Sefton-Green, UCL Press, London.

Sheff, D. 1993, *Game Over: Nintendo's battle to dominate an industry*, Hodder & Stoughton, London.

Shuker, R. 1996, 'Video games: Serious fun', *Continuum*, v.9, n.2, pp.125-45.

Snyder, I. 1996, *Hypertext: The electronic labyrinth*, Melbourne University Press, Melbourne.

—— 1997, 'Hyperfiction: Its possibilities in English', *English in Education*, v.31, n.2, pp.23-33.

Tobin, J. 1998, 'An American *otaku* (or, a boy's virtual life on the Net)', in *Digital Diversions: Youth culture in the age of multimedia*, ed. J. Sefton-Green, UCL Press, London.

Victorian Parliamentary Family and Community Development Committee 1998, Inquiry into the Effects of Television and Multimedia on Children and Families in Victoria, discussion paper, http://avoca.vicnet.net.au/~fcdc/curr.htm

Walkerdine, V. 1998, Violent boys and precious girls: Regulating childhood at the end of the millennium, unpublished paper.

Wark, M. 1994, 'The video game as an emergent media form', *Media Information Australia*, v.71, pp.21-29.

—— 1996, 'In the shadow of the military-entertainment complex', *Continuum*, v.9, n.1, pp.98-117.

Christopher Hickey and Lindsay Fitzclarence

chapter 10

If you listen, you will hear: Building relationships using "conversational flow"

I have since come to believe that the greatest gift one person can give another is such careful listening. It is in hearing with care the detailed specificity of the other that the specificity of each of us is made possible (Davies 1993, p.xiii).

Behind labels such as "generation X" and the "options generation" (Mackay 1997) there is a strong inference that young people's lives today are profoundly different to their predecessors. Amid contemporary transformations of cultural, political, economic and educational practices there is widening concern about how young people are coping. Social concern about young people's capacity to gain employment, participate in lasting relationships, be healthy and, above all, be happy, is the focus of much contemporary thought and effort. Social commentators, such as Mackay (1997), Sacks (1996) and Tulgan (1995) provide new insights into what appears to be an increasing fracture between the lives and needs of young people and traditional understandings of their socialisation and developmental passages. Interestingly, it is young people who are thought to be in "crisis", not the institutions that socialise them (notably, families, sports and schools). Through the contemporary indicators of suicide, drug abuse, violence, sexual promiscuity, non-conformity and vagrancy, young people are increasingly positioned as "at risk". At issue here are the fundamental self-knowledges and identities with which young people make their transition into the adult world. Of particular concern to us is the extent to which young people are increasingly becoming "products" of the analyses that describe them. Without the necessary social resources to understand and interpret their beliefs and behaviours, young people are likely to see themselves as victims of the contemporary (postmodern) social world. McGillion (1998) highlights this pattern in his discussion of the Young People and the Future report that was commissioned by the Australian Catholic Bishops:

Young people are constantly barraged with negative images of themselves, are pressed to experiment with sex, drugs and alcohol, and are disproportionately affected by economic rationalist imperatives that view a degree of unemployment as ... Young people hear that they do not care about anything or anyone other than themselves; that they lack discipline and respect; that they are unemployed because they are lazy and do not want to work (McGillion 1998, p.6).

The meaning of what it is to be a "good citizen" in contemporary western society is currently being reconstituted. Whereas traditional (read modern) notions of citizenship have been understood along the lines of equality, community and cooperation, postmodern articulations of "successful" human participation appear increasingly "marketised", globalised and individualised. It is our belief that in spite of the so-called "communications revolution" people are becoming increasingly disconnected from each other and their physical community. Indeed, Hallowell (1993) argues that the conditions of "globalisation" conspire to fragment and isolate people in ways that have not been experienced in the past. Commenting on the forms of social redefinition thought to arise from the "postmodern turn", Hallowell claims that, "we live in times that conspire to "disconnect us, one from another, from institutions, from ideas and from ideals, so that the individual is precariously alone" (p.196).

In particular, there is evidence of marked disconnection between the generations. Mackay (1997) has noted a major disjunction between the post-war generation of "baby boomers", people born in the 1950s and 1960s, and their children born in the 1970s and 1980s, a group he titles the "options generation". This differentiating between the generations reinforces the view that the processes of socialisation for the two generations have been quite different. Here we encounter a difficult interpretative/methodological problem, that is, how the values, attitudes, beliefs and general social mores of one generation are to be studied and represented by members of a different generation. Our method for engagement is through a process of narrative inquiry. The logic behind this approach is not new. It taps into a long tradition that has employed ethnographic inquiry to represent the life worlds of young people in and outside schools. Within this discourse young people are seen to be particularly problematic in that they are often portrayed as risk-takers who cause damage to themselves and others, act irresponsibly and, when in gangs or groups, have a tendency to become violent and aggressive. We take this discourse as a warrant for research that explores young peoples' knowledges, commitments and understandings from the point of view of young people. In the interest of nurturing a greater sense of connectedness with this group, there is a burgeoning need to engage in new conversations with them.

The primary aim of this chapter is to introduce a method designed to nurture effective communication between individuals within their particular social groups and across the different generations. Underpinning this is our belief that individuals need to overcome the social barriers associated with isolation, alienation and marginalisation if they are to develop feelings of connectedness. In the backdrop of what Hallowell (1993) sees as the isolating tendencies of a globalised society, there clearly emerges a strong warrant for new methods of facilitating productive forms of interpersonal communication. This is particularly relevant to the many young people who we believe are "shutting-off" rather than "reaching-out" in times of need and/or crisis. Drawing on the principles of affiliation and narrative, the method of "conversational flow" provides a range of interventionist strategies that aim to nurture active listening, uninterrupted speech and engagement with emotional content.

Communication breakdown: a spotlight on young males

Despite best intentions, the power differential that exists between adults and young people often acts to circumvent the flow of interaction between them. This may go part of the way to explaining why so many teachers, parents and sports coaches seem frustrated with the general lack of engagement they are able to establish with young people. Given the great difficulty many adults have communicating emotional issues with other adults, it is not surprising that, in the presence of a power differential, young people are unlikely to seek adult counsel in dealing with emotional and personal issues. Anecdotally, it appears that this is particularly so for young males. Mackay (1993) argues that in the shadow of the women's movement, beginning in the 1960s, little has been done to understand and reshape the contemporary forms of masculinity. Males, he argues, have not chosen to engage in any process of redefinition and rather have taken a "business as usual" approach to the socialisation of boys to men. Of course, the transition from boyhood to manhood, should not be simply viewed as "men's business". Many females clearly have major investments in this process, as mothers, grandmothers, daughters, sisters, lovers, friends and teachers.

Contemporary studies of socialisation practices highlight important differences in the socialisation process for girls and boys, and for young women and men. Research conducted by social commentators such as Connell (1995) and Miedzian (1991) suggests that many young males often receive mixed and competing views of their position in contemporary society. While young males should not feel exclusively inflicted by social change, the resources available to them for dealing with such changes are arguably less developed than those available to their female counterparts. Within his "New Women and Old Men" thesis, Mackay (1993) argues that the lack of a coherent framework to guide young males growing up in "new times" means that the processes of enculturation are either left to serendipity or forged in the traditional (hegemonic) constructions of masculinity. Traditional constructions of masculinity, we argue, are clearly illuminated in the contexts of high-profile male contact sports.

Our work in studying interconnections between masculinity and sport reveals that for many young males the knowledges and practices they construct through their engagement with sport continue to be influential. Behind rhetorical claims that sport is the breeding ground for healthy young males, appears growing recognition that a "shadow" exists (Fitzclarence, Hickey & Matthews 1997; Messner 1992; Messner & Sabo 1994; Rowe & Lawrence 1990). As the spotlight of social inquiry is used to illuminate the values and practices frequently (re)produced within dominant male sporting cultures, problematic images reveal a less than glowing picture of this social institution. For example, this is a social space where violence is frequently tolerated (and even expected), where women are second rate, and where "yobbish" behaviour is rationalised under the maxim that "boys will be boys" (Miedzian 1991). There is also growing anecdotal and empirical evidence that many of the attitudes and behaviours that are considered "reasonable" within the culture of sport parallel forms of social disharmony and deviance. For example, Messner and Sabo (1994) have highlighted the way violence, aggression and sexism have directly manifested themselves from the culture of sport into the wider community. Daily tabloids are littered with stories on male athletes who engage in antisocial, intimidatory and violent behaviour in their day-to-day lives. The acceptance of aggression and borderline violence in sport clearly infiltrates the broader aspects of social existence.

Another primary socialising site in which young people learn about themselves as both individuals and members of a community exists in the context of schooling. Given that over

70% of young Australian's see school through from Prep to Year 12 it is inevitable that their experiences and interactions within this context(s) will play a pivotal role in their constructions of self and other. Keeping young people in schooling has long been held as a desirable social objective (Miller 1990), underpinned by assumptions of advanced academic development and prolonged social mentoring. However, in recent times it seems that many schools are struggling to provide the sort of leadership and curriculum capable of delivering on these aspirations. One of the resounding themes that emerges from this struggle involves many teachers' inability to develop constructive connections with their students (Kenway & Willis et al. 1997). It is here that we believe Judith Rich Harris's (1998) work provides an important corrective to some of our most fundamental assumptions about the socialisation of young people. Harris shifts the socialisation spotlight from adults being the primary influence in young people's development to peers. She argues that while children are prepared by parents for their initial entry into wider society, it is the peer group that provides the *ongoing* socialising force. Harris's placement of peers in this primary category is both controversial and suggestive (Gladwell 1998; Bretag 1999). Her work reinforces our own conclusions of the need for a close examination of peer group socialisation processes and their role in shaping the construction of personal values, beliefs and commitments.

The pedagogic implications of Harris's argument are potentially far reaching. The long-time influence of developmental psychology in the formation of educational pedagogy has favoured a view of social development with the teacher as the central change agent. By logical extrapolation, it has long been assumed that good students are the product of good teachers. Of course, the converse is also thought true: that bad students are products of bad teaching. What this does, albeit unwittingly, is place teachers under the same set of "nurture assumptions" that are imposed on parents. This, we believe, places a set of unfair and unrealistic impositions on teachers. For us, there are two important oversights in this relational equation. First, it neglects the role of the peer group in the way young people construct and enact their identity. It is erroneously assumed, in accordance with current learning theory, that where student and teacher voices are in conflict or dispute it is the teacher's voice that will prevail, on account of their wisdom and experience. Our research reveals the extremely problematic nature of this assumption (see Hickey & Fitzclarence 2000). Second, there is no pedagogy that genuinely installs teachers (baby boomers) as the chosen mentors of the young person's (options generation) world. The following testimony from a young and (previously) enthusiastic Health and Physical Education teacher illustrates the sort of desperation that teachers can feel when their pedagogic resources are exhausted:

> I have been questioning myself as a teacher of late. I've just had a gutful of the kids at the school. The only thing that keeps me going is the money, but now I don't even think that makes it worthwhile. The discipline has got worse and I find [the students] very demoralising, sarcastic and insolent. It's mainly the Year 9 and 10 boys. They have NO respect for teachers, let alone females! They have such an "image" they're trying to fulfil – tough, "manly", surfie, cool, cold, spaced out … Most of them are so untouchable, unteachable … It's just plain hell being with them.
>
> Western Australian high school teacher

In this case it is clear that emotional demands have started to take their toll on the capacity to provide rational professional judgment. The problem is that formal education has staked its primary claim on the importance of the advancement of intellectual capacities (Sharp &

White 1968; Sharp 1985). In our opinion, current leaning theory and practice privileges intellectual ways of knowing at the expense of other ways of understanding and expressing ideas and feelings about the world. Embedded in this orientation is an ideological blind spot in recognising the socialisation and pedagogical implications of teachers being outnumbered at ratios of around 30:1 in the schooling environment. In our attempts to infuse the emotional and irrational in order to counteract the over-emphasis on the rational we have turned to work within narrative therapy.

In the following discussion we outline a methodological approach for working with young people which takes account of these various issues of socialisation and communication – both across and within different social and cultural groupings. Our particular focus is on developing a methodology/pedagogy to foster communication, and some strategies to enhance the "conversational flow" between groups.

Developing "conversational flow"

Foremost in the implementation of the "conversational flow" model is a need to overcome some of the structural barriers to effective interpersonal and group communication. Among these are an individual's fear of humiliation or reprisal, shyness, a lack of assertiveness, self-doubt, an inattentive audience, fear of isolation, and a reluctance to make the personal public. While it is difficult to overcome all of these barriers, where such problems restrict the potential for connection among individuals, there is an unambiguous warrant for active intervention. To this end, "conversational flow" is a process strategically designed to, 1) facilitate active listening, 2) nurture open-ended discussion and 3) work constructively with emotional content. The method combines two different strategies that are engaged simultaneously to facilitate the development of "real conversation" in a manner that "flows". In the context of this model, "flow" is applied in the spirit of a second-order cybernetics which views conversation as a dynamic and (nonlinear and non-hierarchical) mutually generative process between participants (Becvar, Canfield & Becvar 1997).

In the first instance, interaction is nurtured between participants on the basis of some "prior affiliation". This strategy builds on the notion of "affinity groups" (see Mackay 1993) where participants with similar interests and perspectives are grouped together to discuss particular issues. Mackay believes that the presence of affinity within a group is a considerable advantage in the process of nurturing conversation. What this does is remove structural incompatibility (such as, assailant from victim, superordinate from subordinate, young from old) and provide participants with a level of comfort or commonality within which to build conversation. Of course, this does not presuppose that all participants will naturally agree on particular issues. Indeed, there will be leaders and followers within such groups, just as there are in any collection of people. There will be those who are submissive, those who are argumentative and those who are flippant. Within the conversational flow model, such attributes are seen as part of the ebb and flow of natural conversation around which an affinity group will gradually energise. To be sure, affinity is formed around equality and camaraderie, not compliance!

Second, the method invokes an interventionist approach to facilitate active listening. The idea of active listening is built around the application of a structure that acknowledges everyone's right to speak, but controls when they can enact this right. Participants who are not in the "speaking group" are forced to internalise and/or store up their questions and comments. This approach, as used in the context of family therapy (see Jenkins 1990), forces participants to listen to the uninterrupted conversations and narratives of others. This has the effect of deleting impulse comments, hostile surges and negative instantiations, which, if unchecked, interrupt and/or stifle the flow of conversation. We believe that many people are not good listeners and rarely subject themselves to engaging the attitudes, feelings and experiences of others. Picking up on Mackay's thesis, we believe that one of the reasons why many young people do not verbalise their problems and anxieties, or seek the counsel of older people is because they do not believe they will get a fair and considered hearing. Hearing that they are "being silly", that they "should grow up" or that "it's not that bad" is a benign substitute for being heard and respected. Once developed, the skills of active listening can be simultaneously generous and illuminating.

The technique we are describing involves a process of "externalising" experience. Meaning making that is rendered private and internal is often limited in scope and confused in practical expression. For example, young males who have grown up accepting and rehearsing machismo behaviours, often encounter the limits of such behaviours when they are old enough to work, drive and drink legally and embark on intimate relationships. With the relative freedoms and opportunities that this stage of life brings, there is often the need for a readjustment of both behaviour and personal understandings. The process of turning private and idiosyncratic understanding into more public and self-conscious knowledge necessitates engaging in conversation.

"Conversational flow" in action

What follows is a brief example of a workshop conducted with a group of final-year pre-service primary school (generalist) teachers at Deakin University. The workshop was implemented to pick up on some of the discussions on "gender in sport" that had arisen during previous tutorials conducted during the semester-long unit entitled 'Physical and Health Education'. Broadly speaking, discussions about gender in sport were contested along the gender lines of the 36 students (13 males and 23 females) in the tutorial group. The workshop was designed to facilitate discussion among this group of young people (mean age 20.7 years) and provide strategic opportunities for particular points of view to be heard. Discussion about "gender in sport", provoked around the following vignette, was audio-taped and later transcribed.[1]

> It's a Sunday afternoon, August 1, and in Canberra a football game between Ainslie and Campbelltown is played at the Ainslie Oval. Kevin "Cowboy" Neale, a "legend" of the strong St Kilda team of the late 1960s and early 1970s, coaches Ainslie. Only a couple of hundred people are in attendance, a small number for a major league game. A rugby league game between Canberra and Penrith is being playing at the same time at Bruce stadium and this might be a contributing factor for the small attendance.

> During the first quarter there is an "incident" on the Campbelltown half-forward line whereby a Campbelltown player is left lying motionless while his team mates remonstrate with no. 22 for Ainslie. Campbelltown people sitting in the stand are angry and agitated at what has happened, and consider that it is an illegal "off the ball" incident. At this point the umpires do not take any direct action against any players

> After a short time, as the game proceeds, the injured player is slowly assisted from the ground. He is bleeding badly from the nose and mouth and his escort provides

support to his jaw. Both men walk directly from the oval and to the back of the Campbelltown coaching box where an elastic bandage is wrapped around the injured player's head and jaw. Once this is completed the player and escort walk slowly from the ground. There is clearly some concern in this process as the player does not even collect a tracksuit or change of clothes; he remains in his football gear, including his boots.

While the game proceeds, two Campbelltown officials meet to discuss the incident and inquire whether or not the game is being videotaped. When they discover that there is a tape of the game one of them declares, "good we'll get him charged!" After this exchange one of the men moves to comfort a young woman who is visibly upset. After a short time the woman proceeds into the clubrooms to collect the player's clothes. Once she has completed this task she also leaves the ground.

At quarter time, in Ainslie's team huddle, the coach speaks calmly about the team game plan and directs his attention to a couple of players specifically. During this address no. 22 stares blankly off into the distance, showing no sign of any engagement with anything that is being done or said. All that is visible in no. 22's behaviour are signs of complete detachment. During the coach's address there is no mention of the incident; however, the final comments are something like "you've been good and hard at the ball. Make sure you don't relax and lose any intensity!"

Almost two weeks after this game the following report appeared in the *Canberra Times* (Lloyd 1998). Headed 'Neale sacked, fires parting shot at Ainslie committee' the article outlined the details of the coach's dismissal. At the end of the article the following details were recorded.

"Campbelltown's Nathan Lenton has been advised not to play football again after breaking his jaw against Ainslie two weeks ago. Lenton, 25, spent nine days in Calvary hospital after the game – including five days in intensive care – and has had two operations to try to repair his jaw. He had several metal plates inserted and specialists advised him not to play football, or any other contact sport, again.

"Ainslie's Saleem Kassem was reported for allegedly striking Lenton in that game. The charge is yet to be heard, after the tribunal again held over the case for a further two weeks at its hearing on Tuesday night" (p.18).

Postscript: The ACTAFL tribunal finally met on 28 August and suspended Kassem for 10 weeks.

The workshop for engaging conversational flow was built around the formation of three groups.[2] Immediately following a reading of the vignette by the facilitator, all students were asked to independently choose one word that best encapsulated how the story made them feel. This method ensured that each person took something tangible into the following discussion. At the same time it helped formalise discussion around a common focus. Following this, the participants were asked to record other words or phrases that represented their feelings about the incident described in the vignette. Two affinity groups were then formed along gender lines. Group one comprised five males who volunteered to discuss issues raised in the vignette in light of their respective experiences as footballers. Group two was made up of five females who openly revealed an antagonism toward football. This group was formed when "Sally"[3] announced that she would like to participate as a group member on the platform and that, "it (football) is a ridiculous game that allows men to get away with things that would be seen as violent and criminal in any other aspect of society". "Claire", "Brigette", "Lani" and "Kay" agreed with Sally and volunteered to form group two. Group three comprised all members of the class. It was not until the final phase of the workshop that members of the third group, known as the reflecting team, were invited to speak. Indeed, the first two groups did not engage in any direct dialogue prior to this phase, but instead were provoked to listen to each other's perspectives in order to advance general understanding of the issues raised.

"Dominic", "Paul", "Dave", "Bruno" and "James" spent much of their initial 10-minute discussion time talking about the actions of the assailant and debating the merits of the 10-week suspension that had been ultimately bestowed upon him. Dominic, Paul and James felt that while the incident had been unfortunate it was a part of the game and that the allocated 10-week penalty was reasonable punishment. In discussing the assailant, the word "unlucky" appeared 11 times in the transcript of their discussion. Paul typifies this in his response to James's comment that the assailant was unlucky to have inflicted such a severe injury. "Yeah, it just happens, there's 20 other blokes running around wanting to knock their blocks off and he's the one that gets caught. So he's a bit unlucky on that front." Dominic concurred: "It's just a spur of the moment thing. I mean you don't think about it when you're playing; you see someone there and you hit them. You don't think about it." Dave and Bruno were less convinced about this line of argument and/or rationalisation. The basis of their concern was that the alleged incident had taken place behind play and was therefore unacceptable. Bruno argued, "(e)veryone knows they can get hurt when they play football. You accept that. But I don't think it's right for someone to hit someone behind play". The group seemed to be coming to a general agreement that the fact that the incident had taken place "off the ball" rendered it "cowardly" and justified a 10-week suspension, when their allocated 10 minutes was complete.

The second group began their discussion focusing on what group one had been talking about. Between their own thoughts and feelings about the issues, and their reflections on the previous group's discussion, the second group had no problem initiating discussion. Lani opened the discussion denouncing the "excuses" she perceived the males had been making for the assailant. "It's just violence. I mean it's unnecessary in anyone's language and just should not happen." The females were in agreement that the act was violent and totally unacceptable in any context, and were appalled that the males seemed to justify it on the grounds that it happened on a football field. Their only point of contest during this line of discussion revolved around Lani's claim that football "is a stupid game that promoted violence in society and should be banned completely". Both Brigette and Kay rejected this as going too far. "I like football. My boyfriend plays and I like to go and watch him. I don't like it when he gets hurt but most stuff is not serious and he rarely misses games because he's hurt, and injured and that." Kay agreed that she liked watching football and even confessed, "I know it's a bit hypocritical but I even like the fights (pause for her chuckles). I don't like seeing people, even the opposition players, getting like, seriously hurt though". The last part of the second group's conversation centred on the female who had been so seriously distressed following the incident that had taken place on the field. "She must have been freaking out. Like here's her husband or boyfriend, or whatever, getting carted off to the hospital with bandages holding his face together. God, I'd have been feeling sick if it was my boyfriend", said Claire. The group agreed that although she was not physically hurt, the female in the story also needed help and support but that it wouldn't be forthcoming. Brigette summed this up, saying, "The bloke who is hurt is off to hospital, his girlfriend is off after him and everyone's attention is back on the game". There was clear confirmation for this comment among all members of the group.

The model is designed to allow the first group to become the focal point of discussion one more time before opening up to the reflecting team. Like the second group, they commenced their discussion responding to specific issues raised by the previous group. "One thing we obviously didn't mention earlier was the girlfriend. But I mean when someone's been hurt or that, you just don't think about those things. You just don't", explained Bruno. "Yeah", agreed James, "like I barrack for the Brisbane Lions and Michael Voss broke his leg really bad. I'm sitting there thinking the season's over for Vossy and how much we're going to miss him. I'm not thinking about his girlfriend and how she might be feeling. It's just how it is". There was broad agreement that while it was a bit of an over-sight on their behalf, they wouldn't really expect that concern about a player's girlfriend, mother or sister would be natural part of their reaction to such an incident. Bruno qualified this on the basis of proximity: "If it happens to someone on your team you probably think about his girlfriend a bit later. But if it's someone on the other team you wouldn't think about their family or anything like that." Extending this line of discussion, Paul announced that if it happened to someone on the other team, the only comments that would be made about such an incident were likely to be celebratory. "Like the boys would probably say 'well done, you got him a beauty' and stuff like that. Like I remember I had this guy who was agitating me, I lined him up and crunched him. It was near the ball and that so it wasn't illegal. I just had an opportunity and got him. He didn't get up! Everyone was coming up to me after the game saying, 'well done', 'what a beauty' and you know, 'that was great' and stuff like that." The remainder of the conversation continued around the testimonies of what each participant had done or seen in this context. Each of the incidents described was arbitrated as "reasonable or unreasonable" on the grounds of whether or not it had happened in the "normal" course of play.

The final 10 minutes involved all participants in a discussion reflecting on the form and substance of the three previous discussions. As is the case with most group discussions, not everyone got a chance to speak as people began to debate issues and question and answer one another. The facilitator was forced to intercede a number of times to keep the discussion on track and dilute the build-up of acrimony between some participants. Notable inclusions in this discussion were narratives volunteered by two participants. The first, a female, recounted an incident where her father had been badly injured playing football and how the remnants of an assault (which occurred "off the ball" in a grand final) were still visible some 20 years later. Folklore has it that the assailant was bought into the opposition grand final team to intimidate and cause injury. She was concerned that such practices illustrated the scope for violence that existed in the context of football. The other narrative was offered by a young male who recounted his experience as a victim of a violent attack in a hotel. He retold how he and two of his friends had been beaten and kicked as they left a local hotel one night. Central to his story was his description of the perpetrators as opportunistic and cowardly. He presented himself and his two friends as people who didn't seek trouble and were beset upon for no other reason than the fact that they were there. On the basis of his personal experience, he felt some empathy with the victim in the vignette. He was disappointed that relatively little of either group's attention had been given to the victim; not only to the physical injuries that he had sustained, but more importantly, to the emotional damage that such an incident is likely to cause to him and the people that care about him.

Some observations

Underpinning our interest in the processes of conversation is our concern that the lack of genuine connection between people is often underscored by their inability to converse in ways that are mutually generative and supportive. Where young people feel, for whatever reasons, that communication about an issue or event is not worthwhile with a particular audience (namely, their parents and/or teachers), it is reasonable that they will conceal the information. They may seek opportunities to discuss such issues or events in more supportive environments (among friends) or simply not choose to talk about it at all. The latter is a very easy option for someone to take, who may be feeling anxious or vulnerable. The less they choose, or are afforded genuine opportunities, to talk about such things the more disconnected they will become. In the downward spiral of "I can't explain it" and "s/he doesn't listen", the vicious cycle of disconnectedness begins. Where such division exists between teachers and students, in the context of education, there is bound to be conflict and/or a general lack of empathy or understanding. Short bursts of this sort of breakdown are probably inevitable, but a prolonged lack of connection is destined to have ramifications for both the individual and society. At a time when young people have new and difficult challenges to confront and sort through, the warrant for teachers to develop new forms of communication is compelling.

According to White (1991), one of Australia's foremost narrative therapists, the process of sharing and externalising narrative enables us to make personal experiences and understandings the object of scrutiny and analysis. The externalising process, involves turning subjective understandings into more objectified perspectives. In the process, the participants are able to unravel, across time, the basis on which people make particular choices and engage in particular behaviours. As a result of the externalising process, the various impacts of particular choices and behaviours can be the focus of reflection and discussion. Importantly, the narrative method encourages the generation of alternatives for making choices and enacting one's relationships. Specifically, the method involves identifying what are known as "unique outcomes". This term refers to the exploration of alternative stories that may exist within each person's biography. The detection of such alternatives opens the way towards the self-conscious choice of alternative ways of "being in the world". To this end, the method is designed to assist people to assume responsibility for finding solutions to their problems and conflicts.

Applied specifically to education, the methods that underpin "conversational flow" open gateways into the territory of alternative pedagogies and as a result offer alternative ways of being and acting in the world. To explain this, we need to further develop the spatial metaphor. As a form of narrative this method works within and across two "landscapes" of understanding and meaning making. Understandings of the chronology of events are "mapped" as part of the "landscape of action". Associated feelings and emotional responses are known as part of the "landscape of consciousness".

The "landscape of action" is characterised by a focus on:
- the description of a situation, moment or event within a sequence of events;
- references to situations, moments or events within the context of past, present and future; and
- options for alternatives – the counter plot.

The "landscape of consciousness" is characterised by a focus on:
- the person's reflection of the events within the landscape of action. The review of events is revealing of:
  - the nature of preferences and desires;
  - the character of personal relationships;
  - the make-up of intentional states;
  - the composition of preferred beliefs; and
  - the nature of commitments.

The narrative process can be made specific and concrete through the mapping of the dual landscapes. For example, in the study of antisocial behaviour in the context of schooling, the method described here would attempt to identify understandings of particular events in sequence and connect these with tangible consequences and emotional reactions. Thus, the method "externalises" the experiences, commitments and reactions of different people to a particular set of behaviours. From this vantage point, the approach connects individuals which opens the way to identifying alternative patterns of behaviour.

Within the context of the workshop described in this paper, the adoption of the conversational flow method was clearly beneficial in providing a strategic outlet for discussing issues that would never have been aired or would have been truncated in more traditional pedagogic forums. Not only did the groups enjoy the opportunity to speak free of interruption and rebuttal, but there was something empowering for them in knowing that their thoughts and perspectives were being listened to. For instance, the males were enticed to talk about the role of important "others" (namely, girlfriends, wives, mothers, etc.) in their second conversation. By their own admission, they recognised that they had not considered this viewpoint before. While their musings did not reveal any clear sense of a clemency, the fact that they discussed such issues and acknowledged some of the wider implications of violence, is something to build on.

Conclusion

In this chapter we have proceeded from the assumption that power differentials constrain open and creative dialogue. Given that education is built on hierarchies of power, it follows logically that communication problems and breakdowns are built into the very structures of classroom and staffroom relations. This issue is well described by White (1995) when he asserts that:

> Whenever there are inequalities in power between groups, conversations that take place in the name of dialogue usually take place on the terms of the dominant group. This is not a criticism of the motives of the dominant group. I don't know how such an outcome could be avoided when the playing field is not level. How could those people in the dominant group be conscious of their taken-for-granted privilege? (White 1995, p.63)

White's question is instructive. It suggests that the formal processes of education lack self-consciousness about the processes of silencing, withholding, withdrawal and resistance that have been normalised and implicit within dominant pedagogies. To this end, the method described in this chapter is designed to overcome some of the effects that produce breakdowns in communicating. As such, they have been designed to disrupt the dominant patterns of exchange associated with hierarchical relations. Using such methods is not easy. For educators, it requires giving up some of the status and privilege of having the dominant and active voice. For students, it involves an act of trust that their words and ideas will be taken seriously. In the end, we believe that these risks and challenges are worth taking if we are to move towards more authentic, transformative and equal forms of communication within education and beyond.

References

Becvar, R., Canfield, B. & Becvar, D. 1997, *Group Work: Cybernetics, constructivism and social constructivist perspectives*, Love, Denver/Sydney.

Bretag, T. 1999, 'Danger in taking peer group pressure too far', *The Australian*, 13 Jan., p.11.

Connell, R.W. 1995, *Masculinities*, Allen & Unwin, Sydney.

Davies, B. 1993, *Shards of Glass: Children reading and writing beyond gendered identities*, Allen & Unwin, Sydney.

Fitzclarence, L., Hickey, C. & Matthews, R. 1997, 'Getting changed for football: Challenging communities of practice', *Curriculum Perspectives*, v.17, n.1, pp.69-73.

Gladwell, M. 1998, 'Do parents matter?', *The New Yorker*, 17 Aug., pp.54-64.

Hallowell, E. 1993, 'Connectedness', in *Finding the Heart of the Child*, eds E. Hallowell & M. Thompson, Association of Independent Schools in New England Inc., Braintree, MA.

Harris, J.R. 1998, *The Nurture Assumption*, The Free Press, New York.

Hickey, C. & Fitzclarence, L. 2000, 'Peering at the individual: Problems with trying to teach young males not to be like their peers', *The Australian Educational Researcher*, v.27, n.1, pp.71-91.

Jenkins, A. 1990, *Invitations to Responsibility*, Dulwich Centre Publications, Adelaide.

Kenway, J., Willis, S. with Blackmore, J. & Rennie, L. 1997, *Answering Back, Remaking Girls and Boys in Schools*, Allen & Unwin, Sydney.

Lloyd, D. 1998, 'Neale sacked, fires parting shot at Ainslie committee', *The Canberra Times*, 13 Aug., p.18.

Mackay, H. 1993, *Reinventing Australia*, Angus & Robertson, Pymble.

—— 1997, *Generations: Baby boomers, their parents and their children*, MacMillan, Sydney.

McGillion, C. 1998, 'Bishops focus on the perils of being young', *The Age*, 17 Sept., p.6.

Miedzian, M. 1991, *Boys Will Be Boys: Breaking the link between masculinity and violence*, Virago, London.

Miller, A. 1990, *For Your Own Good: Hidden cruelty in child-rearing and the roots of violence*, The Noonday Press, New York.

Messner, M. 1992, *Power at Play: Sports and the problem of masculinity*, Beacon Press, MA.

Messner, M. & Sabo, D. 1994, *Sex, Violence and Power in Sports: Rethinking masculinity*, Crossing Press, Cambridge, MA.

Rowe, D. & Lawrence, G. 1990, *Sport and Leisure*, HBJ, Sydney.

Sacks, P. 1996, *Generation X Goes to College: An eye-opening account of teaching in postmodern America*, Open Court, Chicago.

Sharp, G. 1985, 'Constitutive abstraction and social practice', *Arena*, n.70.

Sharp, G. & White, D. 1968, 'Features of the intellectually trained', *Arena*, n.15.

Tulgan, B. 1995, *Managing Generation X: How to bring out the best in young talent*, Santa Monica, CA.

White, M. 1991, 'Deconstruction and therapy', *Dulwich Centre Newsletter*, n.3, pp.21-40.

—— 1995, 'Schools as communities of acknowledgment, a conversation with Michael White', *Dulwich Centre Newsletter*, nos 2 & 3, pp.51-66.

Notes

1 This vignette was compiled while the authors were researching the relationships among sport, masculinity and education.

2 This method has been adapted from the ideas developed in narrative therapy as practiced, for example, by Alan Jenkins in his work with abusive males, and Michael White and David Epston in their work in family therapy.

3 All names used in the vignette are fictitious.

Karen Malone

chapter 11

Dangerous youth: Youth geographies in a climate of fear

"They put me in the back of the police van and drove me around the park for a couple of hours occasionally beating me" states a 17-year-old youth caught doing pranks at a local school the night before muck-up day,[1] " I was bleeding. I broke my front teeth when I fell over and they handcuffed me. They found a picture of my mate and me in my wallet and they said you're a gay boy aren't you. When I said no, they hit me. I was scared – I felt helpless. When they finally let me out of the van they threw my wallet back at me and laughed, it was empty, the picture and my money was gone and they had stuck it together with super glue".

Lucas, 17

Dangerous youth

Stories, told by young people, about being harassed and physically abused by police for minor misdemeanours are becoming commonplace in Australian society (Tait 1994; White 1994). Being bullied is becoming synonymous with the definitive experience of growing up in our cities. There are no doubts Lucas was involved in an unlawful activity, along with the group of 30 other young males and females who superglued locker doors shut as a childish prank. But is losing two front teeth, being physically and verbally abused, handcuffed and made a hostage for two hours in the back of a van a justified response? Lucas transgresses the child/adult world – adults, with their power as boundary enforcers, toy with his vulnerability as a child, and meet his childish prank with forceful hostility.

Labelled as *dangerous* or *unpredictable* and positioned as *other*, a young person in public space is regularly persuaded, using bullying tactics or threats of incarceration, to move on. Under constant gaze, youth invariably find themselves embroiled in struggles of legitimacy and appropriation in regard to their status in public place (Allen 1994; Polzot 1997; Iveson 1998). A recent study revealed that 80% of young people interviewed had been stopped by police in a public space, such as the street, train station or shopping mall for minor or undisclosed misdemeanours (White 1994). Roughed up in the back of a police van, sometimes taken in for questioning, other times just verbally abused on the street and told to move on, many of these young males and females stopped by police were still in school uniform. Community support for these and other policing methods has been encouraged through some media outlets amid calls for the introduction of youth curfews and further restrictions to public space. Internationally, these practices have not passed without notice. The United Nations Australian review on the status of the Convention on the Rights of the Child (CRC)[2] recently stated,

> ... young people being refused access to commercial premises on the basis that they are likely to behave irresponsibly and be disruptive, [and] police in various localities establishing curfews which require all children to be home after a specific time are examples of discriminatory practices and an infringement of children's civil rights (HREOC 1997).

Influenced by underclass ideology, society demonises "youth" in media and police campaigns as deviant, barbaric and unclean, a threat to social and physical order (Eckersley 1992; Guilliatt 1997). Consequently, young people have come to view the environment as a hostile place. No longer is it the transient landscape where the child plays ambiguously with fantasies of childhood and the logic and demands of being an adult. While shopkeepers concern themselves with how a teenager sits on a bench or kicks a can around the street, and feel anger and distress by what is deemed as inappropriate or antisocial behaviour – the teenager is likely to be oblivious to or dismissive of their concerns. As children, their playfulness in the public domain was viewed as childhood antics, yet as teenagers we fear them – what has changed?

In a recent newspaper article 'Just whose fear is this?' John Mangan, youth reporter for *The Age*, wrote:

> *Next time you're walking past a group of teenagers, some of the news reports of the past week might come to mind – the gang of young women attacking people on Melbourne trains, the recently convicted man in Sydney who murdered a British tourist, the wild teen party in Perth that was broken up by baton-wielding police. Whether you're a teenager, or someone who just has to share a pavement with teenagers, images of violence might be enough to make you think about crossing the road or taking the long way home (The Age, 20/5/1998, p.16).*

Is this fear justified? Mangan argues the fear is not. He claims that behind these media images of dangerous adolescent gangs and juvenile delinquents haunting the suburbs in packs lies a less dramatic and frightening reality. Juvenile crime rates in Victoria have been stable for many years. As far as the statistics go, you are more likely to be assaulted by a 30-year-old drug dealer than the eyebrow-pierced, baggy-pantsed youth hanging out on the local street corner. So from where does the fear and mythmaking about dangerous youth emerge? Why do three or four young people hanging out on a street corner instil a fear of a *gang* while a group of mothers waiting at the school gate does not? And, what are the consequences of these fears on young people's capacity to feel able to move freely in public space? As a country that has ratified the CRC (see UNGA 1989) this is certainly our civil duty.[3]

During the past four years the Growing Up In Cities project, an Australian study of young people's use and perceptions of their neighbourhood, has highlighted the emerging impact of a *climate of fear* on young people's spatial experiences. Based on the principles of CRC and the Habitat 2 Agenda, Growing Up In Cities is a UNESCO-MOST-sponsored project currently being conducted in a number of cities around the globe. This chapter discusses results emanating from two research sites in Australia and reflects on the research methodology.

Mapping geographies of youth

In recent times, research studies about young people in public space have tended to focus on the impact of regulatory practices and policies – border maintenance – with groups of visible young people (usually males). These studies are usually located in highly contested public arenas, such as shopping malls and inner-city shopping precincts (see White 1994; White & Alder 1994; Wyn & White 1997; YAPA 1997; Heywood & Crane 1998). In contrast, our study maps geographies of power and resistance as they are played out in young people's local neighbourhoods, where they congregate in contested public arenas. Of particular interest to the researchers are 10- to 15-year-olds. This is an age group in which it is felt young persons are most susceptible to the changing conditions of their local neighbourhood and a time when they begin to use their neighbourhood as a resource to play and socialise outside of parental regulations. It is also an age where sexuality and difference become more apparent, identity development is important, and transgressions between childhood play and adult spatial behaviour are learnt. Public space, therefore, becomes the stage for display and exhibition, for trying on and exploring new identities. It is the context in which to explore the adult world in a playful way and is an important part of children's social and spatial development. The GUIC project is built on the premise that the well-being of children and youth is the ultimate indicator of a healthy environment, a democratic society and good governance. Further, it is our responsibility as adults to provide safe, healthy and peaceful environments where children and youth can develop their sense of place and participate freely in community life (UNICEF 1997).

Constructing a sense of place is about experiencing an environment and not just living in it. A street or footpath is the physical expression of an urban design – it is transformed into a living environment when I walk along it. Whether that street space provides mobility, access and enhances my quality of life is not dependent on just the physical characteristics attributed to it by the designer, but on how I feel when I experience that street – safe, fearful, interested or bored. Therefore, to study a person's sense of place and spatial identity, we must explore the relationship between the physical design of the space, the behaviour of the individual when negotiating the space, and their perceptual lived experience. To accomplish this, the GUIC research design is multi-method and incorporates physical and social science methods supported by a multidisciplinary research team comprising educators, anthropologists and urban planners. The methods used include interviews, time schedules, roaming range maps, drawings, neighbourhood tours, self-taken photographs, behaviour observations and focus groups.[4] In this chapter, two case studies are presented and discussed. The data were obtained using these multi-method tools. The first case study presents data from an intensive two-year study of 44 young people growing up in a low socioeconomic neighbourhood, Braybrook, in the western suburbs of Melbourne. The second is a broader study of a large regional city, Frankston, in the southeastern suburbs of Melbourne. Frankston City has eight distinct neighbourhoods that were researched simultaneously over a six-month period. One hundred young people participated in this city study.

Case one: Braybrook

"Vandalism of trees and buildings", says Betty an elderly resident who has lived in the neighbourhood for 40 years, "is a result of alienation. Young people have been disenfranchised by the lack of access to recreational and support facilities, this has resulted in alienation and a lack of respect for the area ..."

Betty, interview 1996

The neighbourhood for many young people in Braybrook exists as a melange of myths and legends embedded over time as cultural codes in the environment. These codes exist in a historical and sociocultural landscape that was physically constructed in response to slum clearance in inner-city Melbourne and a postwar housing boom over a five-year period between 1951 and 1956. Built from cheap building materials with a limited life expectancy, the 488-hectare fibro housing estate, quickly fell into disrepair and became, as did many estates of this era, a site of urban poverty (see Winter & Bryson 1998). Originally, it was home for newly arrived refugees from Europe and Britain. Forty years later, the demographics have changed drastically. Now over 30% of residents come from non-English-speaking backgrounds, predominantly Asian. The social stigma and the subsequent marginalisation of being a non-working-class neighbourhood, a vanguard of the *underclass*, has, unlike many of the houses, survived the test of time.

McDonald (1997, pp.3-4) describes the underclass as:

... a social group or class of people located at the bottom of the class structure who, over time, have become structurally separate and culturally distinct from the regularly employed working class and society [and are] in general almost permanently confined to living in poorer conditions and neighbourhoods.

Represented as key figures in conservative accounts of the underclass are the irresponsible welfare-draining single mother and the feckless young man (McDonald 1997). "We get it rammed down our throats by the newspapers that the western suburbs are deprived, illiterate and breed crime and are full of no-hopers ... if you live in an area you're lumped with it", proclaims Harry, a local Braybrook resident. Both McDonald (1997) and Davis (1990) express grave concerns about the concept of underclass. They believe it acts as a red herring to divert attention from the real causes of poverty and that it allows underclass theorists to focus their attention on blaming *dangerous youth* (and their sole parents) and using them as a scapegoat for the ills of modernist society.

Both "youth" (specifically allegedly "disaffected" youth) and the assumed "underclass" have remained powerful metaphors for societal decay and the focus for "respectable fears", often with limited, or mythical justification (Davis 1990, p.70).

Fear, marginalisation and *moral* decay

The young people who live in Braybrook represent for outsiders the archetypal metaphor of social and moral decay; they are members of the minority underclass and the disaffected youth. Evidence of vandalism, graffiti, youth crime and drug trafficking convince even the uninitiated that this is a dangerous place where decay, disorder and violence are gnawing away at the social fabric. The empty streets, the shuttered shop windows and the deserted, treeless parks help to create an air of anxiety and fear. From behind closed doors and venetian blinds, residents survey the streets. Most of these residents are young people home alone, watching television, baby-sitting siblings or talking with friends. They are, as Betty stated earlier, alienated, disenfranchised and disconnected from their physical surrounds. The intent of the study was to find out why.

"It's trashy and there's nothing for kids to do, cause there's needles everywhere, everyone, nearly everyone does drugs", states Sara, a 13-year-old female resident of Braybrook. This young woman's description of the neighbourhood is not unlike many recounted by young people growing up in the neighbourhood. Generally, young people described their area as boring, if not dangerous and occasionally, as Sam's story below reveals, street action can be viewed from behind the safety of your lounge room window.

> My street is boring and quiet and nothing much happens except, well, yesterday when a fire bomb was thrown from a passing car at the house next door. I saw it from my lounge room window. And do you know it only took the fire brigade 15 minutes to arrive but the police didn't come for over 30 minutes.
>
> Sam, 15, interview 1997

Asking young people to draw or map their neighbourhood is one method used by GUIC researchers to determine young people's perceptual and real relationship to their neighbourhood environment. Young people in Braybrook often responded to the task by creating images that were based on social rather than physical characteristics of the area. Relph (1976) and others suggest that a sense of place is represented by a person's ability to construct physical images of a place. The mental map or drawing can be analysed by the researcher as a means for understanding how the participant experiences their surrounding environment and the importance attributed to particular elements. For example, a map or drawing of the neighbourhood can incorporate a range of five kilometres, one street or the view from the kitchen window. It may be detailed, with every street and shop name in the neighbourhood, or only show the streets leading out of the neighbourhood. It may highlight a particular place that is significant and represent it as being larger than other images in the drawing. For children, this is often the local school, park or their friend's house.

The drawings from the young people in the Braybrook area were consistently very contained in range (usually just their street or their house). Many of the young people did not include any physical elements of the environment, only images of things that presented dangers for them such as syringes, drugs, bongs, cigarettes and fast cars. To further explore the representation of the physical environment, a number of the participants were asked over the period of a week to take photographs of their neighbourhood. Again, these images illustrated a limited view of the neighbourhood. The subjects of the photographs were predominantly the inside of their houses – pets, family, friends, bedroom, backyard, the view from their lounge room window, even the screen of their television.

To determine if significant places existed in the neighbourhood for young people, they were asked to write a list of every place they knew and circle their favourite and most frequented place. Favourite and most frequented places correlated for young women – both were home and home sites. Males' favourite destinations were commercial facilities, and the most frequented places were community centres, with the local community sports centre being the most likely destination. In all our discussions, not one young person identified natural or structured play environments (such as playgrounds or nature reserves) as a likely destination.

Time schedules provided a useful tool to see if a correlation existed between the places the young people identified as their favourite and where and how they actually spent their time. Analysing males' time schedules, it was evident that even though many of the males spent time at the community sports centre and listed playing sport as a favourite activity, very few of them actually played a sport. In fact, the males spend most of their time watching television, messing around with friends or hanging around in the street near their houses. When asked what they did when messing around with their friends, young men replied "hung around outside the sports centre" or "stayed at home".[5]

To add further substance to the analysis of young people's time use, we then asked them to identify with whom they spent most of their spare time. The results illustrated that gender and ethnicity were a determining factor in young people's time use and leisure companions. Most young people nominated friends as the person they spent the most time with, but a large percentage (almost half) of the young males spent their time alone. Of the young males who spent time alone, most were from non-English-speaking backgrounds and of Asian origin. Many of the Asian males had similar patterns of spatial behaviour and time use – they spent their out-of-school time alone in their homes. Female Asian youth, on the other hand, were perceived to be *at risk* when left alone, were most often billeted to grandparents or other relatives in neighbouring suburbs when parents were not going to be at home. In contrast, young Somalian males, who were accustomed to socialising in their community, preferred to congregate together in their leisure time. Because of the limited space in their homes and lack of privacy (many Somalian homes had up to 12 family and extended family members), the males socialised on the streets. Described as dark, large and menacing (by local community members) these gatherings of young, confident males who physically impacted on the bland monotone environment evoked fear in local residents. Police patrols stepped up in the neighbourhood with the increase of Somalian refugee numbers. The ensuing consequence was conflict over space use.

> Police often discriminate against us, they pick on us. Once we were walking on the street with a friend and a policeman in a car stopped and asked me my name and address for no reason. He said to me don't speak bloody African language. This made me my feel really angry because he didn't respect my language or culture. He pushed my friend over when he came to help me.
>
> Abdulah, 16, interview 1997

During the interviews young people also constructed maps of their roaming range. These maps illustrated that many of the young people had bounded or geographically contained roaming ranges. Their use of the neighbourhood environment generally included no more than one or two blocks from their homes. Young people were also asked to identify on the map places they avoided. Many identified certain streets where house occupants were seen as potentially dangerous and a local reserve where syringes and other drug-related debris was likely to be found. Their maps contradicted the earlier view that they had limited knowledge of the physical structure of the neighbourhood – in fact they had a heightened social sensibility. But this sensibility was not in terms of their use or connection to the environment – as would be represented on a mental map – but their ability to find safe passage through dangerous social and physical elements.

Streets were recognised by one-third of the young people as the place where they felt most in danger. Both young women and men listed drugs, alcohol, physical and verbal abuse as the primary cause of their fear in the streets, due, in the majority of cases, to adults or adult activities (drug taking, drunkenness, policing). Violence, drug use and trafficking, while being presented by the young people as a major concern for them, is apparently not seen by outsiders as a problem for young people in the area.

> *Acting Detective Inspector John Johnson said ... "There is nothing in our statistics to reflect that crime against youth is a major problem in Braybrook" ... He said he was surprised by the results of the UNESCO study ... "We have had times in years gone by when there have been problems with crimes against youth but that is very, very much resolved"* ('Crime against youth "under control"', by Melissa Arch, *The Footscray Mail*, 20/7/98, p.18).

Young people often described their neighbourhood by highlighting stories of dangerous events – the time the child was abducted from the street, the house that was burnt down, the hotel owner who was shot by drug dealers, the person who contracted HIV/AIDS from stepping on a syringe. To further explore these stories of danger and fear, the research team spoke with parents. Influenced by the exaggeration or "beat up" of youth and drug-related issues by the media and the police, parents told us they feared if young people were in public spaces they were likely to get caught up in deviant behaviour either as victims or perpetrators. Parents told us that they recited stories of violence to dissuade their children from hanging around the streets – many of the stories, confessed the parents, were either imaginary or historical. Acting on the advice of parents, and as a safety strategy to overcome being victimised in the streets, young people either limited their movements or only moved around in groups. Due to public perceptions that young people congregating in groups represented a *gang*, adopting this safety strategy often meant policing agents or local residents targeted them. To avoid detection, they often resorted to hanging around in dangerous places (for example, in the alleyway behind shops or in secluded areas of the park). This action increased the likelihood of young people being bullied by older youth or mixing with drug dealers who were also looking for places to hide from authorities. Overall, the study in Braybrook revealed that the consequence of conflicts over power, control and resistance in the public domain meant the majority of youth seldom ventured far from the safe haven of their homes.

Case two: Frankston

> I suppose I am guilty of judging young people – not being very tolerant. It's just the way they look, hanging around in groups, untidy, smoking – they look like trouble. When I think about it though I guess they aren't doing anything wrong – it's just that they look like they could.
>
> Mary, local councillor, council meeting 2000

Lack of tolerance in a city where young people come from diverse social backgrounds and physical locales contributes to high levels of tension and conflict in public space. Since the township was established in 1854, Frankston City has long been an ephemeral community – functioning for divergent purposes. From being a seaside host to the rich city folk on lengthy weekends at the turn of the century, a gateway to a postwar building boom on the Mornington Peninsula, it now struggles to be a self-contained city with its own employment and retail opportunities. For many outsiders and city dwellers, Frankston is *the end of the line* – the last stop on the southbound suburban train. The flatness of the land between the city and Frankston meant the train line was established in 1882 well in advance of more hilly suburbs to the northeast. A 90-minute train ride at the turn of the century, it now takes less than 50 minutes to come from Melbourne. The train station and its role as the connecting link to the greater metropolis is an interesting metaphor for the city, which we found to be very inversely focused.

Historically, Frankston was always an important railway junction where travellers waited for trains or carriages to Mornington and other parts of the Peninsula. They were usually on their way to honeymoons or family holidays at the beachside. It was a bustling township where travellers brought supplies and relaxed in a town not dissimilar to many English resorts – out of the smog and pollution of a highly industrial city it promised a milder climate, sea breezes and a healthy lifestyle. A number of wealthy families built mansions in the hilly region to the south of the town, creating a clear class boundary and two quite separate regions. The working-class town of inner Frankston was where the shopkeepers lived and worked. Frankston South and Mount Eliza were home to upper-class residential weekenders. As geographical and cultural divides, these boundaries still exist – accentuated by the green and lush environment of the southern end of the town with its rolling hills and bay views and the congested, inverted city centre and suburban sprawl spreading inland.

Young people who attend the local schools and congregate in the town centre are a mix of social class, ethnic background and geographical locations. Attracted to the town centre to escape their empty suburban neighbourhoods, the city provides the opportunity for young people seeking independence and excitement, socialisation and interaction with the broader community. But young people in the town are viewed with suspicion and hostility. This is intensified by a legendary reputation as a city at war with its youth. This legend is a fixation from the late 1970s, when Frankston became the focus of national media after rioting youth took to the streets to protest against police brutality. Local residents and outsiders recall this local legend, with its retelling contributing to perceptions that Frankston is a rough town and its young people are menacing and rebellious.

Researching the perceptions and experiences of young people growing up in Frankston was logistically a difficult task. With eight distinct neighbourhoods and a large youth population, it meant conducting a broadscale but intensive study spread over an expansive geographical area. With the focus of the study being to provide data for the local council which was developing a community safety strategy for the city, it was important for the data to be representative of the whole youth cohort, as well as being neighbourhood-specific. Using the GUIC multi-method approach, the research team also included a peer interview phase into the project design to expand the scope of possibility for youth participation.

Drugs, safety and moral panic

Boredom has been identified as being a significant contributor to young people becoming involved in risk-taking behaviour (Patterson & Pegg 1999). Risk-taking can include consuming illegal substances with possible consequences of being drawn into a vibrant drug culture or it can mean hanging around dangerous locations at night waiting for buses or alternative rides home. For a number of young people living in Frankston, the lack of leisure and recreational opportunities in their local neighbourhoods means they congregate in the town centre and compete for the limited facilities available there. Places and activities identified by young people as most attractive to them include messing around at the skateboard ramp (located on the periphery of a major car park), meeting friends at McDonalds, hanging around the shopping centre or attending an underage disco. Young people noted that each of these activities present two major risks for young people. First, because it meant travelling into the town centre, and second, because there was bullying and violence associated with competition over limited resources. When asked why McDonalds was such an attractive place for socialising with friends they were unanimous in their response. It was bright, clean and safe (this was particularly emphasised by the females who used the toilet facilities because they felt unsafe in public toilets),[6] and the management was sympathetic to the needs of young people. In contrast, when we asked young people what their favourite places were in their *local neighbourhood* over half said their favourite place was in the town centre – nothing in their neighbourhood was interesting for them.

The shopping mall looms like a magnet, attracting young people from even the most fringe neighbourhood in the city. Because of the paucity of reliable buses at night and weekends and the degraded condition of the transit station (the focus of street heroin trade in the city), most young people interviewed relied on parents to drive them into the city and pick them up. Mapping the participants roaming range correlated with this. The majority of young people (around 60%) stayed within a two-kilometre radius of their home – essentially never moving outside of their neighbourhood without adult supervision. Neighbourhood leisure activity usually consisted of hanging around the street or in their homes or the homes of friends. Young people who did rely on public transport were concerned about their safety, especially at night when the station was deserted, but said it was a risk they had to take if they wanted to get home.

Mobility is a critical issue for young people living in a regional city, with a significant urban sprawl, and not just for recreational reasons. To access educational facilities many young people have to travel on public transport everyday. All the buses and trains meet and depart from the transit station in the centre of the city. Young women said they felt particularly vulnerable when at the station, even though there were lot of people around.

> Everyday when I get off the train on my way home from school I see them at the station. Young mothers smashed on drugs. They sit in the walkway. It is so sad. They hassle you for money – I try not to look. I always feel unsafe at the train station – I am lucky I have a friend who travels with me.
>
> Becky, 16, interview

Young people identified the streets as a place where they felt unsafe because they were hassled by junkies and beggars. "I suppose because we are young the junkies pick on us – when I come in to town with my mum I never get offered drugs" (Mary, 14, interview 1999). Young people felt junkies targeted them. Drug trafficking and illicit drug use is a major problem in the city. Following a nationwide trend of increased heroin use, the new *takeaway ethic* underpinning heroin distribution[7] has resulted in robust street-based heroin markets in the city centre. The consequences of these explicit dealing practices have been increased crime and violence, loitering and needle litter. Young people reported feeling particularly vulnerable late at night when the shops were closing and they had to walk through the darkened streets to catch a bus or while waiting on a street corner for a late pick-up. At closing time the town centre empties of shoppers and shopkeepers very quickly. Due to all the restaurants and hotels being located on the other side of city, a young person can find that within 10 minutes of the shops closing they are alone in the darkened city streets. Young people reiterated these fears when over half of them identified increased law and order to clean up the *druggies* as the number one recommendation for improving the city centre.

> We need more security guards to get rid of the druggies, no drugs in public toilets and to stop all syringes everywhere.
>
> Karl, 15, interview 1999

> To make the centre safe we need surveillance cameras, lights and mirrors in the alleyways.
>
> Susan, 12, interview 1999

There was evidence of animosity towards young people (especially young males) by store-keepers and shoppers who often referred to them as *delinquents* and *thieves*. The national media has been quick to seize the opportunity to draw parallels between young male teenagers' choice of clothes and music and the universal *home-boy* figure, a figure that originates from the inner-city black American home-boy gangs and represents a global icon for the unpredictable menacing violent predator. There has been a lot of discussion on what constitutes a gang in an Australian context. The use of the term gangs or gang warfare instantly conjures up images of armed youth involved in illegal behaviour, including anything from sexual harassment, intimidation to drug dealing, robbery and murder. What constitutes a gang as opposed to a group of young people meeting together? According to Mathews:

> *A youth gang is a group of three or more youths whose membership, though often fluid, consists of at least a stable core of members who are recognised by themselves or others as a gang and who band together for social, cultural, or other reasons and impulsively or intentionally plan and commit antisocial, delinquent, or illegal acts* (Mathews 2000, p.7).

According to the *Fear of Crime* report released by the National Campaign Against Violence and Crime in 1998, "homies" were the group most mentioned by participants of all ages who caused fear in public places.

> *You see six of them, baseball caps on backwards, they're probably as innocent as anything, but they've got sometimes a vibe about them … it's not if there's one or two [of them , it's if there's a gang. I don't necessarily think they'd do anything to me, but it goes through my head, "what are you up to?"* (NCAVAC 1998, p.22).

Increased police foot patrols in the city around the time of our study was, according to a police spokesperson, a response to local shopkeepers lodging complaints about young people, saying they scared away customers by being noisy and loitering outside their shops. Young people told us they had noticed the increased visibility of police and felt it was an improvement – hardly the response of a group of criminally intent homies. Police recently commented to the researchers that since increasing foot patrols they had found the majority of people engaging in antisocial behaviour in the streets were not young people but young adults (24- to 30-year-olds) usually drunk or on drugs.

Young people identified natural places, particularly the beach, as a place they would not frequent. While "Dolphin City" is the promotional name for Frankston City, paradoxically, the natural resource of the beach has been detached from the town centre by inverted town planning which allowed the postwar building boom to turn its back on the beach and develop inland. Going through alleyways and hotel car parks is the only way to access the once attractive riverfront and tea-tree lined foreshore. Once a haven for waterbirds, it now harbours drunks from the hotel, drug users looking for a quiet place to inject and "petrol heads" who coat the bitumen with oil so they can do burnouts and donuts in hotted up cars. The local kiosk owner at the pier recalls a number of occasions when she felt her life was in danger from junkies and petrol heads fighting in public. She is constantly picking up used syringes and warning families and young people to be careful. She was not surprised when the researchers commented that the young people felt unsafe at the foreshore.

> They would be wise not to hang around, especially at night. After 20 years I am ready to call it quits … it is just getting worse, the drug problem is terrible. Syringes everywhere – it is a disgrace.

Drugs, bullying, violence and lack of available and reliable transport are major issues for young people growing up in Frankston. Ironically, the two main features that were so fundamental in Frankston's early history for creating flow and vitality, the train station and the beach, have become formidable sources of concern, anxiety and danger for young people. Additionally, lack of tolerance and understanding has lead to the marginalisation of young people in public places. Adults' fear of youth, constructed through negative media hype, stereotyping and moral panic, has diverted attention from the source of the unsafe situation and allowed young people to be the easy scapegoat.

Consequences of a "climate of fear"

Contrary to media and community perceptions that young people are a threat to social order, the research found that the majority of young people spend very little time in, and have limited access to, public spaces. The neighbourhood, we learn, previously the site of spontaneous and autonomous child/youth play, is becoming less appealing for young people due to a lack of facilities and the impact of inverted urban planning. In the case of Braybrook, the inversion is the retreat of dominant society (the public) from the centre to the periphery, from the streets to their homes, which has allowed the marginal other (the criminals) to take over the streets.

Concluding our findings about the neighbourhoods, it became clear that fear and initiation of sanctioning measures to regulate and exclude young people from the public domain has resulted in a form of self-policing. By mapping youthful geographies, we found a situation not dissimilar to Foucault's (1979) panopticon phenomena. Young people, such as Foucault's imaginary inmates of the panopticon, do not know when they are under surveillance; they may or may not be being watched: in response, they police themselves. They negotiate the risks and read the environment from a harm minimisation and self-preservation perspective. How can I stay safe but not be hassled? A sentiment supported by James, Prout and Jenks (1998, p.56) when they exclaim "Modernity's child, at school, on the street and even at home becomes its own policemen".

The politics of repressive interventions, such as the campaigns and policing practices employed in the local neighbourhoods of the study, represent a response to public fear and an attempt to eliminate ambiguity in borders between categories of adult/child and public/private spaces. Young people through categorisation find themselves located in a liminal zone – too old for playgrounds, too young to be valued consumers (Sibley 1995; Valentine 1996). When they transgress between these categories, as Sibley (1995) explains, it becomes a source of anxiety for the boundary markers:

Adolescents may be threatening to adults because they transgress the adult/child boundary and appear discrepant in "adult" spaces … teenagers demonstrate that the act of drawing the line in the constructions of discrete categories interrupts what is naturally continuous (Sibley 1995, p.34).

Sibley's view has been supported by a number of youth researchers in Australia (Bessant 1994; Wyn & White 1997; Malone & Hasluck 1998), who have questioned popular representations of the category "youth" because of its repressive and exclusionary intent. Constructing a group in the category of *other* supports the maintenance of boundaries and boundary enforcement. But these boundaries are not just constructed at a metaphysical level: built environments in the politics of border maintenance assume symbolic importance as policing markers: young people may only enter if they conform to specific normalising interventions constructed by hegemonic culture. In the built environment, the liminal zone is the street (in the case of Frankston the street includes the transition zone from the suburban street to the city centre), representing the link between the margins and the inner sanctum. As a site of control, to eliminate border crossing, the street becomes highly contested terrain.

According to Loukataitou-Sideris (1996) fear, suspicion, tension and conflict between social groups cause the segregation of space in terms of legitimate and illegitimate users. Appearing in late modernity, and determined in terms of class, ethnicity and age, this emerging global phenomenon of segregated space is being policed through increased regulatory practices and policies (James, Prout & Jenks 1998). Sibley (1988, p.410) identifies these forces of segregation as the purification of space "… constructed through the maintenance of territorial boundaries and frontiers". Purification aims to secure protection from and superiority over the unclean "other". Consequently, public spaces become strongly classified with clear boundaries, internal homogeneity and order, and the concern is for boundary maintenance, "… in order to keep out objects or people who do not fit the classification" (Sibley 1992, p.109).

Borrowing from the physical and social sciences, the multi-method research approach used in the Growing Up In Cities project endeavours to explore the relationship between young people, their environment and the impact of their transgressions in public space. Methodologically, the research reveals the multiplicity of the youth environmental experience. It also presents, to embellish recent studies of youth conflict in public space, a case for the inclusion of neighbourhood studies mapping the spatial range of young people flowing in and out of public spaces. It explains the usefulness of scrutinising how and why young people cross the boundaries from the periphery to the centre – not just the impacts of their transgressions.

Substantively, the research reveals that stereotypical views of urban youth as mindless, uncouth, dangerous predators have been greatly exaggerated by the media and the police, and further, that adults give mixed messages to young people. We advise them to stay in groups for safety, then we view them in groups with suspicion and fear. The study reveals that moral panics fuelled by this climate of fear bring boundaries into focus by accentuating differences, excluding those deemed dangerous, as other, and parade the power of mainstream values. And, once in the inner-sanctum, we find young people are often ill-prepared for the conflicts, tensions and contestation that competing views of what is appropriate behaviour can engender. Bounded, intolerant and fearful, the public inadvertently places young people in dangerous situations. Whether it is hiding in the alley, standing on an abandoned street corner or being roughed up by police in the back of a van – young people exist in a climate of fear.

References

Allen, M. 1994, '"See you in the city": Perth's citiplace and space of surveillance', in *Metropolis Now*, eds K. Gibson & S. Watson, Pluto Press, Leichhardt.

Bessant, J. 1994, 'Questioning popular representations of "youth"', *Family Matters*, v.38, August, pp.38-39.

Davis, M. 1990, *City of Quartz*, Vintage Press, London.

Eckersley, R. 1992, *Apocalypse? No! Youth and the Challenge to Change*, Australia's Commission for the Future, essay series n.1, July.

Foucault, M. 1979, *Discipline and Punishment: The birth of the prison*, Vintage Books, New York.

Guilliatt, R. 1997, 'Hey you ... boy!', *Good Weekend*, 22 Nov., pp.16-20.

Hasluck, L. & Malone, K. 1999, 'Location, leisure and lifestyle: Young people's retreat to home environments', in *Contemporary Perspectives on Family Research*, series ed. F. Berardo, v.1, JAI Press, Connecticut.

Heywood, P. & Crane, P. with Egginton, A. & Gleeson, J. 1998, *Out and About: In or out? Better outcomes from young people's use of public and community space in the City of Brisbane, v.2: Policies, implementation strategies and tools*, Brisbane City Council, Community Development Team West, Brisbane.

HREOC 1997, *Submission by the Human Rights and Equal Opportunity Commission to the Inquiry by the Joint Standing Committee on Treaties Into the Status of the United Nations Convention on the Rights of the Child in Australia*, July, Commonwealth Government, Canberra.

Iveson, K. 1998, Public cultures and public space, paper presented at the Planning as if Young People Mattered forum, Sept., Royal Australian Planning Institute, ACT.

James, A., Prout, A. & Jenks, C. 1998, *Theorising Childhood*, Polity Press, London.

Loukataitou-Sideris, D. 1996, 'Cracks in the city: Addressing the constraints and potentials of urban design', *Journal of Urban Design*, v.1, n.1, pp.91-104.

Malone, K. 1999, 'Growing Up In Cities as a model of participatory planning and "place-making" with young people', *Youth Studies Australia*, v.18, n.2, pp.17-23.

Malone, K. & Hasluck, L. 1998, 'Geographies of exclusion: Young people's perceptions and use of public space', *Family Matters*, n.49, Autumn, pp.21-26.

Mathews, F. 2000, Youth gangs on youth gangs, paper presented at the First National Youth Service Models Conference, 12–15 March, Adelaide.

McDonald, R. 1997, *Youth, the "Underclass" and Social Exclusion*, Routledge, London.

NCAVAC 1998, *Fear of Crime: The fieldwork research volume 2*, Commonwealth of Australia, Canberra.

Patterson, I. & Pegg, S. 1999, 'Nothing to do: The relationship between "leisure boredom" and alcohol and drug addiction: Is there a link to youth suicide in rural Australia', *Youth Studies Australia*, v.18, n.2, pp.24-28.

Polzot, L. 1997, 'Young people and police in public space', *Youth Issues Forum*, Winter, pp.30-32.

Relph, E. 1976, *Place and Placelessness*, Pion Ltd, London.

Sibley, D. 1988, 'Purification of space', *Environment and Planning D: Society and Space*, v.6, n.4, pp.52-65.

—— 1992, 'Outsiders in society and space', in *Inventing Places: Studies in cultural geography*, eds K. Anderson & K. Gale, Longman, Melbourne.

—— 1995, *Geographies of Exclusion*, Routledge, London.

Tait, D. 1994, 'Cautions and appearances: Statistics about youth and police', in *The Police and Young People in Australia*, eds R. White & C. Alder, Cambridge University Press, Melbourne.

UNGA 1989, *Convention on the Rights of the Child*, adopted by the General Assembly of the United Nations, Paris, 20 Nov.

UNICEF 1997, *Children's Rights and Habitat: Working towards child-friendly cities*, UNICEF, New York.

Valentine, G. 1996, 'Children should be seen and not heard: The production and transgression of adults' public space', *Urban Geography*, v.17, n.3, pp.205-20.

White, R. 1994, 'Street life: Police practices and youth behaviour', in *The Police and Young People in Australia*, eds R. White & C. Alder, Cambridge University Press, Melbourne.

White, R. & Alder, C. (eds) 1994, *The Police and Young People in Australia*, Cambridge University Press, Melbourne.

Winter, I. & Bryson, L. 1998, 'Economic restructuring and state intervention in Holdenist suburbia: Understanding urban poverty in Australia', *International Journal of Urban and Regional Research*, v.22, n.1, pp.21-28.

Wyn, J. & White, R. 1997, *Rethinking Youth*, Sage Publications, London.

YAPA 1997, *No Standing: Young people and community space project research report*, YAPA, Sydney.

Notes

[1]   "Muck-up day" is the last day of school for students finishing high school. It has the reputation of being a day where the students throw water bombs and eggs, and generally let off steam.

[2]   Australia ratified the Convention on the Rights of the Child in 1992 therefore committing itself to a regime of auditing against the conventions principles.

[3]   Two articles in the CRC of particular significance: Article 15: State Parties recognise the rights of the child to freedom of association and to freedom of peaceful assembly, Article 31: State Parties recognise the right of the child to rest and leisure, to engage in play and recreational activities appropriate to the age of the child and to participate freely in cultural life and the arts.

[4]   There is not enough room in this chapter to discuss each method individually although they will be discussed in the context of presenting data. Information on the methods can be found in earlier published work by the author including Malone 1999.

[5]   See Hasluck and Malone (1999) for a further discussion on the relationship between young people's leisure choices and the restrictions of the physical and social environment of a neighbourhood.

[6]   It was common knowledge among the young people that there had been quite a number of drug overdoses in the shopping mall and public toilets.

[7]   See the recently released Pennington Report, *Drugs: Responding to the Issues, Engaging the Community*, Stage One Report April 2000 produced by the Victorian Drug Policy Expert Committee for further details on the impacts of shifting trends in drug consumption and distribution in Victoria.

Lyn Yates

chapter 12

Representing "class" in qualitative research

In 1993, with Julie McLeod, I began a seven-year qualitative, longitudinal study of young people in Australia. The 12 to 18 Project[1] was intended as a longitudinal study to investigate the development of young people's gendered identity in Australia now, and schooling's contribution to social inequalities: the way in which different schools interact with and produce differentiated outcomes for different types of young people. It was a project inspired by the fact that we had both spent many years studying education, gender formation, inequalities, changing cultural and policy discourse and wanting to design a new type of study to take us further with these interests. It was also a study whose design was influenced by two film series, both of them also concerned, in different ways, with representing social differences and development of individual identity and outcomes over time.

The better known of these film series is the British *7 Up* series, which has followed boys and girls from different class backgrounds from age seven through 14, 21, 35 and 42. That project is exciting because the close focus on individuals over time allows the viewer to think about individuality but also class patterning. However, in relation to one of our key areas of interest, social inequality and schooling, it has a problem shared by many qualitative research studies. It is quite difficult to distinguish family and school effects in these films, in that we largely get glimpses of rich kids at rich schools; poor kids at poor schools (though, rather better than much ethnographic literature, it also does include one or two middle kids at middle schools). The films have been criticised (including by their maker) as being initially designed with too little attention to gender and race. Class was taken as the overwhelming issue of interest.

Our other inspiration was Gillian Armstrong's series of documentary films based on three working-class Adelaide schoolgirls.[2] In the first of this series, made in the 1970s, the girls were 14. In the most recent film, *Not Fourteen Again*, which was released in cinemas in 1996, these girls have aged to their mid-30s, and two of them have 14-year-old daughters. This film includes a lot of footage from the earlier films, and it shows in the background some broad changes affecting what might be seen as the same "class" of people two decades apart. In the 1970s, the working-class teenagers dressed and spoke "roughly", dropped out of school early, had babies at 18. In the 1990s, both they and their daughters are less distinguishable by accent or dress as belonging to a particular class – there is the influence of television and of certain things being more widely available; and of different broad patterns of schooling, contraception, life events. It is not that class differences of some sort have ceased to exist, but their forms have changed, both at the level of the structure of jobs, and in terms of cultural forms. (Indeed one of these social and cultural shifts is apparent in the making of the film itself. In the most recent film, but not in the earlier ones, Gillian Armstrong shows herself in the story, alongside the other women, rather than as someone who preserves her own privacy while being a voyeur on others.)

Historically, "class" has been an important lens through which young people have been differentiated, studied, represented and explained by researchers, but today there is considerable uncertainty about whether that lens can continue to be used, and considerable ambiguity about what it would mean to do so. This chapter discusses why, today, researchers might want to continue to grapple with this issue; some analytical and methodological problems in doing so; and examples of some ways in which the design and the evidence from the 12 to 18 Project are attempting to contribute to reflections about "class" in a time when much has changed and when many different ways of understanding young people, social inequalities, and educational processes have entered the interpretive literature.

Why bother with "class"?

Because I will soon go on to discuss some of the slipperiness and difficulty of trying to focus on class, in Australia, on the cusp of the 21st century, I want to begin by explaining why I think it is worth talking about; why I do not want to begin by assuming that a focus on gender or ethnicity will make such a discussion redundant, and why I am not wanting to treat qualitative research as something whose only agenda is to produce "rich descriptions" of a myriad of individual cases.

In Australia, the statistical picture shows that "socioeconomic status" (or SES, usually judged by a combination of factors such as parents' occupation and education; locality; income level) is one of the strongest predictors of school retention rates, achievement at school, extent to which students continue to university or to further education, types of courses and careers and universities they go on to enter (Lamb 1998; Teese 2000). It is true that patterns can also be shown in terms of other categorisations, such as gender, ethnicity, rurality, disability and, most strongly of all, with Aboriginality,[3] but even with some of these patterns, many analyses continue to stress the way in which some form of consideration of class is important. For example, in the burgeoning debate about whether it is boys rather than girls who are disadvantaged at school, many commentators have noted that working-class girls do considerably worse than middle-class boys (MCEETYA 1995; Teese et al. 1995; Yates 1997). In terms of education, especially university participation, the effect of class in who is there and how they behave is an observable experience as well as a statistical fact – at least for those coming from non "middle-class" origins. And yet a few years ago, when Gilah Leder and I reviewed a number of major Australian databases on student pathways (Yates & Leder 1996), we found that a number of state education authorities had made the decision not to collect evidence of SES in terms of analysing the outcomes data. Similarly, reviewing the policy funding of research on girls and education, I have often noted how much attention has been devoted to this issue in the two decades from the mid-1970s, and how little to the issue of class and poverty (Yates 1995, 1998a). In the press too, while there is regular coverage of education as a competitive arena in gender terms (have the girls or the boys got the top results this year?) and in terms of supposed "school" effects, rarely does a newspaper article even mention, far less discuss, the way in which results are heavily patterned by difference between the western and eastern parts of a city.

There is some political embarrassment in acknowledging social inequalities of this type, but there is also, for researchers, an analytical difficulty in what it is we are trying to study or represent, especially in qualitative research. At a common-sense level, and especially in terms of extremes, we believe we can identify "working-class boys", or "middle-class girls". But if we construct studies around those we assume represent these, to what extent are we studying class rather than simply assuming it; and what sort of explanatory idea lies behind or arises from the attempt to deal with class/gender/ethnicity, etc. in combination?

Historically, the idea of "class" has been used in many ways and in many contexts. Sometimes it is used in the Marxist sense, as a relational concept, and as a means of understanding group interests which are structured in opposition to each other (that is, where the interests and outcomes of the groups are not simply different, unequal, but have a structured relationship to each other). In recent times, the work of Pierre Bourdieu has been particularly influential here, since it is work that is not only concerned with the contemporary forms of the structured relations of social groups to each other, but sees the workings of the education system as a central mechanism within this (for example, Bourdieu & Passeron 1977; Bourdieu 1998a, 1998b). This is a more powerful concept than the classificatory use which is more common today, where it is used simply as a means of classifying differences of economic and symbolic capital, and as a basis for tracing educational and life opportunities in terms of these. However any attempt to recapture a relational, structural sense of the differences must confront the shifts from industrial society (owners of the means of production versus factory workers) to the post-industrial, globalised, knowledge- and service-based economies of the present. They must also confront the problem of what "class" looks like once women and domestic life are more fully integrated into the picture (Birkelund, Broch-Due & Nilsen 1999). For social theorists, attempting to understand changes in the economy, technology, culture, nationhood, the meaning of what "class" is as part of that pattern is posed as a question. In the literature on gender, ethnicity and race, "class" often comes in as a way of not "essentialising", or a way of trying to signal differences which are not reducible to a single one (Weis & Fine 1993) And in the feminist literature on class (as well as in an earlier literature dominated by male sociologists of education), discussion of "class" can be a way of understanding the psychology of individuals from different backgrounds, as well as of attempting to recuperate the pain in the autobiographical experiences of the researcher whose origins were a long way from their current social milieu (for example, Reay 1996; Mahoney & Zmrocezek 1997; Skeggs 1997; Steedman 1993; Walkerdine 1989, 1990).

For the 12 to 18 Project, a project concerned with identity, biography, educational and social inequalities, any one of these discussions suggests "class" to be an issue which may be highly salient but which is also problematic. The issue of whether class is a relevant category of representation and analysis enters into consideration of the following:

- How do we represent the meanings, constructions, values, imperatives that each individual subject is working with?
- How do we understand their engagements with schooling and the schooling/biography effects over this time?

- How do we describe (analytically categorise) the processes and patterns of inequality, exclusion, power, social formation embedded in these young people's understandings and experiences, and how, similarly, do we think about possibilities of change?

To sum up, both the statistical evidence and everyday experience suggest that the patterns and outcomes of young people's relation to education is affected by their background in ways not simply accounted for by using categories like gender. The autobiographically-based literature on education also suggests that some elements of this type are a strong part of subjective and emotional experience/formation. But how to theorise/categorise/be more specific about what is being identified as "class" is an issue, given, on the one hand, the significant changes from industrial to post-industrial or knowledge forms of society, and, on the other, given the rise to prominence of other candidates for analytical primacy (gender, race, ethnicity).

Some analytic problems in setting up qualitative projects on "class", inequality and schooling

Since the 1970s, a lot of useful work has been done on the production of inequalities via the microprocesses of schooling: looking at knowledge and assessment and the creation of success and failure through these; looking at the development of identities and subjectivities; coining and making use of immensely powerful concepts like "cultural capital" and "resistance". However, as a number of recent commentators have noted, some problems and gaps are evident in much of this body of work. Here I want to outline four of the major problems.

The problem of empiricism: of ethnographies which "read off" processes from an untheorised selection

A common approach (as Watson 1993 notes) has been to focus on what is seen as a classic working-class group, and to read their practices for evidence of the processes of class, schooling and the reproduction of social inequality. Here the problem is the extent to which the experience of that group can be taken to represent processes occurring more broadly and to represent the experiences of other groups; and also the problem of imputing significance within what is observed.

The problem Watson identifies has actually been in some respects worsened by the recent fascination with autobiography as part of the research process. Both in their selection of "working-class" groups to study, and in the stories they tell, there is a tendency to be trying to tell the story of the researcher's own pain as a working-class girl or boy – a story located in the 1950s, 1960s or 1970s rather than today, and in which the central contrast tends to be a binary of "working class" to "middle class" rather than an attention to different forms and possibilities in both. Some tendencies of this kind are seen in work by Walkerdine and Lucey (1989); and Reay (1996). Similarly, in a recent work entitled *Formations of Class and Gender: Becoming Respectable*, Beverley Skeggs (1997) challenges feminism for its lack of attention to class, and constructs a book based on a study of working-class women in the north of England undertaking child-care courses. From this she argues that respectability was a key issue in the processes of female working-class formation – but does not reflect on the extent to which this may be an artefact of the particular group she has decided to study. The point here is that identification of the group to be studied is as much an issue as what is imputed from the study, and we need to beware of practices of romantically recreating "the working class" in their 19th century guise by sociologists and anthropologists going out to select samples who look like the ones they are familiar with.

To illustrate Watson's second point, that there is a danger of simply reading off all of the practices of the group studied as all causally explaining inequality, we might consider the changing debate about gender inequality. In the heyday of the legitimacy of concerns about girls, virtually every feature of girls' practices in school (the way they applied themselves to their work, their rule-following, their quietness) was read as an example of their disadvantaging in the processes of education and life pathways. Articles assumed that how boys approached mathematics, or computing was advantageous, and was the model to be followed. Now, in the wake of a different public debate about feminism having gone too far, the same range of practices are being read in reverse ways, that is that boys' practices are deficit (Yates 1997). In both cases there has been an insufficiently theorised reading of the practices.

The problem of focusing on extremes

As Watson (1993) has also pointed out, an adequate understanding of the processes and possibilities of schooling in interaction with social class is unlikely to come from only studying the extremes: how the most privileged succeed, and how the least privileged fail. There are two problems here. The very large group of students and families that are in the middle are left untheorised and under-researched. Second, this approach tends to leave the popular field of "school effectiveness" studies (that is, studies of the comparative possibilities of schools or of different approaches to schooling) to researchers who are sociologically naïve. Focusing on "the middle" is important for a number of reasons – the large number of schools and students in this group; the changing structure of jobs and the difficulty of classifying many of these (the problem of the new middle class for example); and because the "middle" group of schools and of students may offer insights about possibilities of success and failure through schooling not available when the sample is the over-determined advantaged and disadvantaged.

The problem of the rapidly changing form of the economy and labour force, and what this means for "class" analysis

Given that jobs and employment possibilities are changing rapidly, how adequately are studies tracking and theorising what schooling is doing here? Again, the extremes are relatively clear-cut; but is "class" being "reproduced" now? For example, in the labour force we have seen the demise (in numbers and in conditions) of certain categories of jobs (public sector work, bank tellers, sales assistants, teachers); and the rise of others (hospitality and the celebrity chefs, for example; some jobs in e-industries and in finance). The significance and status and effects of completing Year 12 now mean something different from what they did two decades ago (Yates & Leder 1996).

It does not need subtle research to show that schools (or groups) with extreme drop-out rates are losing out, or that schools whose students go en masse to the most prestigious courses in the most prestigious universities are in some sense winning – but the bulk of the population are not in these two groups, and in looking within these for what schools are doing relative to social inequality, it may be misleading to focus only on the schools that produce the best tertiary entrance scores, or which have the highest retention rates. (In our study, for example, there are noticeable differences between the schools in terms of the opportunities they offer to enter training courses, and more broadly, in terms of the types of jobs and courses to which students are oriented.)

To take another example, of changing contexts and their relevance for thinking about processes of "reproduction", in recent work on youth and "pathways" Johanna Wyn and Peter Dwyer have commented that it is more common to find young women taking a more flexible approach in their post-school education and pathways (while keeping an end goal in mind), whereas young men often focus intently on a particular qualification or pathway as the thing that must be gained (Wyn & Dwyer 2000, see also Wyn in this volume). Today, they argued, it is the former attitude that may be more strategic, given the rapidity and frequency of change. Now for some time, research has suggested that at school boys are more likely to be "strategic" in their choice of subjects (for example, in continuing with mathematics because of its utility to future work, regardless of whether they like the subject), whereas girls are seen as more likely to choose subjects they are interested in. It may be that the changing form of the economy alters the relative pay-off of these processes – that patterns repeated at school may not reproduce patterns beyond school.

How do we analyse "class" relative to other social forms, such as gender, ethnicity?

In an overview of changing structures and processes of assessment in schooling, Patricia Broadfoot argues that the changing forms continue to reproduce the same class outcomes (Broadfoot 1996). She entirely ignores the heated debate about gender and assessment, that has not only been a significant public issue for policy-making, but where there is some evidence that relative outcomes of the groups have had some change (see MCEETYA 1995; Yates 1997b; Arnot, David & Weiner 1999). Again this raises questions about what is "class" in the contemporary economy. We might talk about class being gendered, or about gender taking classed forms, but we need to think about both the specificity of different groups, and also about what patterns and processes of power, privilege, disadvantage are being produced and recast here.

The 12 to 18 Project: design issues

We wanted to approach our own qualitative project with some sensitivity to the issues I have outlined. The study is one where we have followed 26 main students, located initially at four different secondary schools, from the beginning of this time to the first phase of post-school life (Yates & McLeod 1996; McLeod & Yates 1997, 1998). Twice each year we interview them, often with their friends, in lengthy and semi-structured interviews which we tape and videotape. In relation to the issues outlined above, important methodological features of the 12 to 18 Project as a way to explore class in some qualitative way are: 1) a recognition that the interpretive work must be close, open and ongoing in its interrogating of meaning and empirical observation against a range of broader theorising of social forms and processes today; and 2) a structuring to enable but not foreclose comparative possibilities and judgments, and to give more attention than previously to groups and schools "in the middle".

The project we designed was small-scale and qualitative. The type of contribution it might potentially make to the issues I have outlined is by offering some further inductive evidence as to the meaning (or, potentially, inappropriateness) of "class" in the subjectivity and biographies of young people in interaction with school. To talk of some "inductive" quality is, in some respects, disingenuous. As Lather (1991) has said, every research act, and especially "interpretation", is an act of inscription, not merely description. To name something as "class" is to inscribe it in a particular way. But to acknowledge the constructing acts of the researcher should not be to assume that all research is equally inscribing rather than discovering the world. There is, certainly, an inescapable situatedness to one's conceptual tools and empirical object of study, and a lack of finality to what one discovers – both because there are other stories to be told and because there is a reflexiveness in the culture itself to the interpretations initially made. But the design of a project may be better or worse in enabling some further insight to be gained as compared with the assumptions and knowledge from which the research begins:

> *every act of research is simultaneously empirical (it confronts the world of observable phenomena) and theoretical (it necessarily engages hypotheses about the underlying structure of relations that observations are designed to capture)* (Wacquant, talking of the work of Pierre Bourdieu in Bourdieu & Wacquant 1992, p.35).

An important design feature of the 12 to 18 Project was that the interviewing, classification (including any coding), interpretations and writing would all be carried out by the two principal researchers. Two issues matter here. Given heightened feminist and qualitative methodological interest in recent years in the constructing activity of the researcher, and in the relations of the research act, we believe it is important for us to be directly involved in and exposed at length to the act on which we need to reflect. For this project we (Julie McLeod and myself) have both participated in almost all of the 200 interviews. For half of these we have had an opportunity to listen and observe the other rather than be the interviewer; and in all cases we take audio and videotape records which we can revisit and mutually discuss. Using qualitative methods to try to discuss broader concepts such as class or gender or subjectivity necessarily involves an interpenetration of theory and the empirical experience. As Bourdieu and Wacquant (1992) argue, this is as important a component of a reflexive sociology as is dwelling on the researcher's autobiographical situatedness, yet the current conditions of academic life in Australia and of research funding regimes, work against the type of intensive work that is theoretically required, namely:

> *the practical organisation and carrying out of data collection – or, to be accurate, data production – are so intimately bound up with the theoretical construction of the object that they cannot be reduced to "technical" tasks left to hired underlings, survey bureaucracies, or research assistants* (Bourdieu & Wacquant 1992, p.29).

The second important design feature of the 12 to 18 Project was its selection of sites and subjects for study. The initial sites of the study were four schools: two provincial and two metropolitan schools; and including one elite private school, one ex-technical school in a poorer area, and two high schools. The selection of school sites was done with considerable care. We wanted an opportunity to be listening to students who might be classified (in ABS terms, for example) as having similar backgrounds, but who were attending different schools in our study; and students who were of different class, ethnic, gender situations but at the same school. We were wanting opportunities to disaggregate home and school; to avoid conflation of school and "habitus"; to not take one group in one locality and one school environment as a unitary embodiment of "working-class" experience. On the other hand, in terms of selecting the students for ongoing study at the four schools, our methods were rather rough. We selected equal numbers of girls and boys, and other than that simply tried to include "a range". We tried to include articulate and inarticulate, and hoped for some range of ethnicity, but our methods here were not precise. We did not ask questions about parent's occupation or ethnicity before we began. This was deliberate. We were not setting out to read off what students already classified in a particular way looked like. We were not aiming simply to provide illustrative "rich" examples for already theorised processes. We were aiming to build from the students themselves a new sense of how they constructed subjectivity and school experience, and to take a fresh look at whether and/or how "class" was part of this.

Finally, in terms of the location of this study, we set out to include examples at the more familiar extremes of elite experience (elite home, elite school) and working-class experience (poor homes, school in poor area); but also to have a large proportion of students and schools in the study who do not represent these extremes. Our interest here is not only the more familiar issue of what happens to someone from a less elite background attending an elite school; or from a middle-class background attending a "disadvantaged" school. Our interest is also whether some of the differentiations, processes of identity formation, and educational outcomes that can be seen in the schools in the middle, can be illuminated by the broader theories of class and education, or whether this is not such a salient concept there.

Biographies, school processes and effects, and the question of "class" – some work in progress

We began the 12 to 18 Project in 1993, when the students involved were in Grade 6, and are completing the interviewing in 2000 when almost all the students have left school. Neither the interviewing nor the analysis of the overall material from the project is complete, so in the remainder of this chapter, I will be pulling out only some aspects of the work to date to illustrate some ways we are trying to work on issues I have been discussing. What I am trying to illustrate is some ways we are trying to reflect on "class" by moving between close readings of individual transcripts, comparisons within and across schools, and reflections on debates in theory and the broader literature. Other examples of ways of drawing on the material from this project can be seen in the chapter by Julie McLeod in this volume, and in other publications from the project (McLeod & Yates 1997, 1998; Yates & McLeod 1996; Yates 1999a, 1999b; McLeod 1998, 2000).

On "distinction" and relational effects

The most familiar part of previous work on class as it relates to education (e.g. Young 1971; Bernstein 1975; Bourdieu & Passeron 1977; Connell et al. 1982) stresses the close fit between "middle-class" modes, know-how, ways of speaking and what schools want and reward, and, conversely, the disjunction between what working-class kids bring to school and what schooling does. The 12 to 18 Project was not set up to directly observe educational interactions. Its focus was on the meanings students were giving to their experiences in school and the building of their sense of themselves and their future that was part of this.

One of the first things we could note, was how students were reading (that is, constructing) what their respective schools were doing.

We cannot understand the symbolic violence of what were once hastily designated as the "ideological state apparatuses" unless we analyse in detail the relationship between the objective characteristics of the organisations that exercise it and the socially constituted dispositions of the agents upon whom it is exercised (Bourdieu 1998b, p.3).

The schools at the two extremes in our study not only offered a different curriculum, but their respective curricula were being read by students in ways that exaggerated and reproduced certain differences. At the private school, students saw themselves as benefiting by having a well-equipped school ("Like in a state school you probably wouldn't have two really well kept ovals and a swimming pool and tennis courts, netball courts, basketball courts, stuff like that") and a wider than normal range of "options", though the breadth in this case was in the arts and participation was not optional but compulsory. The students in Year 7 did only a single computing period per week, and no other technical subjects. Students commented on how poor the teaching of computing was ("that was shocking", "it was like a free period", "I don't think he's ever like used a computer before"), but not one student commented generally about the lack of technical and manual studies. Here, what students brought to the school, what the school itself did, and how the school was located in its community and its history, all mutually constitute a way of making invisible what might otherwise be seen as a lack – the school's relatively impoverished computer offerings.

At the technical school in our study, there was, by contrast, a plethora of impressive equipment, a large range of computing and technically-oriented studies, and some innovative teaching in those areas which the students enjoyed. In addition to English, mathematics, science, social education, languages, physical education and home group, students, in the course of their first year, studied textiles, home economics, systems technology, information technology, keyboarding, 3D art, sheetmetal and woodwork! Most of these technical-manual subjects were included in students' nominations of their favourite subjects, and when they were asked their views of other schools, they nominated the lack of such subjects as a negative:

> Christine: And then if it's like in an all girls school you don't get to do the subject like sheetmetal work and all that. And they're some of my favourite subjects, so …
>
> Ellen: You don't have like woodwork, sheetmetal and all that.
>
> Christine: Like there's a whole tech work you wouldn't know.
>
> Year 7 girls, 1994

However, despite this enthusiasm, school was constructed by these students (and their parents) as an institution with a clear hierarchy of valued knowledge:

> Interviewer: What do you think this school thinks is important?
>
> Keren: Maths … kind of science, maths, social ed and English … They sort of think them subjects are the main ones, even though, you know, most people don't like the main subjects.
>
> Year 7 girl, 1994

In these two examples, taken from the two extremes of the four schools in our study, we see differentiations being made which tend to reconstitute and constitute both the subjective identities and trajectories of the individual students and the social order (see also Teese 1998).

By the fourth year of the study, the ways students talked about certain things had been shaped by their particular school in a way that would tend to reproduce further the relative positioning of the students who entered it. At the most elite school, every student responded to a question about unemployment by saying that it was basically due to people not trying hard enough to get work; while at a high school in a suburb nearby, every student responded by saying unemployment was due to general economic conditions, or immigration, or things other than the individual's own efforts. In other words, the first students had learnt/had reinforced to some extent to "misrecognise" their own social advantages and to take up an unsympathetic stance to those who lacked these. The students in the second school had learnt/had reinforced a stance of progressive fatalism that had them competing less vigorously for school success.

In other words, in relation to some of the issues I raised in the first part of this chapter, we are seeing here some sense of what it means to talk of class as part of subjectivity, but also as a relational process that is not simply to do with what attributes and advantages an individual possesses but is part of a much broader network of relationships between individuals and between institutions. Schools and students are mutually part of this process.

But what of the further question: what relevance does this have to young people and schools "in the middle", and how do we take account of difference and non-conflation of what students bring to school and what emerges from their interaction with school?

Another school in the study is a high school, in the same town as the technical school mentioned above, a town with a very prominent range of private schools. The students here constantly tell us of ways in which this school measures up to the private schools. In every interview students respond to a question about how the school compares with other schools, by mentioning that the school has a boat shed, and takes part in a rowing competition with private schools. In the interviews with different students in our study (which there is not space to quote at length in this chapter), it is apparent that the values and the distinctions of the kind outlined enter into the definitions of self, the experiences of success and failure, the expectations about the future, whether the student is in the over-determined extreme (the students at the poorer school who see themselves as part of another world than students from the private schools, where they would never fit in); whether the student comes from a background somewhat higher or lower than the broad positioning of the school they enter (the student who enters the elite school from a less elite background and gradually takes on the value that unemployment is the result of lack of effort; the student who enters the same school and who feels his ethnicity implicitly places him as an "other" in that context, and who eventually changes schools); or the students in the high school which values rowing who must engage in constant disciplinary work to try to keep up with the "distinction" of students and private schools whose history and class positioning can take this for granted. The repeated comments of different students at this middle high school ("they expect a lot from us, because they're saying the school has a good reputation") remind us of Diane Reay's comment:

> My father always told his children, "you are just as good as anybody else". We all knew that encoded in that phrase was a subtext that we were not (Reay 1996, p.453).

These are some examples of meanings being formed, meanings that contribute to identities, trajectories, outcomes – but in terms of thinking about "class" they are not the whole of the story. It may, after all, matter (in terms of power, relative social positioning) if students do not acquire high facility with computer technology.

On "difference" and social change

The discussion in the previous section illustrated one way of taking up the interview material from our study – looking for points of comparisons and difference between the students at different schools and from different kinds of backgrounds. To some extent, this was a discussion grounded in previous forms of class analysis in relation to schooling. An alternative way of using our material is to begin with a close reading of an individual story over time, to think about what sense "class" makes as an analytic category in explaining individual experiences, compared with such matters as gender and ethnicity, and to attempt "inductively" to be listening for themes that may be different from those of a previous period and a previous generation. Here I have space only for very brief summary indications of some work in progress.

When we first interview her, at age 12, Sue[5] is working hard helping her mother run a caravan park, cooking, looking after younger siblings, dealing with a stepfather who makes her uncomfortable, but whom she does not want to talk about. She wants to do well at school, ideally to become a kindergarten teacher or a chef, but she is uncertain about her ability, and talks about the future in terms of "taking it as it comes" – a common theme among the students from this school, and these issues grow stronger as she proceeds through school. Read in terms of the British feminist literature on working-class women, we would emphasise this fatalism, self-doubt, that thread through Sue's story. Read through Bourdieu's eyes, we could pick out the themes of her puzzlement about what school really wants of her. Over the years of interviews, she mentions hopes of particular jobs, but also retreats and expresses doubt that she will make it. She seems deeply unsure of her ability, especially academic ability. But, her way of talking about these things belies what seems like a strong determination to keep in there, to keep taking the next step. Unusually for this school, Sue is still there in Year 12, and actually does complete school and enter a tertiary course.

Over the six years we have interviewed Sue, her home life also experiences changes. Her mother returns to the local technical college to study to become a youth worker. The family move from the caravan park, and the unwanted man is no longer in their life.

How should we interpret the dynamic that has produced Sue's path through school? Is this just the story of this individual, or is this part of a pattern of change involving many working class women, at least in this part of Australia?

The British feminist work helps us to notice the psychology, emotions and family dynamics of the class experience. What it often tends to obscure is any generational changes in this class experience or location. In our study, we have been struck by the extent to which a number of girls from roughly "working class" backgrounds are managing their lives through their teenage years: handling a boyfriend who may have left school, or be in trouble with the law, even seeing him every night, and yet not letting that stop them keeping their own studies afloat; filling their lives with a huge range of activities: paid work, sport, domestic chores, boyfriend, study, and yet handling all of these. In a number of cases, these girls seem to have recognised opportunities of the newly reconstituted labour market – the significance of the hospitality industry for example; in others they keep very traditional dreams of becoming a respectable teacher of young children.

In another paper (Yates 1998b) I have taken up the stories of three boys from non-mainstream ethnic backgrounds in our study. Through those stories we are again able to see something of the shaping of subjectivity as well as broader social outcomes from the interactions of what students bring to school and what particular schools (and schooling overall) are doing. In one case, the boy comes from a culture which values formal academic work and displays of success, but is sent to a high school whose peer culture values informality. The school is "culturally inclusive" in terms of having a very mixed student body and generally non-racist in the values students acquire, but there is a disjunction between the "habitus" of this boy, and the way this particular school culture works. Yet another boy in our study, also from a different ethnic and religious group, gets on quite happily at the same school. At the elite school, a boy who is marked as racially different, despite his proficiency with the formal curriculum and "cultural capital" that the school values, is so unhappy with what he sees as its lack of tolerance of difference, that he leaves it.

In these stories, the question of what sense it makes to talk of "class" in representing them, is complex. In the case of the boy at the high school who is at sea with his peers and the expectations of school, there is certainly a mismatch of cultural "know-how", but it is not one of class difference in any traditional sense of that term – this boy's family were doctors in his own country. On the other hand, the parents' lack of resources to assess different school options in this culture is related to their class as well as immigrant positioning in this country. At the elite school, the problem is not one of "dispositions" on the part of the boy of the type that class theorists write about, but of racism and bodily difference – though the inscription of these by the school and the mainstream student body may well be understood as part of their class formation. But in terms of educational pathways and outcomes, in his case the class location of his parents means that they are able to handle and diffuse the problem by finding another elite school that is more appropriate for him.

Concluding remarks

Methodologically, the usefulness of considering "class" in terms of a qualitative, longitudinal study such as this one is that it forces us to keep on considering the relationship between the individual story (the individual psychology, subjectivity, choices, outcomes) and the broader patterns of social arrangements which constitute and are constituted by those individual stories. In terms of the problematic issues I set up at the beginning, the examples from the project that I have offered are not a neat pinning down of what class "means", of how we should draw the lines, of whether key structures and oppositions can be identified. But working with the concepts and theories associated with "class" does, I think, help to illuminate "individual" ways of being, and relationships between individuals and education, that are still important to consider in research on young people, in Australia, in this post-industrial world.

References

APC 1997, Australian Press Council Adjudication No. 910 (February 1997), http://www.austlii.edu.au/other/apc/910.html

Arnot, M., David, M. & Weiner, G. 1999, *Closing the Gender Gap: Postwar education and social change*, Polity Press, Cambridge, MA.

Bernstein, B. 1975, *Class, Codes and Control*, vol.3, Routledge, London.

Birkelund, G.E., Broch-Due, A.K. & Nilsen, A. (eds) 1999, *Ansvar og Protest: Kjonn, klasse og utdanning i senmoderniteten*, University of Bergen Press, Bergen.

Bourdieu, P. 1979, *Distinction: A social critique of the judgement of taste,* trans. R. Nice, Harvard University Press, Cambridge, MA.

—— 1998a, *Practical Reason*, Polity Press, Oxford.

—— 1998b, *The State Nobility: Elite schools in the field of power*, trans. L.C. Clough, Polity Press, Oxford.

Bourdieu, P. & Passeron, J.C. 1977, *Reproduction in Education, Society and Culture*, Sage, Newbury Park.

Bourdieu, P. & Wacquant, L. 1992, *An Invitation to Reflexive Sociology*, University of Chicago Press, Chicago.

Broadfoot, P.M. 1996, *Education, Assessment and Society: A sociological analysis*, Open University Press, Buckingham.

Connell, R.W., Ashenden, D., Kessler, S. & Dowsett, G.W. 1982, *Making the Difference: Schools, families and social division*, Allen & Unwin, Sydney.

Lamb, S. 1998, 'Completing school in Australia', *Australian Journal of Education*, v.42, n.1, pp.5-31.

Lather, P. 1991, *Getting Smart: Feminist research and pedagogy with/in the postmodern*, Routledge, New York.

Mahoney, P. & Zmrocezek, C. 1997, *Class Matters: 'Working class' women's perspectives on social class*, Taylor & Francis, London.

McLeod, J. 1998, Friendship, schooling and gender identity work, paper presented at the annual conference of the Australian Association for Research in Education, University of Adelaide, Dec.

—— 2000, 'Subjectivity and schooling in a longitudinal study of secondary students', *British Journal of Sociology of Education*, v.21, n.4.

McLeod, J. & Yates, L. 1997, 'Can we find out about girls and boys today, or must we just settle for talking about ourselves. Dilemmas of a feminist, qualitative longitudinal research project', *Australian Education Researcher*, v.24, n.3, pp.23-42.

—— 1998, 'How young people think about self, work and futures', *Family Matters*, v.49, pp.28-33.

MCEETYA (Ministerial Committee on Employment, Education, Training and Youth Affairs) (Australia) 1995, Proceedings of the Promoting Gender Equity Conference, ACT Department of Education, Canberra.

Reay, D. 1996, 'Dealing with difficult differences: Reflexivity and social class in feminist research', *Feminism and Psychology*, v.6, n.3, pp.443-56.

Skeggs, B. 1997, *Formations of Class and Gender: Becoming respectable*, Sage, London.

Steedman, C. 1993, *Landscape for a Good Woman*, Virago, London.

Teese, R. 1998, 'Curriculum hierarchy, private schooling and the segmentation of Australian secondary education 1947–1985', *British Journal of Sociology of Education*, v.19, n.3, pp.291-304.

—— 2000, *Academic Success and Social Power: Examinations and inequality*, Melbourne University Press, Carlton South.

Teese, R., Davies, M., Charlton, M. & Polesel, J. 1995, *Who wins at school? Girls and boys in Australian secondary education*, Melbourne University Department of Education Policy and Management, Melbourne.

Walkerdine, V. 1989, *Democracy in the Kitchen: Regulating mothers and socialising daughters*, Virago, London.

—— 1990, *Schoolgirl Fictions*, Verso, London.

Watson, I. 1993, 'Education, class and culture: The Birmingham ethnographic tradition and the problem of the new middle class', *British Journal of Sociology of Education*, v.14, n.2, pp.179-97.

Weis, L. & Fine, M. 1993, *Beyond Silenced Voices: Class, race and gender in United States schools*, State University of New York Press, New York.

Wyn, J. & Dwyer, P. 2000, 'New patterns of youth in transition in education', *International Social Science Journal*, v.164, pp.148-59.

Yates, L. 1995, 'Not re-thinking the grand intellectual', *Australian Educational Researcher*, v.22, n.1, pp.119-25.

—— 1997, 'Gender equity and the boys debate: What sort of challenge is it?', *British Journal of Sociology of Education*, v.18, n.3, pp.337-47.

—— 1998a, 'Education', in *Australian Feminism: A companion*, eds B. Caine, M. Gatens, E. Grahame, J. Larbalestier, S. Watson & E. Webby, Oxford University Press, Sydney.

—— 1998b, Dreams of the future in an era of change: Longitudinal qualitative research speaks back to policy studies, paper presented to American Educational Research Association conference, San Diego.

—— 1999a, 'Transitions and the Year 7 experience: A report from the 12 to 18 Project' *Australian Journal of Education*, v.43, n.1, pp.23-41.

—— 1999b, 'How should we tell stories about class and gender and schooling today?' in *Ansvar og Protest: Kjonn, klasse og utdanning i senmoderniteten*, eds G.E. Birkelund, A-K. Broch-Due & A. Nilsen, University of Bergen Press, Bergen.

Yates, L. & Leder, G. 1995, 'The Student Pathways Project: A study of large databases and gender equity', *Unicorn*, v.21, n.4, pp.39-47.

—— 1996, *Student Pathways: A review and overview of national databases on gender equity*, ACT Department of Education and Training, Canberra.

Yates, L. & McLeod, J. 1996, '"And how would you describe yourself?" Researchers and researched in the first stages of a longitudinal research project', *Australian Journal of Education*, v.40, n.1, pp.88-103.

Young, M.F.D. (ed.) 1971, *Knowledge and Control*, MacMillan, London.

Notes

[1]   The *12 to 18 Project* has been supported by funding by the Australian Research Council, with additional support from La Trobe University; University of Technology, Sydney; and Deakin University.

[2]   These were *Smokes and Lollies* (when the girls were 14); *Fourteen's Good, Eighteen's Better* (at 18); *Bingo, Bridesmaids and Braces* (at 25); and *Not Fourteen Again* (when they were in their mid-30s, and two of them had 14-year-old daughters). This last film was released in 1996, when we were in year three of our project.

[3]   All of these terms or categorisation are highly problematic ones (see Yates & Leder 1995, 1996).

[4]   A notable exception is the coverage of the Year 12 Mt Druitt High School results published by Sydney's *Daily Telegraph* 8/1/97. See Australian Press Council Adjudication No. 910 (APC 1997).

[5]   "Sue's" interviews are discussed in another context and in some more depth in the chapter by McLeod in this volume.